SECOND EDITION

Learn C on the

osh®

SECOND EDITION

Learn C on the Macintosh®

Dave Mark

ADDISON-WESLEY PUBLISHING COMPANY

Reading, Massachusetts • Menlo Park, California • New York • Don Mills, Ontario
Wokingham, England • Amsterdam • Bonn • Sydney • Singapore • Tokyo
Madrid • San Juan • Paris • Scoul • Milan • Mexico City • Taipei

Library of Congress Cataloging-in-Publication Data

Mark, Dave.
    Learn C on the Macintosh / Dave Mark. — 2nd ed.
      p. cm.
    Includes bibliographical references and index.
    ISBN 0-201-48406-4
    1. Macintosh (Computer)—Programming.   2. C (Computer program language)   I. Title.
QA76.8.M3M36771861995
005.265—dc20   95-23299
                                                              CIP

Sponsoring Editor: Martha Steffen
Project Manager: John Fuller
Production Coordinator: Ellen Savett
Cover design: Andrew M. Newman
Text design: Wilson Graphics and Design (Kenneth J. Wilson)
Set in 10 point Palatino by Vicki L. Hochstedler

1 2 3 4 5 6 7 8 9 -MA- 9998979695
First printing, September 1995

Addison-Wesley books are available for bulk purchases by corporations, institutions, and other organizations. For more information please contact the Corporate, Government, and Special Sales Department at (800) 238-9682.

This book is dedicated to Deneen J. Melander and Daniel J. Mark —
LFUEMNMWWA,OK? . . .

Contents

*O*ne of the best decisions I ever made was back in 1979 when I hooked up with my buddy Tom and learned C. At first, C was just a meaningless scribble of curly brackets, semicolons, and parentheses. Fortunately for me, Tom was a C guru, and with him looking over my shoulder, I learned C quickly.

Now it's your turn.

This time I'll be looking over your shoulder as you learn C. My goal is to present every aspect of C the way I would have liked it explained to me. I've saved up all the questions I had as I learned the language and tried to answer them here.

Learning to program in C will open a wide range of opportunities for you. C is one of the most popular programming languages in the world today. Recessions may come and go, but there's always a demand for good C programmers. Whether you want to start your own software company or just write programs for your own enjoyment, you will discover that C programming is its own reward. Most of all, C programming is fun.

I hope you enjoy the book. If you make it to MacWorld on either coast, stop by the Addison-Wesley booth and say hello. I'd love to hear from you. In the meantime, turn the page, and let's get started. . . .

D. M.
Arlington, VA

Acknowledgments

*I'*d like to take a paragraph or two and thank some people whose names didn't make the cover, but who made this book possible. First of all, I'd like to thank Keith Rollin, whose technical review made this book so much better. Thanks, Keith. I owe you big!

Next, I'd like to thank all the folks at Addison-Wesley for their time, dedication, and just plain hard work. People like Keith Wollman, Martha Steffen, Kaethin Prizer, John Fuller, and Ellen Savett do the work that gets this book from my Mac into your hands.

Next, I'd like to thank Greg Galanos, Greg Dow, Berardino Baratta, Avi Rappoport, and the rest of the folks at Metrowerks for their support. Not only did they provide the copy of CodeWarrior you'll use to run all the examples in this book but they answered all my questions when Keith wasn't available.

Thanks to Stu Mark who put together the CD in back of the book and alternated between bass, drums, and lead guitar to keep me from getting bored. Stu, I'm lucky to have you for a brother!

A special thanks to Deneen and Daniel for letting me burn the midnight oil without complaint. And thanks to Hersh, Beth, Jackson, and Caroline Porter for being such great friends and neighbors.

Finally, I'd like to thank the man who was there at the beginning, the man who introduced me to the wonders of C, my good friend Tom Swartz. Thanks, Tom.

Chapter 1

Welcome Aboard

Welcome! By purchasing this book/disk package, you have taken the first step toward learning the C programming language. As you make your way through the book, you'll learn one of the most popular and powerful programming languages of all time. You will be glad you took this step.

Before we start programming, there are a few questions worth addressing at this point.

What's in the Package?

Learn C on the Macintosh is a book/disk package. The book is filled with all kinds of interesting facts, figures, and programming examples, all designed to teach you how to program in C.

In the back of the book you'll find a compact disc filled with important information. Though it may look like a normal audio CD, you won't want to pop this disc into your compact disc player. Instead, you'll place the disc into a CD-ROM drive connected to your computer.

Like a giant floppy disk, the *Learn C* CD-ROM is filled with files. First and foremost, it contains everything you'll need to run each of the book's programming examples on your own computer. As you look through the disc, you'll find a customized version of CodeWarrior, one of the most popular Macintosh development environments, along with each of the programs presented in the book, so you don't have to type in the examples yourself. We've also included a boatload of cool shareware and commercial software demos. Such a deal!

By the Way

> If you don't have a CD-ROM drive, try to borrow one from a friend or borrow a friend's CD-ROM equipped computer. You'll only need the CD-ROM drive long enough to copy CodeWarrior and the book's programs from the *Learn C* CD to the hard drive inside your computer.

Why Learn C?

There are many reasons for learning C. Perhaps the biggest reason is C's popularity as a programming language. C is probably the hottest programming language around. In fact, most of the best-selling Macintosh applications were written in C. If you are just getting started in programming, C is a great first programming language. If you already know a programming language, such as BASIC or Pascal, you'll find C a worthy addition to your language set.

C is everywhere. Almost every computer made today supports the C language. Once you learn C, you'll be able to create your own programs for fun and profit. You can use C to create utilities, games, and tools that do exactly what you want them to do. You can even use C to write the next great spreadsheet, word processor, or utility. Who knows? You might even make $80 gazillion in the process!

Whatever your reasons, learning to program in C will pay you dividends the rest of your programming life.

What Should You Know to Get Started?

For the most part, the only prerequisite to using this book is a basic knowledge of the Macintosh. Do you know how to double-click on an application to start it up? Does the scrolling list in Figure 1.1 look familiar? Do you know how to use a word processor like MacWrite or Microsoft Word? If you can use the Macintosh to run programs and edit documents, you have everything you need to get started learning C.

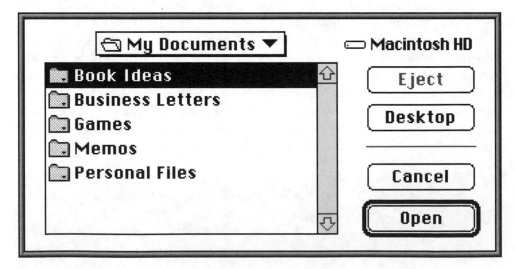

Figure 1.1 Scrolling through a list of documents.

If you know nothing about programming, don't worry. The first few chapters of this book will bring you up to speed. If you have some programming experience (or even a lot), you might want to skim the first few chapters, then dig right into the C fundamentals that start in Chapter 4.

What Equipment Will You Need?

Although it is possible to learn C just by reading a book, you'll get the most out of this book if you run each example program as you read how it works. To do this, you'll need a Macintosh with a 68020, 68030, 68040, or PowerPC processor; at least 8 megabytes of memory; System 7.1 (68K-based Macintosh computers) or System 7.1.2 (for Power Macintosh computers) or later; and, of course, a CD-ROM drive so you can install your new programming environment.

The Lay of the Land

This book was designed with several different readers in mind. If you're new to programming, you'll want to read every chapter. As you make your way through the book, try not to skip over material you don't understand. Ask. Make a commitment to finish this book. You can do it!

If you have some programming experience but know nothing about C, read Chapter 2, then skim through Chapter 3. If Chapter 3 is cake to you, jump right to Chapter 4. You'll probably find that the concepts presented in the first few chapters are pretty straightforward. Read at your own speed until you reach a comfortable depth. The farther into the book you get, the more complex the concepts become.

If you get stuck, there are a lot of places you can turn to for help. On-line services, such as eWorld, CompuServe, and America Online, all feature Macintosh development forums filled with friendly folks who are usually more than glad to help someone just getting started. If you have access to the Internet, you can subscribe to newsgroups, such as "comp.lang.c" and "comp.sys.mac.programmer.-help," where you'll be able to post your questions and, hopefully, find answers to them. Better yet, find a friend who's been down this road before, someone you can get together with, face-to-face, to help you through the tougher concepts.

Whether you have programming experience or not, you might find it helpful to have a copy of a good C reference by your side as you make your way through this book. Two particularly useful books are *The C Programming Language* by Kernighan and Ritchie (affectionately known as K&R) and *C: A Reference Manual* by Harbison and Steele (also known as H&S). K&R is the granddaddy of all C references and is the book that got me started in C programming. Although K&R

tends to be a little dense, it is filled with great sample code. As you master each new concept in this book, take a look at how K&R treats the same subject.

H&S covers much of the same ground as K&R but at a slightly different level. If you can swing the cost, consider picking up both of these books. They'll prove to be valuable additions to your C programming library. You'll find descriptions of both books (along with a bunch of others) in the bibliography in Appendix G.

The Chapters

This book is made up of 12 chapters and 7 appendixes. Chapter 1 provides an overview of the book and gets you started down the right path.

Chapter 2 introduces the disk portion of this book/disk package. You'll learn about CodeWarrior, the C programming environment you'll use to run all of the programs in this book. You'll install CodeWarrior on your hard drive and test the software to make sure it's installed properly. You'll also run your first C program. Regardless of any programming experience you already have, don't skip Chapter 2!

Chapter 3 is for those of you with little or no programming experience. Chapter 3 answers some basic questions, such as Why write a computer program? and How do computer programs work? We'll look at all the elements that come together to create a computer program, elements such as source code, a compiler, and the computer itself. Even if you're a seasoned Pascal programmer, you might want to read through this chapter, just to review the basics.

Chapter 4 opens the door to C programming by focusing on one of the primary building blocks of C: the function. You'll run some sample programs and discover one of the cruelest, least-liked, yet most important parts of programming: the syntax error.

Chapter 5 explores the foundation of C programming: variables and operators. When you finish this chapter, you will have a fundamental understanding of programming. You'll know how to declare a variable and how to use operators to store data in the variable.

Chapter 6 introduces the concept of flow control. You'll learn how to use C programming constructs, such as `if`, `while`, and `for`, to control the direction of your program. You'll learn how your program can make decisions based on data that you feed into it.

Chapter 7 starts off with the concept of pointers, which you'll use in almost every C program you write. Pointers allow you to implement complex data structures, opening up a world of programming possibilities.

Chapter 8 introduces data types. You'll learn about arrays and strings and the common bond they share. At this point, you are in real danger of becoming a C guru. Careful!

Chapter 9 tackles data structures. You'll learn how to design and build the right data structure for the job. Your knowledge of pointers is sure to get a workout in this chapter.

Chapter 10 teaches you how to work with disk files. You'll learn how to open a file and read its contents into your program. You'll also learn how to write your program's data out to a file.

Chapter 11 is a potpourri of miscellaneous C programming issues. This chapter tries to clear up any programming loose ends. You'll learn about recursion, binary trees, and something not every C programmer knows about: C function pointers.

Chapter 12 prepares you for your next step along the programming path: the *Macintosh C Programming Primer*. You'll learn a little about what makes Macintosh programs special, as well as find out how you can write your own programs that sport that special Macintosh look and feel.

Appendix A is a glossary of the technical terms used in this book.

Appendix B contains a complete listing of all the examples used in this book. This section will come in handy as a reference as you write your own C programs. Need an example of an `if-else` statement in action? Turn to the examples in Appendix B.

Appendix C is another useful reference. It describes the syntax of each of the C statement types introduced in the book. Need an exact specification of a `switch` statement? Check out Appendix C.

Appendix D provides a description of the **Standard Library** functions introduced in this book. The Standard Library is a set of functions available as part of every standard C development environment, no matter what type of computer it's being used with. Need to know how to call one of the Standard Library functions introduced in the book? Use Appendix D.

Appendix E describes the differences between the version of CodeWarrior that came with this book and the commercial version.

Appendix F provides answers to the exercises presented at the end of each chapter.

Appendix G is a bibliography of useful programming titles.

Conventions Used in This Book

As you read this book, you'll encounter a few standard conventions intended to make it easier to read. For example, technical terms appearing for the first time are in **boldface**. You'll find most of these terms in the glossary in Appendix A.

By the Way

> Occasionally, you'll come across a block of text set off in its own little box, like this. These blocks are called *tech blocks* and are intended to add technical detail to the subject being discussed. For the most part, each tech block will fit in one of three categories: "By the Way," "Important," and "Warning." As the names imply, these blocks have different purposes. "By the Way" tech blocks are intended to be informative but not crucial. "Important" tech blocks should be read beginning to end and the information within tucked into a reasonably responsive part of your brain. "Warning" tech blocks are usually trying to caution you about a potentially disastrous programming problem you should be on the lookout for. Read and heed these warnings.

All of the source code examples in this book are presented using a special font, known as the `code font`. This font is also used for source code fragments that appear in the middle of running text. Menu items, or items you'll click on, appear in **Chicago font**.

At the end of each chapter from Chapter 4 on, you'll find a set of exercises designed to reinforce the concepts presented in that chapter. Go through each of the exercises. It will be time well spent. As mentioned earlier, Appendix F contains answers to selected chapter exercises.

Strap Yourself In . . .

That's about it. Let's get started. . . .

Chapter 2

Installing and Testing CodeWarrior Lite

Tucked into the back of this book is a CD containing a special version of Code-Warrior, one of the leading Macintosh programming environments. CodeWarrior Lite provides you with all the tools you'll need to work with the programming examples presented in the book.

Installing CodeWarrior Lite

When you insert the *Learn C* CD in your CD-ROM drive, the main *Learn C* CD window will appear on your desktop. In the center of that window is the CodeWarrior Lite Installer icon (Figure 2.1). Double-click on that icon to launch the installer.

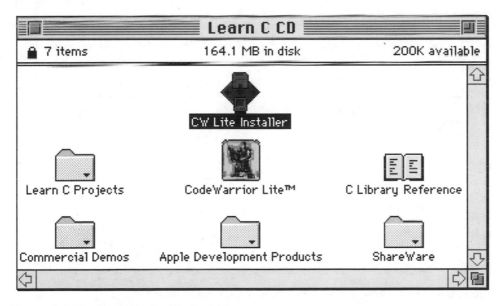

Figure 2.1 The CodeWarrior Lite Installer

By the Way

> If you already own a reasonably recent version of CodeWarrior, you may want to skip the installation of CodeWarrior Lite. If that is the case, just drag the `Learn C++ Projects` folder from the top level of the CD onto your hard drive. If you do run into problems, try removing the full CodeWarrior from your hard drive and install CodeWarrior Lite instead.

When you start the installer, the first thing you'll see is the CodeWarrior Lite information screen. Click on the **Continue** button. Next, a license agreement will appear in a scrolling window. Read the license agreement (it's *sooo* interesting); then click on the **Continue** button. This time, you'll be presented with a list of possible installation configurations (Figure 2.2). In this version of CodeWarrior, there's only one configuration, named "Standard Install," which requires about 18 megs of free hard drive space. If you've got the space, click the **Install** button. Otherwise click **Quit** and go make some room.

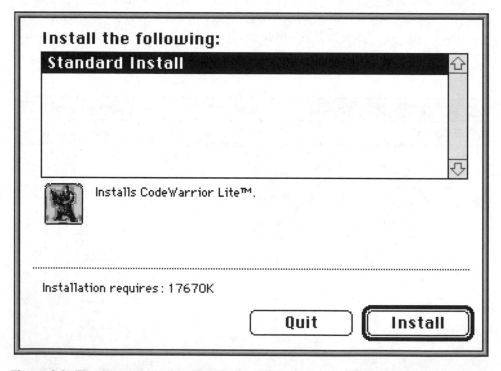

Figure 2.2 The CodeWarrior Lite installer. Do you have enough free space on your hard drive?

Figure 2.3 The 02.01 - hello folder.

After the installation is complete you will still need to do one thing: At the top level of the *Learn C* CD is a folder named Learn C Projects that contains all of the book's programs. Drag this folder from the CD onto your hard drive. Once you have done this you will no longer need the CD (although you'll want to keep it as a souvenir!).

File	Code	Data	目 🐛	
▽ **source**	0	0	• ▾	⇧
hello.c	0	0	• ▸	
▽ **libraries**	0	0	▾	
MacOS.lib	0	0	▸	
ANSI (2i) C.68K.Lib	0	0	▸	
SIOUX.68K.Lib	0	0	▸	
MathLib68K (2i).Lib	0	0	▸	
5 file(s)	0	0		

Figure 2.4 The hello.μ project window.

Testing CodeWarrior Lite

Now that CodeWarrior Lite is installed, let's take it for a spin. Open the `Learn C Projects` folder on your hard drive; then open the subfolder named `02.01 – hello`. You should see a window similar to the one shown in Figure 2.3. The two files in this window contain the ingredients you'll use to build your very first C application.

Double-click on the file `hello.μ`. A window just like the one shown in Figure 2.4 should appear. This window is called the **project window**. It contains information about the files used to build our double-clickable application. Since this information is stored in the file `hello.μ`, this file is also known as a **project file**. A file that ends in the characters `.μ` is likely a project file.

Warning

> If you got a message telling you that the document `hello.μ` could not be opened, restart your Mac and try again. If this still doesn't work, try rebuilding your desktop. To do this, restart your Mac and then press the command (⌘) and option keys simultaneously. Keep holding both keys down until the Mac asks you if you'd like to rebuild your desktop. Click on **OK** and go watch TV for a few minutes.
>
> If a window with the title `hello.c` appeared instead of the one shown in Figure 2.4, you double-clicked on the wrong file. Quit CodeWarrior and double-click on the file `hello.μ` instead of `hello.c`.

```
hello.c

#include <stdio.h>

int main( void )
{
    printf( "Hello, world!\n" );

    return 0;
}

Line: 7
```

Figure 2.5   The source code window with the source code from the file `hello.c`.

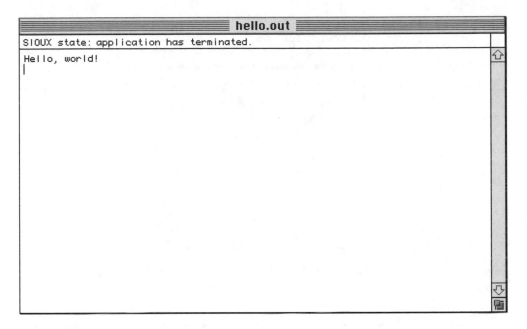

Figure 2.6 The window created by the `hello` program.

The project window in Figure 2.4 is divided into two parts, each marked by a down-pointing triangle on the extreme left side of the window. The first part (labeled `source`) names the files that contain the project **source code**. Source code is a set of instructions that determine what your application will do and when it will do it. This project contains a single source code file, named `hello.c`.

Let's take a look at the source code in `hello.c`. Double-click on the label `hello.c`, being careful not to double-click on the word `source`. A source code window will appear containing the source code in the file `hello.c` (Figure 2.5). This is your first C program. This program tells the computer to display the text "`Hello, world!`" in a window. Don't worry about the how or why of it right now. We'll get into all that later on. For now, let's turn this source code into an application.

Go to the **Project** menu and select **Run** (alternatively, you could have typed ⌘R). If you look closely, you'll see numbers appear in each row of the project window. Then, a new window, labeled `hello.out`, will appear on the screen.

Actually, this window doesn't belong to CodeWarrior. When you selected **Run** from the **Project** menu, CodeWarrior converted your source code into a double-clickable application named `hello` and then ran `hello`. The application `hello`, in turn, created the new window (Figure 2.6). Once this window appears, you know you've successfully installed CodeWarrior Lite.

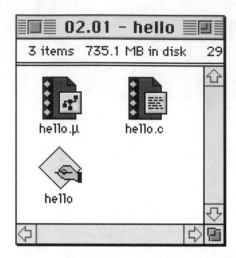

Figure 2.7 The folder 02.01 – hello, with the addition of the hello application.

Once you are done admiring your handiwork, select **Quit** from the **File** menu. You'll be asked if you want to save the results of your program. If you click on the **Save** button, the results produced by your program are saved as a text file, which you can then open by using CodeWarrior or your favorite word processor. For now, select **Don't Save** and let's move on.

Back in the Finder, take another look at the folder 02.01 – hello. Notice that there's now a third file in the folder—the application hello (Figure 2.7). Congratulations! You've just built your first C application!

What's Next?

Now that you've installed CodeWarrior, let's take a little closer look at the programming process. Get comfortable and turn the page. Here we go. . . .

Chapter 3

Programming Basics

Before we dig into the specifics of C programming, we'll spend a few minutes reviewing the basics of programming in general. We'll answer such basic questions as, Why write a computer program? and How do computer programs work? We'll look at all of the elements that come together to create a computer program, such as source code, a compiler, and the computer itself.

If you've already done some programming, skim through this chapter. If you feel comfortable with the material, skip ahead to Chapter 4. Most of the issues covered in this chapter are not specific to C.

Reasons for Programming

Why write a computer program? There are many reasons. Some programs are written in direct response to a problem too complex to solve by hand. For example, you might write a program to calculate the constant π to 5000 decimal places or to determine the precise moment to fire the boosters that will bring the space shuttle home safely.

Other programs are written as performance aids, allowing you to perform a regular task more efficiently. You might write a program to help you balance your checkbook, keep track of your baseball card collection, or lay out this month's issue of *Dinosaur Today*.

All of these examples share a common theme. All are examples of the art of programming.

Programming Languages

Your goal in reading this book is to learn how to use the C programming language to create programs of your own. Before we get into C, however, let's take a minute to look at some other popular programming languages.

Some Alternatives to C

As mentioned in Chapter 1, C is probably the most popular programming language around. There's very little you can't do in C, once you know how. On the other hand, a C program is not necessarily the best solution to every programming problem.

For example, suppose that you are trying to build a database to track your company's inventory. Rather than writing a custom C program to solve your problem, you might be able to use an off-the-shelf package, such as FileMaker Pro or 4th Dimension, to construct your database. The programmers who created these packages solved most of the knotty database management problems you'd face if you tried to write your program from scratch. The lesson here: Before you tackle a programming problem, examine all the alternatives. You might find one that will save you time or money or that will prove to be a better solution to your problem.

Some problems can be solved by using HyperCard or AppleScript. Take some time to learn about both of these products. Using HyperCard, you can very quickly put together an application (known as a stack) that features all the standard Macintosh gadgets (like buttons, checkboxes, and scroll bars). If you choose, you can customize your stack by using a programming language called **HyperTalk**. The nice thing about HyperCard is that it is very easy to use. HyperCard *does* have its limits, however. Although you might build a HyperCard stack to keep track of your business contacts or, perhaps, to track your growing wine collection, you won't be able to build a more sophisticated, general-purpose application, such as PageMaker or ClarisWorks.

Like HyperCard's HyperTalk, AppleScript is a programming language. Instead of controlling HyperCard stacks, however, AppleScript interacts with **scriptable programs.** One of the best examples of a scriptable program is the Finder. Using AppleScript, you can make the Finder do some pretty cool things. You can ask the Finder to find a specific file, to arrange all open windows just so, or even to drag the current selection to the trash (careful with that one!).

By the Way

Want to mess with AppleScript? Everything you need to do just that is on the CD in back of the book. Search for the AppleScript extension on the CD, install it in your `System folder`, and then reboot your Mac. Next, copy the Script Editor and the Scriptable Text Editor onto your hard drive. The Script Editor lets you create and run AppleScript programs. The Scriptable Text Editor makes a perfect target for your scripts.

Once you get everything installed, launch the Scriptable Text Editor and type some text into the text editing window that appears. Next, launch the Script Editor, type in this script, and click on the **Run** button:

```
tell application "Scriptable Text Editor"
     get number of words in front window
end tell
```

If all goes well, a window named the result will appear, containing the number of words in your Scriptable Text Editor window. If you are interested in learning more, there are a number of good AppleScript books out there. Personally, I like Danny Goodman's *AppleScript Handbook*.

Some applications feature their own proprietary scripting language. For instance, Microsoft Excel lets you write programs that operate on the cells within a spreadsheet. Some word processing programs let you write scripts that control just about every word processing feature in existence. Although proprietary scripting languages can be quite useful, they aren't much help outside their intended environments. You wouldn't find much use for the Excel scripting language outside Excel, for example.

What About Pascal?

There are a lot of programming languages out there. In the late 1970s and early 1980s, C's popularity was still growing, and the undisputed ruler of the programming universe was Pascal. Pascal remains an excellent programming language, but it has now fallen far behind C in popularity. To prove this to yourself, go to your favorite bookstore and compare the number of C books and Pascal books (assuming you can still find a Pascal book). Better yet, dig out the employment section from last Sunday's paper and count the number of computer ads calling for C or C++ experience (we'll get to C++ in a minute) versus those calling for Pascal experience. These two exercises should convince you that you are on the right track.

What About C++?

If there is a pretender to the programming language throne, it has to be a language called C++ (pronounced C-Plus-Plus). Simply put, C++ is an object-oriented version of C and is extremely popular with both Macintosh and Windows programmers. Someday, you will want to learn C++. Thankfully, you can learn C first, and all that C knowledge will count toward your C++ education. Learn C now and spend some time practicing your newfound craft. Once you have some C experience under your belt, make learning C++ your next priority.

The Programming Process

In Chapter 2, you installed CodeWarrior and went through the process of opening a project, converting the project's source code into a real, double-clickable application. Let's take a closer look at that process.

Writing Your Source Code

No matter what their purposes, most computer programs start as source code. Your source code will consist of a sequence of instructions that tell the computer what to do. Source code is written in a specific programming language, such as C. Each programming language has a specific set of rules defining what is and isn't "legal" in that language.

Your mission in reading this book is to learn how to create useful, efficient, and, best of all, legal C source code.

If you were using everyday English to program, your source code might look like this:

```
Hi, Computer!
Do me a favor. Ask me for five numbers, add them together,
then tell me the sum.
```

If you wanted to run this program, you'd need a programming tool that understood source code written in English. Since CodeWarrior doesn't understand English but does understand C, let's look at a C program that does the same thing:

```c
int main( void )
{
    int    index, num, sum;

    sum = 0;

    for ( index=1; index<=5; index++ )
    {
        printf( "Enter number %d --->", index );
        scanf( "%d", &num );
        sum = sum + num;
    }

    printf( "The sum of these numbers is %d.", sum );
```

```
    return 0;
}
```

If this program doesn't mean anything to you, don't panic. Just keep reading. By the time you finish reading this book, you'll be writing C code like a pro.

Compiling Your Source Code

Once your source code is written, your next job is to hand it off to a **compiler**. The compiler translates your C source code into instructions that make sense to your computer. These instructions are known as **machine language,** or **object code**. Source code is for you, machine language/object code is for your computer.

CodeWarrior uses the project file to keep track of all your source and object code. As an example, the project file shown in Figure 3.1 contains the names of three files. The first two files contain C source code. The third file, known as a **library**, contains object code. Think of a library as a source code file that has already been compiled.

A library starts life as source code. The source code is compiled and the resulting object code stored in a file. This object code can then be included in other projects. By using a library, you get access to some useful source code without having to go through the time and effort of recompiling the source code into object code.

When you ask CodeWarrior to run your project, CodeWarrior steps through each of the files referenced by your project file (Figure 3.2). If a file contains source code, the source code is sent to a compiler, and the resulting object code is copied into the project file. If the file is a library, the compilation step is skipped, and the library's object code is copied into the project file. Once all the object code is in place, it gets combined (in a process known as **linking**) and copied into your application file. Finally, CodeWarrior runs your application.

If the compilation process seems confusing to you, don't worry. Each programming example comes complete with step-by-step directions that show you how to compile your code. Once you feel more comfortable with the programming process, give this section another read.

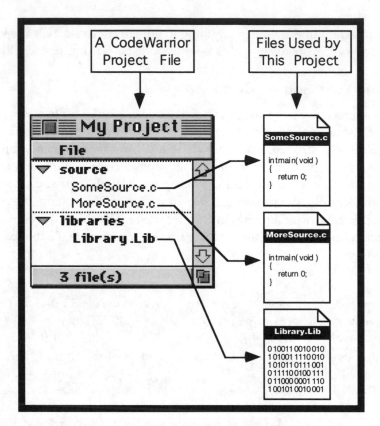

Figure 3.1 A CodeWarrior project file containing three files.

Let's take a look at a real-life example. In Chapter 2, you opened a project file named hello.μ. Figure 3.3 shows the hello.μ project window. The project window lists all the files that CodeWarrior uses to build the hello application. Notice that the list is divided into two parts. The top part lists the project's source code files (there's only one), and the lower part lists the project's libraries (there are four).

Each of the five files listed in the project window is found on your hard drive. You'll find the file hello.c in the same folder as the project file (hello.μ). The four library files are located with the rest of the CodeWarrior files, in various subfolders of the folder named Libraries ƒ. To convince yourself of this, use the Finder's **Find** command to search for these libraries on your hard drive. They were copied onto your hard drive when you installed CodeWarrior.

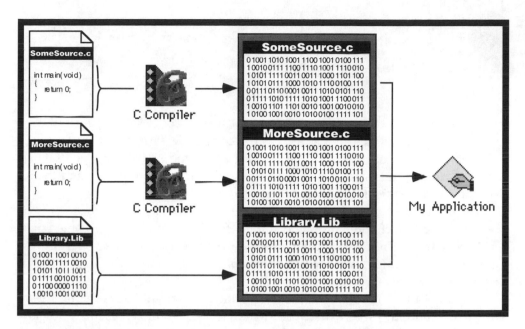

Figure 3.2 CodeWarrior sends source code through a compiler to generate object code, then copies the object code into the project file. Object code from libraries bypasses the compilation step.

File	Code	Data		
▽ **source**	**0**	**0**	•	▼
hello.c	0	0	•	▶
▽ **libraries**	**0**	**0**		▼
MacOS.lib	0	0		▶
ANSI (2i) C.68K.Lib	0	0		▶
SIOUX.68K.Lib	0	0		▶
MathLib68K (2i).Lib	0	0		▶
5 file(s)	**0**	**0**		

hello.μ

Figure 3.3 The `hello.μ` project window, before compilation.

Warning

> When you find the libraries, don't move them or mess with them in any way. CodeWarrior knows where these libraries live and won't be able to run your project if it can't find them.

When you select **Run** from the **Project** menu, CodeWarrior steps through each of the project's files. In the case of `hello.c`, CodeWarrior first checks to see whether `hello.c` has been modified since the last time it was compiled. If it has, the source code in `hello.c` is passed to CodeWarrior's C compiler, and the resulting object code is stored in the file `hello.`μ.

In the case of each of the four libraries, CodeWarrior first checks to see whether the object code from the library file has already been copied into `hello.`μ. If it has not been copied, the object code gets copied over. This process is known as **loading**. Source code gets compiled and libraries get loaded (insert silly drinking reference here).

Figure 3.4 is a snapshot of the project window after all the project files were updated. Notice that where there used to be a solid block of zeroes, there are now all kinds of numbers. The `Code` column tells you how much object code is stored in `hello.`μ for each file in the project. For example, the object code for the file `hello.c` is 28 bytes long, and the object code for the library `MacOS.lib` is 31,554

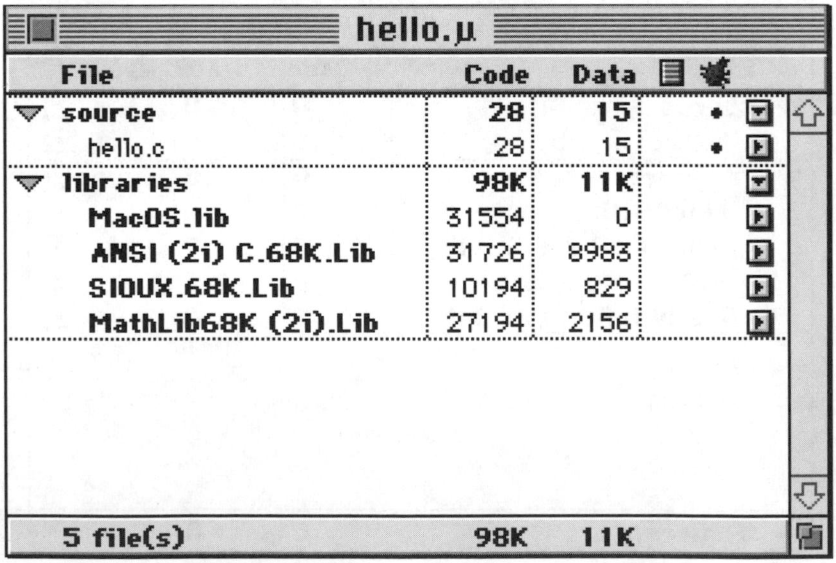

File	Code	Data		
▽ **source**	28	15	•	▾
hello.c	28	15	•	▸
▽ **libraries**	98K	11K		▾
MacOS.lib	31554	0		▸
ANSI (2i) C.68K.Lib	31726	8983		▸
SIOUX.68K.Lib	10194	829		▸
MathLib68K (2i).Lib	27194	2156		▸
5 file(s)	**98K**	**11K**		

(window title: hello.μ)

Figure 3.4 The updated project window.

bytes long. Why such a big difference? The source code in `hello.c` is tiny. As you get farther along in the book, watch that number start to climb!

By the Way

> You'll find these same four libraries in every one of the programs in this book. Together, these libraries contain everything needed to create the window that appears every time you run one of the book's programs.

The row labeled `source` summarizes the numbers for all the source code in the project. The row labeled `libraries` summarizes the numbers for the project libraries. If you add the code sizes for all four libraries, you'll get the number 100,668. So where does the number 98K come from? One kilobyte, or 1K, is equal to 1024 bytes; 100,668 divided by 1024 is approximately 98.3. Roughly speaking, 100,668 bytes is around 98K.

As the compiler goes through your source code, it sets aside certain pieces of your source code as data. For example, the text string "Hello, world!\n" is stored in the project file as data, not as part of the object code. As you can see in Figure 3.4, this string takes up 15 bytes of memory (look in the column labeled `Data`). You'll learn all about text strings later in the book.

By the Way

> Since CodeWarrior stores the object code inside the project file on your hard drive, your project files will take up more room with a compiled program than with an uncompiled program. To save space, select **Remove Binaries** from the **Project** menu when you are done with a project. This item tells CodeWarrior to delete any object code it may have stored in the project file. Don't worry; **Remove Binaries** won't affect your source code. It'll just slim down your project file.

Flavors of Object Code

Just as there are many different programming languages, there are many different flavors of object code. In order for your application to run, the object code it was built on must be compatible with the **central processing unit** (also known as the **CPU,** or **processor**), which is the brains of your computer.

IBM PCs and PC-compatibles use processors built by Intel. These processors include the 8086, 80286, 80386, 80486, and the infamous Pentium. Macintosh computers are based on processors from Motorola. These include the 68000, 68020, 68030, 68040, and the PowerPC 601 and 604.

By the Way

Actually, the PowerPC is a joint production, brought to you by Apple, IBM, and Motorola.

Each of these processors understands a specific set of machine language instructions. The 68000 understands 68000 machine language instructions but not 80486 machine language instructions. Similarly, the 80486 does not understand 68000 machine language instructions. That's one reason why you can't just copy a Windows application onto your Mac hard drive and run it. It's also one reason why you can't copy a Mac application onto a Windows machine and run it.

When it introduced the 68020 processor, Motorola started with the 68000 machine language, then added a few new instructions to it. This meant that the 68020 could understand every single instruction in the 68000 machine language. More important, this meant that if a program was compiled into 68000 machine language, it would also run on a 68020.

As Motorola designed each new processor, it stuck with this strategy. The 68030 machine language is a superset of the 68020 (and therefore of the 68000) machine language. The 68040 is a superset of the 68030 machine language. (We'll get to the PowerPC in a minute.)

This means that a program compiled into 68000 machine language can be run by any of the later 68000 family of processors. This concept is known as **backward compatibility**. It's important to note that the reverse is not necessarily true, however. For example, a program compiled into 68040 machine language might contain 68040 instructions that weren't part of the 68000 machine language; therefore, the program wouldn't run on a 68000.

The PowerPC adds a new wrinkle to this situation. When they designed the PowerPC, the Apple, IBM, and Motorola consortium started from scratch. The PowerPC 601 processor has a brand-spanking-new machine language, in no way related to the 68000-series machine language. Fortunately, Apple's remained committed to the concept of backward compatibility. Built into every PowerPC-based Mac is something called the **68000 emulator**. If you run an application built from 68000 object code on a PowerMac, the 68000 emulator translates the 68000 instructions into PowerPC instructions *while the program is running*.

Unfortunately, this translation process does take time, which is why 68000-based programs run slower on a PowerMac than programs compiled using PowerPC object code.

A program compiled into PowerPC machine language and running on a PowerPC is said to be running in **native mode**. Native mode programs run screamingly fast!

As you start writing your own applications, you'll have a few choices to make. Which object code should you base your applications on? If you generate 68000-based applications, they'll run on all Macs, but they'll run slower on the PowerMacs. If you generate PowerPC-native applications, they'll run only on the PowerMacs.

Fortunately, there are several solutions to this dilemma. One solution is to generate two versions of your application: one 68000-based and the other PowerPC-based. Deliver both versions and let your user choose the one that's right. A second solution is to create what's known as a **fat binary**, or **fat application**. A fat binary is an application that contains both 68000 and PowerPC machine language. When you run a fat binary, the Macintosh operating system is smart enough to run the object code that makes sense for the machine you are on. The downside of this approach is that your applications tend to take up a lot more disk space than their skinny counterparts.

What's Next?

At this point, don't worry too much about the details. Although CodeWarrior can easily generate both PowerPC and 68000 object code, the projects on the CD were set up to build 68000-based applications, guaranteeing that they will run on your computer. For now, focus on the basics. Understanding how to write C source code is far more important than the intricacies of the project file.

Ready to get into some source code? Get out your programming gloves; we're about to go to code!

Chapter 4

C Basics: Functions

Every programming language is designed to follow strict rules that define the language's source code structure. The C programming language is no different. The next few chapters will explore the syntax of C.

Chapter 3 discussed some fundamental programming topics, including the process of translating source code into machine code through a tool called the compiler. This chapter focuses on one of the primary building blocks of C programming, the **function**.

C Functions

C programs are made up of functions. A function is a chunk of source code that accomplishes a specific task. You might write a function that adds a list of numbers or that calculates the radius of a given circle. Here's an example of a function:

```c
int main( void )
{
    printf( "I am a function and my name is main!!!\n" );

    return 0;
}
```

This function, called `main()`, prints a message in a window.

Important

> Throughout this book, we'll refer to a function by placing a pair of parentheses after its name. This will help distinguish between function names and variable names. For example, `doTask()` refers to a function, whereas the name `doTask` refers to a variable. Variables are covered in Chapter 5.

The Function Definition

Functions start off with a **function specifier**, in this case:

```
int main( void )
```

A function specifier consists of a **return type**, the function name, and a pair of parentheses wrapped around a **parameter list**. We'll talk about the return type and the parameter list later. For now, the important thing is to be able to recognize a function specifier and be able to pick out the function's name from within the specifier.

Following the specifier comes the body of the function. The body is always placed between a pair of curly braces: { }. These braces are known in programming circles as "left-curly" and "right-curly." Here's the body of main():

```
{
    printf( "I am a function and my name is main!!!\n" );

    return 0;
}
```

The body of a function consists of a series of **statement**s, with each statement followed by a semicolon (;). If you think of a computer program as a detailed set of instructions for your computer, a statement is one specific instruction. The printf() featured in the body of main() is a statement. It instructs the computer to display some text on the screen.

As you make your way through this book, you'll learn C's rules for creating efficient, compilable statements. Creating efficient statements will make your programs run faster with less chance of error. The more you learn about programming (and the more time you spend at your craft), the more efficient you'll make your code.

Syntax Errors and Algorithms

When you ask the compiler to compile your source code, the compiler does its best to translate your source code into object code. Every so often, however, the compiler will hit a line of source code that it just doesn't understand. When this happens, the compiler reports the problem to you and does not complete the compile. The compiler will not let you run your program until every line of source code compiles.

As you learn C, you'll find yourself making two types of mistakes. The simplest type, called a **syntax error**, prevents the program from compiling. The syntax of a language is the set of rules that determines what will and will not be read by the compiler. Many syntax errors are the result of a mistyped letter, or **typo**. Another common syntax error occurs when you forget the semicolon at the end of a statement.

Syntax errors are usually fairly easy to fix. If the compiler doesn't tell you exactly what you need to fix, it will usually tell you where in your code the syntax error occurred and give you enough information to spot and repair the error.

The second type of mistake is a flaw in your program's **algorithm**. An algorithm is the approach used to solve a problem. You use algorithms all the time. For example, here's an algorithm for sorting your mail:

1. Start by taking the mail out of the mailbox.

2. If there's no mail, you're done! Go watch TV.

3. Take a piece of mail out of the pile.

4. If it's junk mail, throw it away; then go back to step 2.

5. If it's a bill, put it with the other bills; then go back to step 2.

6. If it's not a bill and not junk mail, read it; then go back to step 2.

This algorithm completely describes the process of sorting through your mail. Notice that the algorithm works, even if you didn't get any mail. Notice also that the algorithm always ends up at step 2, with the TV on.

Figure 4.1 is a pictorial representation, or flowchart, of the mail-sorting algorithm. Much as you might use an outline to prepare for writing an essay or a term paper,

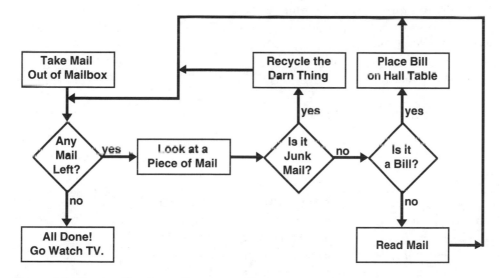

Figure 4.1 An algorithm for sorting your mail.

you might use a flowchart to flesh out a program's algorithm before you start writing the program.

This flowchart uses two types of boxes. Each rectangular box portrays an action, such as taking mail out of the mailbox or throwing junk mail into the trash. Each diamond-shaped box poses a yes/no question. An action box has a single arrow leading from it to the next box to read, once you've finished taking the appropriate action. A question box has two arrows leading out of it: one showing the path to take if the answer to the question is yes and the other showing the path to take if the answer is no. Follow the flowchart through, comparing it to the algorithm as described.

In the C world, a well-designed algorithm results in a well-behaved program. On the other hand, a poorly designed algorithm can lead to unpredictable results. Suppose, for example, that you wanted to write a program that added three numbers and printed the sum at the end. If you accidentally printed one of the numbers instead of the sum of the numbers, your program would still compile and run. The result of the program would be in error, however (you printed one of the numbers instead of the sum), because of a flaw in your program's algorithm.

The efficiency of your source code, referred to earlier, is a direct result of good algorithm design. Keep the concept of algorithm in mind as you work your way through the examples in the book.

Calling a Function

In Chapter 2, you ran `hello`, a program with a single function, `main()`. As a refresher, here's the source code from `hello`:

```c
#include <stdio.h>

int main( void )
{
    printf( "Hello, world!\n" );

    return 0;
}
```

You ran `hello` by selecting **Run** from the **Project** menu. CodeWarrior started by executing the first line in the function named `main()`. In this case, the first line in `main()` was the **call** to the function `printf()`. Whenever your source code calls a function, each statement in the called function is executed before the next statement of the calling function is executed.

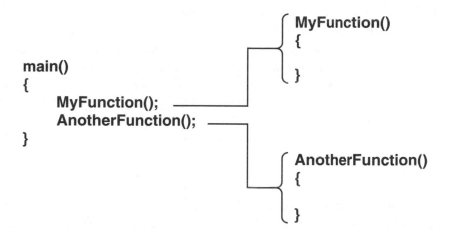

Figure 4.2 When `main()` calls `MyFunction()`, all of the statements inside `MyFunction()` get executed before `main()` calls `AnotherFunction()`.

Confused? Look at Figure 4.2. In this example, `main()` starts with a call to the function `MyFunction()`. This call to `MyFunction()` will cause each statement inside `MyFunction()` to be executed. Once the last statement in `MyFunction()` has been executed, control is returned to `main()`. Now, `main()` can call `AnotherFunction()`.

Every C program you write will have a `main()` function. Your program will start running with the first line in `main()` and, unless something unusual happens, end with the last line in `main()`. Along the way, `main()` may call other functions, which may, in turn, call other functions, and so on.

ISO C and the Standard Library

The American National Standards Institute (ANSI) established a national standard for the C programming language. This standard became known as **ANSI C**. Later, the International Standards Organization (ISO) adopted this standard, and ANSI C evolved into the international standard known as **ISO C**. Part of this standard is a specific definition of the syntax of the C language.

By the Way

Since the term ISO C is still catching on, you'll still hear most C programmers refer to the ANSI C standard. The main difference between the two standards is that ISO C has extra functions in its Standard Library to handle multibyte and wide characters. ISO C or ANSI C—either term is fine. The important thing to be aware of is that a strict C standard does exist.

As we stated earlier, the syntax of a language provides a set of rules defining what is and isn't legal source code. For example, ISO C tells you when you can and can't use a semicolon. ISO C tells you to use a pair of parentheses after the name of your function, regardless of whether your function has any parameters. You get the idea. The greatest benefit to having an international standard for C is portability. With a minimum of tinkering, you can get an ISO C program written on one computer up and running on another computer. When you finish with this book, you'll be able to program in C on any computer that has an ISO C compiler.

Another part of the ISO C standard is the Standard Library, a set of functions available to every ISO C programmer. As you may have guessed, the `printf()` function you've seen in our source code examples is part of the Standard Library. Take another look at the `hello.`μ project window from Chapter 2 (Figure 4.3). In the libraries section, the file `ANSI (2i) C.68K.Lib` contains the Standard Library. Remember, when you see ANSI, think ISO!

We'll spend a great deal of time working with the Standard Library in this book. Once you get comfortable with the Standard Library functions presented here, check out the C Library Reference on the *Learn C* CD. Spend some time going through each of the Standard Library functions to get a sense of the variety of functions offered.

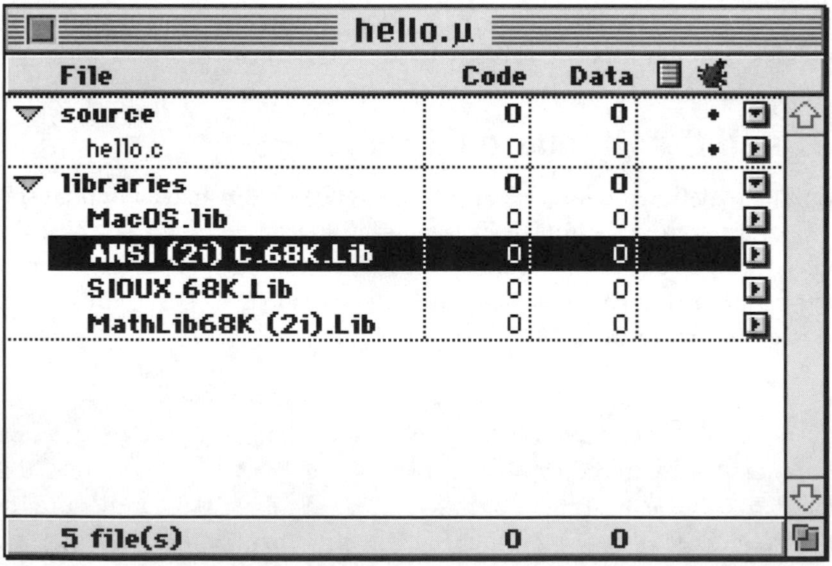

Figure 4.3 The `hello.`μ project window, with the Standard Library highlighted.

Same Program, Two Functions

As you start writing your own programs, you'll find yourself designing many in-dividual functions. You might need a function that puts a form up on the screen for the user to fill out. You might need a function that takes a list of numbers as input, providing the average of those numbers in return. Whatever your needs, you will definitely be creating a lot of functions. Let's see how it's done.

Our first program, `hello`, consisted of a single function, `main()`, that passed the text string `"Hello, world!\n"` to `printf()`. Our second program, `hello2`, captures that functionality in a new function, called `SayHello()`.

> You've probably been wondering why the characters \n keep appearing at the end of all our text strings. Don't worry; there's nothing wrong with your copy of the book. The \n is perfectly normal. It tells `printf()` to move the cursor to the beginning of the next line in the text window, sort of like press-ing the return key in a text editor.
>
> The sequence \n is frequently referred to as a carriage return, or just plain return. By including a return at the end of a `printf()`, we know that the next line we print will appear at the beginning of the next line in the text window.

Opening `hello2.µ`

In the Finder, open the `Learn C Projects` folder, open the subfolder named `04.01 - hello2`, and double-click on the project file `hello2.µ`. A project win-dow named `hello2.π` will appear, as shown in Figure 4.4. If you double-click on the name `hello2.c` in the project window, a source code editing window will ap-pear, containing source code remarkably similar to this:

```
#include <stdio.h>


void SayHello( void );


int main( void )
{
    SayHello();
```

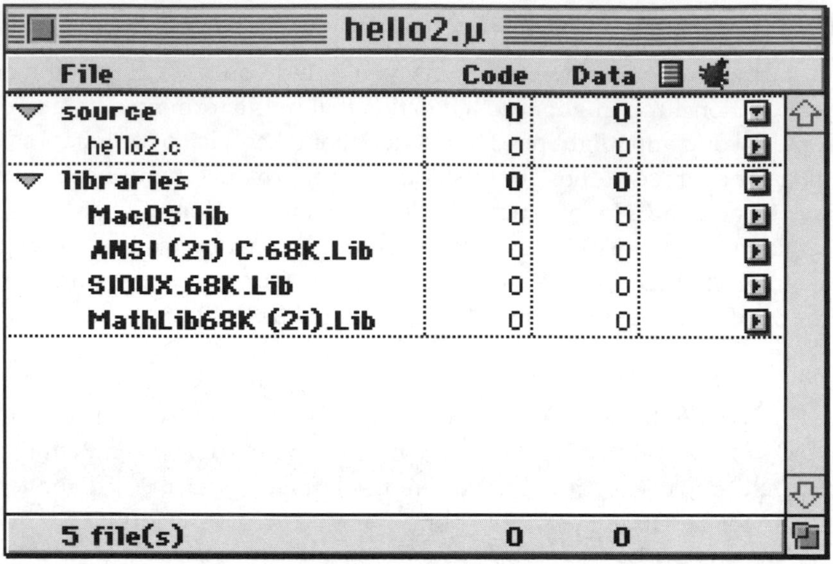

Figure 4.4 The project window for hello.μ.

```
    return 0;
}


void SayHello( void )
{
    printf( "Hello, world!\n" );
}
```

hello2 starts off with this line of source code:

```
#include <stdio.h>
```

You'll find this line (or a slight variation) at the beginning of each one of the programs in this book. It tells the compiler to include the source code from the file stdio.h as it compiles hello2.c. The file stdio.h contains information we'll need if we are going to call printf() in this source code file. You'll see the #include (pronounced pound-include) mechanism used throughout this book, and we'll talk about it in detail later. For now, get used to seeing this line of code at the top of each of our source code files.

The two lines following the #include are blank. This is completely cool. Since the C compiler ignores all blank lines, you can use them to make your code a little more readable. I like to leave a few blank lines (at least) between each of my functions.

This line of code appears next:

```
void SayHello( void );
```

Although this line might look like a function specifier, don't be fooled! If this were a function specifier, it would not end with a semicolon, and it would be followed by a left-curly brace ({) and the rest of the function. This line is known as a **function prototype,** or **function declaration**. You'll include a function prototype for every function, other than main(), in your source code file.

To understand why, it helps to know that a compiler reads your source code file from the beginning to the end, a line at a time. By placing a complete list of function prototypes at the beginning of the file, you give the compiler a preview of the functions it is about to compile. The compiler uses this information to make sure that calls to these functions are made correctly.

By the Way

This will make a lot more sense to you once we get into the subject of parameters in Chapter 7. For now, get used to seeing function prototypes at the beginning of all your source code files.

Next comes the function main(). main() first calls the function SayHello():

```
int main( void )
{
    SayHello();
```

At this point, the lines of the function SayHello() get run. When SayHello() is finished, main() can move on to its next line of code. The keyword return tells the compiler to return from the current function, without executing the remainder of the function. We'll talk about return in Chapter 7. Until then, the only place you'll see this line is at the end of main().

```
    return 0;
}
```

Following `main()` is another pair of blank lines, followed by the function `SayHello()`. `SayHello()` prints the string "`Hello, world!`" in a window, then returns control to `main()`.

```
void SayHello( void )
{
    printf( "Hello, world!\n" );
}
```

Let's step back for a second and compare `hello` to `hello2`. In `hello`, `main()` called `printf()` directly. In `hello2`, `main()` calls a function that calls `printf()`. This extra layer demonstrates a basic C programming technique: taking code from one function and using it to create a new function. This example took the following line of code and used it to create a new function called `SayHello()`:

```
printf( "Hello, world!\n" );
```

This function is now available for use by the rest of the program. Every time we call the function `SayHello()`, it's as if we executed the following line of code:

```
printf( "Hello, world!\n" );
```

`SayHello()` may be a simple function, but it demonstrates an important concept. Wrapping a chunk of code in a single function is a powerful technique. Suppose that you create an extremely complex function, say, 100 lines of code in length. Now suppose that you call this function in five different places in your program. With 100 lines of code, plus the five function calls, you are essentially achieving 500 lines of functionality. That's a pretty good return on your investment!

Let's watch `hello2` in action.

Running `hello2.`μ

Select **Run** from the **Project** menu. You'll see a window similar to the one shown in Figure 4.5. Gee, this looks just like the output from Chapter 2's `hello` program. Of course, that was the point! Even though we embedded our `printf()` inside the function `SayHello()`, `hello2` ran the same as `hello`. Select **Quit** from the **File** menu to exit `hello2`.

Before we move on to our next program, let's get a little terminology out of the way. The window that appeared when you ran `hello` and `hello2` is known as a

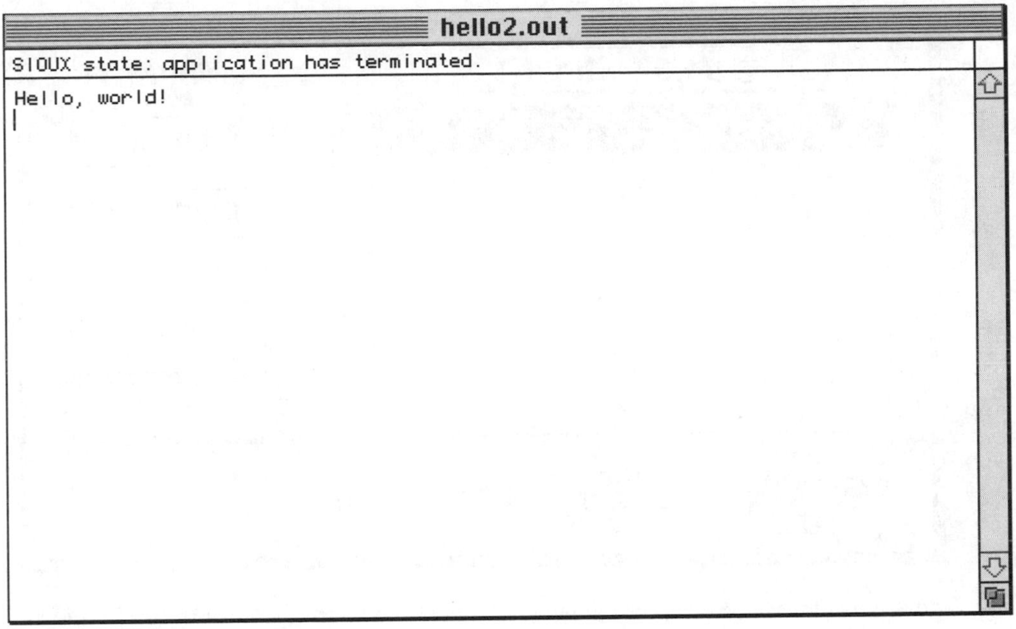

```
                        hello2.out

SIOUX state: application has terminated.

Hello, world!
```

Figure 4.5 The output from `hello2`.

console window. The console window appears whenever you call a function like `printf()`, that is, a routine that tries to display some text. The console window is one of the benefits you get by using the Standard Library. All the programs in this book take advantage of the console window.

The text that appears in the console window is known as **output**. After you run a program, you're likely to check out the output that appears in the console to make sure that your program ran correctly.

Another Example

Imagine what would happen if you changed `main()` in `hello2` to read:

```
int main( void )
{
    SayHello();
    SayHello();
    SayHello();

    return 0;
}
```

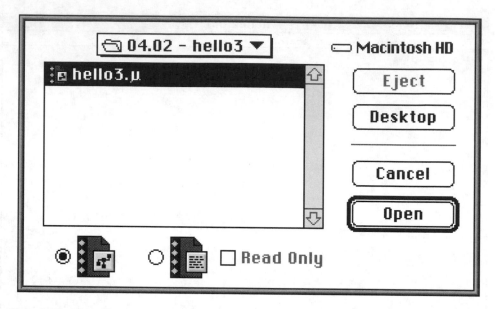

Figure 4.6 This window appears when you select **Open** from CodeWarrior's **File** menu.

What's different? In this version, we've added two more calls to SayHello().
Can you picture what the console will look like after we run this new version?

To find out, close the hello2.μ project window and then select **Open** from
CodeWarrior's **File** menu. When the window shown in Figure 4.6 appears, navigate
into the folder named 04.02 - hello3 and open the project named hello3.μ.

When you run hello3, the console window shown in Figure 4.7 will appear.
Take a look at the output. Does it make sense to you? Each call to SayHello()
generates the text string "Hello, world!" followed by a carriage return.

Once you're done staring at the console window, select **Quit** from the **File**
menu and quit hello3. Note that you are quitting hello3 and not CodeWarrior.

Generating Some Errors

Before we move on to the next chapter, let's see how the compiler responds to errors in our source code. Back in CodeWarrior, double-click on the name hello3.c
in the hello3.μ project window (Figure 4.8). The source code window containing the hello3.c source code will appear.

In the source code window, find the line of source code containing the function
specifier for main(). The line should read:

```
int main( void )
```

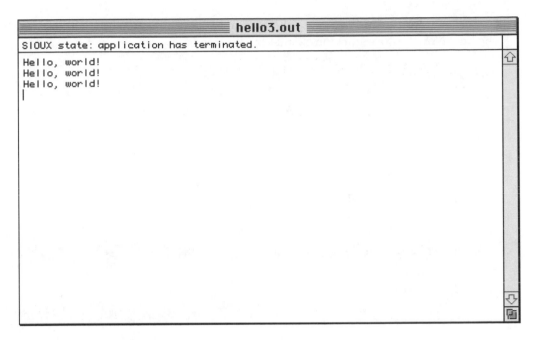

Figure 4.7 The output from hello3.

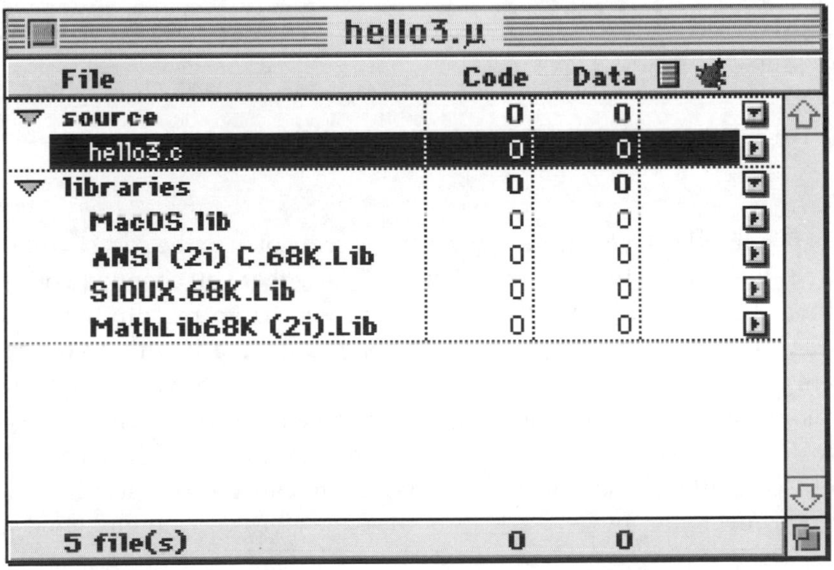

Figure 4.8 The hello3.μ project window, with the source code file hello3.c highlighted.

Click at the end of the line, so the blinking cursor appears at the very end of the line. Now type a semicolon, so that the line reads:

```
int main( void );
```

Here's the entire file, showing the tiny change you just made:

```
#include <stdio.h>


void SayHello( void );


int main( void );
{
    SayHello();
    SayHello();
    SayHello();

    return 0;
}


void SayHello( void )
{
    printf( "Hello, world!\n" );
}
```

Keep in mind that you added only a single semicolon to the source code; select **Run** from the **Project** menu. CodeWarrior knows that you changed your source code since the last time it was compiled and will try to recompile hello3.c. Figure 4.9 shows the error window that appears, telling you that you've got a problem with your source code. Yikes! All that, just because you added a measly semicolon! Sometimes, the compiler will give you a perfectly precise message that exactly describes the error it encountered. In this case, however, the compiler got so confused by the extra semicolon that it reported six errors instead of just one. Notice, however, that the very first error message gives you a pretty good idea of

GENERATING SOME ERRORS

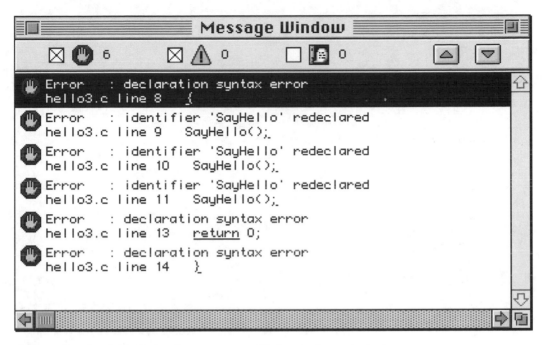

Figure 4.9 Yikes! All this just because you added a single semicolon!

what is going on. It complains about a syntax error on line 8 and then displays a left-curly brace ({). If you click on the line you just modified, then look at the bottom of the source code window, you'll see that the line you added the semicolon to is line 7 and that the very next line (line 8) contains the left-curly brace in question.

Use the mouse and the delete key to delete the offending semicolon at the end of the first line of code. Select **Run** from the **Project** menu again. This time, the code should compile without a hitch. Once the code is compiled, CodeWarrior will run it, proving that your source code is now fixed.

The Importance of Case in C

Many types of errors are possible in C programming. One of the most common results from the fact that C is a **case-sensitive** language. In a case-sensitive language, there is a big difference between lower- and uppercase letters. This means that you can't refer to printf() as Printf() or even PRINTF(). Figure 4.10 shows the error message you'll get if you change your printf() call to PRINTF(). This message is telling you that CodeWarrior couldn't find a function named PRINTF(). To fix this problem, just change PRINTF() to printf() and recompile.

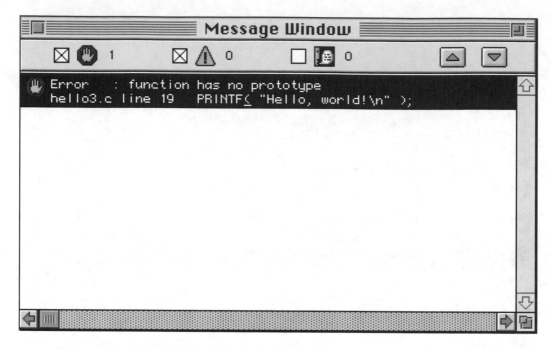

Figure 4.10 The error reported by CodeWarrior for use of incorrect case in call to `printf()`.

What's Next?

Congratulations! You've made it through basic training. You know how to open a project, how to compile your code, and even how to create an error message or two. You've learned about the most important function: `main()`. You've also learned about `printf()` and the Standard Library.

Now you're ready to dig into the stuff that gives a C program life: variables and operators.

Exercises

Open the project `hello2.µ`, edit `hello2.c` as described in each exercise, and describe the error that results:

1. Change the line:

   `SayHello()`

   to say:

   `SayHello(`

2. Change things back. Now change the line:

```
main()
```

to say:

```
Main()
```

3. Change things back. Now delete the { after the line:

```
main()
```

4. Change things back. Now delete the semicolon at the end of this line:

```
printf("Hello, world!\n");
```

so it reads:

```
printf("Hello, world!\n")
```

Chapter **5**

C Basics: Variables and Operators

At this point, you should feel pretty comfortable with the CodeWarrior environment. You should know how to open a project and how to edit a project's source code. You should also feel comfortable running a project and (heaven forbid) fixing any syntax errors that may have occurred along the way.

On the programming side, you should recognize a function when you see one. When you think of a function, you should first think of `main()`, the most important function. You should remember that functions are made up of statements, each of which is followed by a semicolon.

With these things in mind, we're ready to explore the foundation of C programming: **variables** and **operators**. Variables and operators are the building blocks you'll use to construct your program's statements.

An Introduction to Variables

A large part of the programming process involves working with data. You might need to add a column of numbers or sort a list of names alphabetically. The tricky part of this process is representing your data in a program. This is where variables come in.

Variables can be thought of as containers for your program's data. Imagine three containers on a table. Each container has a label: `cup1`, `cup2`, and `cup3`. Now imagine that you have three pieces of paper. Write a number on each piece of paper and place one piece inside each of the three containers. Figure 5.1 shows what this might look like.

Now imagine asking a friend to reach into the three cups, pull out the number in each one, and add the three values. You can ask your friend to place the sum of the three values in a fourth container created just for this purpose. The fourth container is labeled `sum` and is shown in Figure 5.2.

This is exactly how variables work. Variables are containers for your program's data. You create a variable and place a value in it. You then ask the computer to do something with the value in your variable. You can ask the computer

Figure 5.1 Three containers, each with its own value.

to add three variables and place the result in a fourth variable. You can even ask the computer to take the value in a variable, multiply it by 2, and place the result back into the original variable.

Getting back to our example, now imagine that you changed the values in cup1, cup2, and cup3. Once again, you could call on your friend to add the three values, updating the value in the container sum. You've reused the same variables, using the same formula, to achieve a different result. Here's the C version of this formula:

```
sum = cup1 + cup2 + cup3;
```

Every time you execute this line of source code, you place the sum of the variables cup1, cup2, and cup3 into the variable named sum. At this point, it's not important to understand exactly how this line of C source code works. What is important is to understand the basic idea behind variables. Each variable in your program is like a container with a value in it. This chapter will teach you how to create variables and how to place a value in a variable.

Figure 5.2 A fourth container, containing the sum of the other three containers.

Working with Variables

Variables come in a variety **types**. A variable's type determines the kind of data that can be stored in that variable. You determine a variable's type when you create the variable. (We'll discuss creating variables in just a second.) Some variable types are useful for working with numbers. Other variable types are designed to work with text. In this chapter, we'll work only with variables of one type: a numerical type called `int`. (In Chapter 8, we'll get into other variable types.) A variable of type `int` can hold a numerical value, such as 27 or –589.

Working with variables is a two-stage process. First, you create a variable; then you use the variable. In C, you create a variable by **declaring** it. Declaring a variable tells the compiler, "Create a variable for me. I need a container to place a piece of data in." When you declare a variable, you have to specify both the variable's type and its name. In our earlier example, we created four containers, each having a label. In the C world, this would be the same as creating four variables with the names `cup1`, `cup2`, `cup3`, and `sum`. In C, if we want to use the value stored in a variable, we use the variable's name. We'll show you how to do this later in the chapter.

Here's an example of a variable declaration:

```
int    myVariable;
```

This declaration tells the compiler to create a variable of type `int` (remember, an `int` is useful for working with numbers) with the name `myVariable`. The type of the variable (in this case, `int`) is extremely important. As you'll see, a variable type determines the kind and range of values a variable can be assigned.

Variable Names

Here are two rules to follow when you create your own variable names:

- Variable names must always start with an upper- or lowercase letter (A, B, . . . , Z or a, b, . . . , z) or with an underscore (_).

- The remainder of the variable name must be made up of upper- or lowercase letters, numbers (0, 1, . . . , 9), or the underscore.

These two rules yield such variable names as `myVariable`, `THIS_NUMBER`, `VaRiAbLe_1`, and `A1234_4321`. Note that a C variable may never include a space or a character such as & or *. These two rules *must* be followed.

On the other hand, these rules do leave a fair amount of room for inventiveness. Over the years, different groups of programmers came up with additional guidelines (also known as **conventions**) that made variable names more consistent and a bit easier to read.

As an example of this, UNIX programmers tended to use all lowercase letters in their variable names. When a variable name consisted of more than one word, the words were separated by an underscore. This yielded variable names like `my_variable` or `number_of_puppies`.

Macintosh programmers tend to follow a naming convention established by their SmallTalk cousins. We'll use this convention throughout the book:

- We'll form our variable names from lowercase letters and numbers, always starting with a lowercase letter. This yields variable names like `number` or `digit33`.

- When we create a variable with more than one word, we'll start the variable name with a lowercase letter and each successive word in the variable name with an uppercase letter. This yields variable names like `myVariable` or `howMany`.

As mentioned in Chapter 4, C is a case-sensitive language. The compiler will cough out an error if you sometimes refer to `myVariable` and other times refer to `myvariable`. Adopt a naming convention and stick with it: Be consistent!

The Size of a Type

When you declare a variable, the compiler reserves a section of memory for the exclusive use of that variable. When you assign a value to a variable, you are modifying the variable's dedicated memory to reflect that value. The number of bytes assigned to a variable is determined by the variable's type. You should check your compiler's documentation to see how many bytes go along with each of the standard C types.

Some Macintosh compilers assign 2 bytes to each `int`. Others assign 4 bytes to each `int`. By default, CodeWarrior uses 2-byte `int`s.

Warning

> It's important to understand that the size of a type can change, depending on such factors as your computer's processor type and operating system (MacOS versus Windows, for example) and your development environment. Remember, read the manual that comes with your compiler.

Let's continue with the assumption that CodeWarrior is using 2-byte `ints`. The following variable declaration reserves memory (in our case, 2 bytes) for the exclusive use of the variable `myInt`:

```
int    myInt;
```

If you later assign a value to `myInt`, that value is stored in the 2 bytes allocated for `myInt`. If you ever refer to the value of `myInt`, you'll be referring to the value stored in `myInt`'s 2 bytes.

If your compiler used 4-byte `ints`, the preceding declaration would allocate 4 bytes of memory for the exclusive use of `myInt`. As you'll see, it is important to know the size of the each type you are dealing with.

Why is the size of a type important? The size of a type determines the range of values that the type can handle. As you might expect, a type that's 4 bytes in size can hold a wider range of values than a type that's only 1 byte in size.

Bytes and Bits

Each byte of computer memory is made up of 8 **bits**. Each bit has a value of either 1 or 0. Figure 5.3 shows a byte holding the value `00101011`. The value `00101011` is said to be the **binary** representation of the value of the byte. Look more closely at Figure 5.3. Each bit is numbered (above each bit in the figure), with bit 0 on the extreme right side and bit 7 on the extreme left. Most computers use this standard bit-numbering scheme.

Notice also the labels ("Add 1," "Add 2," and so on) that appear beneath each bit in the figure. These labels are the key to binary numbers. Memorize them. (It's easy—each bit is worth twice the value of its neighbor to the right.) These labels are used to calculate the value of the entire byte. Here's how it works:

- Start with a value of 0.

- For each bit with a value of 1, add the label value below the bit.

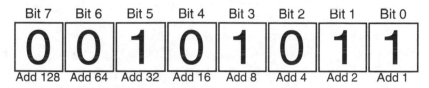

Figure 5.3 A byte holding the binary value 00101011.

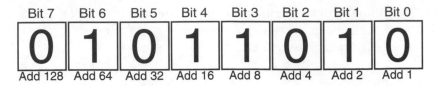

Figure 5.4 What's the value of this byte?

That's all there is to it! In the byte pictured in Figure 5.3, you'd calculate the byte's value by adding 1 + 2 + 8 + 32 = 43. Where did we get the 1, 2, 8, and 32? They're the bottom labels of the only bits with a value of 1. Try another one. What's the value of the byte pictured in Figure 5.4?

Easy, right? Just 2 + 8 + 16 + 64 = 90. Right! How about the byte in Figure 5.5?

This is an interesting one: 1 + 2 + 4 + 8 + 16 + 32 + 64 + 128 = 255. This example demonstrates the largest value that can fit in a single byte. Why? Because every bit is turned on. We've added everything we can add to the value of the byte.

The smallest value a byte can have is 0 (00000000). Since a byte can range in value from 0 to 255, a byte can have 256 possible values.

Important

This is just one of several ways to represent a number using binary. This approach is fine if you want to represent integers that are always greater than or equal to 0 (known as **unsigned** integers). Computers use a different technique, known as **two's complement notation**, to represent integers that might be either negative or positive.

To represent a negative number using two's complement notation:

• Start with the binary representation of the positive version of the number.

• Complement all the bits (turn the 1s into 0s and the 0s into 1s).

• Add 1 to the result.

For example, the binary notation for the number 9 is 00001001. To represent –9 in two's complement notation, flip the bits (11110110) and then add 1. The two's complement for –9 is 11110110 + 1 = 11110111.

The binary notation for the number 2 is 00000010. The two's complement for –2 would be 11111101 + 1 = 11111110. Notice that in binary addition, when you add 01 + 01, you get 10. Just as in regular addition, you carry the 1 to the next column.

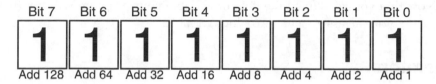

Figure 5.5 Last one: What's the value of this byte?

Don't worry about the details of binary representation and arithmetic. What's important to remember is that the computer uses one notation for positive-only numbers and a different notation for numbers that can be positive or negative. Both notations allow a byte to take on one of 256 different values. The positives-only scheme allows values ranging from 0 to 255. The two's complement scheme allows values ranging from –128 to 127. Note that both of these ranges contain exactly 256 values.

Going from 1 to 2 Bytes

So far, we've discovered that 1 byte (8 bits) of memory can hold one of 2^8 = 256 possible values. By extension, 2 bytes (16 bits) of memory can hold one of 2^{16} = 65,536 possible values. If the 2 bytes are unsigned (never allowed to hold a negative value), they can hold values ranging from 0 to 65,535. If the 2 bytes are **signed** (allowed to hold both positive and negative values), they can hold values ranging from –32,768 to 32,767.

By default, most C data types are signed (allowed to hold both positive and negative values). This means that a variable declared as follows is signed and, assuming a 2-byte `int`, can hold values ranging from –32,768 to 32,767:

```
int    myInt;
```

Important

To declare a variable as `unsigned`, precede its declaration with the unsigned qualifier. Here's an example:

```
unsigned int    myInt;
```

This version of `myInt` (again, assuming 2-byte `int`s) can hold values ranging from 0 to 65,535.

Now that you've defined the type of variable your program will use (in this case, int), you can assign a value to your variable.

Operators

One way to assign a value to a variable is with the = operator, also known as the **assignment operator**. An operator is a special character (or set of characters) representing a specific computer operation. The assignment operator tells the computer to compute the value to the right of the = and to assign that value to the left of the =. Take a look at this line of source code:

```
myInt = 237;
```

This statement causes the value 237 to be placed in the memory allocated for myInt. In this line of code, myInt is known as an **l-value** (for left-value) because it appears on the left side of the = operator. A variable makes a fine l-value. A number (like 237) makes a terrible l-value. Why? Because values are copied *from the right side to the left side* of the = operator. For example, the following line of code asks the compiler to copy the value in myInt to the number 237:

```
237 = myInt;
```

Since you can't change the value of a number, the compiler will report an error when it encounters this line of code (most likely, the error message will say something like "l-value expected").

By the Way

As we just illustrated, you can use numerical constants (such as 237) directly in your code. In the programming world, these constants are called **literals**. Just as there are different types of variables, there are also different types of literals. You'll see more on this topic later in the book.

Look at this example:

```
int   main( void )
{
    int   myInt, anotherInt;

    myInt = 503;
```

```
   anotherInt = myInt;

   return 0;
}
```

Notice we've declared two variables in this program. One way to declare multiple variables is the way we did here, separating the variables by a comma (,). There's no limit to the number of variables you can declare using this method.

We could have declared these variables by using two separate declaration lines:

```
int    myInt;
int    anotherInt;
```

Either way is fine. As you'll see, C is an extremely flexible language. However, there is one rule of thumb you should keep in mind. Although there are exceptions, you'll generally declare all your variables before any other type of statement occurs. Consider this example:

```
int    main( void )
{
   int    myInt;

   myInt = 503;

   int    anotherInt;

   anotherInt = myInt;

   return 0;
}
```

This program will not compile (see the errors in Figure 5.6). Why? A variable (anotherInt) was declared after a nondeclaration statement (myInt = 503). Here's the corrected version:

```
int    main( void )
{
   int    myInt;
   int    anotherInt;
```

```
        myInt = 503;
        anotherInt = myInt;

        return 0;
}
```

This program starts by declaring two `int`s:

```
int     myInt;
int     anotherInt;
```

Next, the program assigns the value 503 to `myInt`:

```
myInt = 503;
```

Finally, the value in `myInt` is copied into `anotherInt`:

```
anotherInt = myInt;
```

After this last statement, the variable `anotherInt` also contains the value 503.

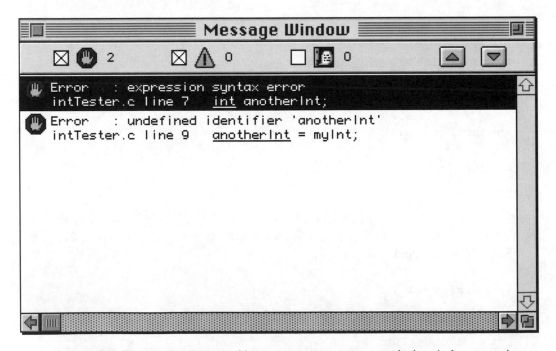

Figure 5.6 These errors occurred because `anotherInt` was declared after an assignment statement.

Here's another version of our program that also compiles:

```
int     main( void )
{
        int     myInt;

        myInt = 503;
        {
            int     anotherInt;

            anotherInt = myInt;
        }
        return 0;
}
```

Wait a sec. This version declares a variable (`anotherInt`) after a nonde-claration statement. So how come it compiles? The left-curly (`{`) after the as-signment statement starts a new block of code, which gives you another opportunity to declare more variables. The right-curly (`}`) ends the block.

Although this may be interesting, it doesn't come up that often. Your best bet is to stick to the strategy of declaring a function's variables at the beginning of the function.

Why go to all this effort just to assign a value to a variable? Think of it as learning to crawl before you can walk. As we cover more and more of the C language, you'll start to see some of the fantastic things you can accomplish. At the beginning of this chapter, we looked at an example that took the values from three containers, added them, and placed the result in a fourth container. That's what this is all about. C variables and operators allow you to manipulate and manage data inside a program. The data might represent your baseball card collection or the flight path of the Mars lander. Variables and operators allow you to massage the data to get the results you want. Have patience and keep reading.

Let's look at some other operators.

The +, –, ++, and –– Operators

The + and – operators each take two values and reduce them to a single value. For example, the following statement will first resolve the right side of the = by adding the numbers 5 and 3.

```
myInt = 5 + 3;
```

Once that's done, the resulting value (8) is assigned to the variable on the left side of the =. This statement assigns the value 8 to the variable myInt. Assigning a value to a variable means copying the value into the memory allocated to that variable.

Here's another example:

```
myInt = 10;
anotherInt = 12 - myInt;
```

The first statement assigns the value 10 to myInt. The second statement subtracts 10 from 12 to get 2, then assigns the value 2 to anotherInt.

The ++ and –– operators operate on a single value only. The ++ operator **increments** (raises) the value by 1, and –– **decrements** (lowers) the value by 1. Take a look:

```
myInt = 10;
myInt++;
```

The first statement assigns myInt a value of 10. The second statement changesthe value of myInt from 10 to 11. Here's an example with ––:

```
myInt = 10;
-- myInt;
```

This time, the second line of code left myInt with a value of 9. You may have noticed that the first example showed the ++ following myInt, whereas the second example showed the –– preceding myInt.

The position of the ++ and –– operators determines when their operation is performed in relation to the rest of the statement. Placing the operator to the right of a variable or an expression (**postfix notation**) tells the compiler to resolve all values before performing the increment (or decrement) operation. Placing the operator to the left of the variable (**prefix notation**) tells the compiler to increment (or decrement) first, then continue evaluation. Confused? The following examples should make this point clear:

```
myInt = 10;
anotherInt = myInt--;
```

The first statement assigns myInt a value of 10. In the second statement, the -- operator is to the right of myInt. This use of postfix notation tells the compiler to assign myInt's value to anotherInt before decrementing myInt. This example leaves myInt with a value of 9 and anotherInt with a value of 10.

Here's the same example, written using prefix notation:

```
myInt = 10;
anotherInt = -- myInt;
```

This time, the -- is to the left of myInt. In this case, the value of myInt is decremented before being assigned to anotherInt. The result? Both myInt and anotherInt are left with a value of 9.

By the Way

This use of prefix and postfix notation shows both a strength and a weakness of the C language. The strength is that C allows you to accomplish a lot in a small amount of code. In the previous examples, we changed the value of two different variables in a single statement. C is powerful.

The weakness is that C code written in this fashion can be extremely cryptic, difficult to read for even the most seasoned C programmer.

Write your code carefully.

The += and −= Operators

In C, you can place the same variable on both the left and right sides of an assignment statement. For example, the following statement increases the value of myInt by 10:

```
myInt = myInt + 10;
```

The same results can be achieved using the += operator:

```
myInt += 10;
```

In other words, the preceding statement is the same as:

```
myInt = myInt + 10;
```

In the same way, the `-=` operator can be used to decrement the value of a variable. The following statement decrements the value of `myInt` by 10:

```
myInt -= 10;
```

The *, /, *=, and /= Operators

The `*` and `/` operators each take two values and reduce them to a single value, much the same as the `+` and `-` operators do. The following statement multiplies 3 and 5, leaving `myInt` with a value of 15:

```
myInt = 3 * 5;
```

The following statement divides 5 by 2 and, if `myInt` is declared as an `int` (or any other type designed to hold whole numbers), assigns the integral (truncated) result to `myInt`:

```
myInt = 5 / 2;
```

The number 5 divided by 2 is 2.5. Since `myInt` can hold only whole numbers, the value 2.5 is truncated, and the value 2 is assigned to `myInt`.

Important

Math alert! Numbers like –37, 0, and 22, are known as **whole numbers,** or **integers**. Numbers like 3.14159, 2.5, and .0001 are known as **fractional,** or **floating-point, numbers**.

The `*=` and `/=` operators work much the same as their `+=` and `-=` counterparts. The following two statements are identical:

```
myInt *= 10;
```

```
myInt = myInt * 10;
```

The following two statements are also identical:

```
myInt /= 10;

myInt = myInt / 10;
```

The / operator doesn't perform its truncation automatically. The accuracy of the result is limited by the data type of the operands. As an example, if the division is performed using `ints`, the result will be an `int` and is truncated to an integer value.

Several data types (such as `float`, introduced in Chapter 8) support floating-point division, using the / operator.

Operator Order
Using Parentheses ( )

Sometimes, the expressions you create can be evaluated in many ways. For example:

```
myInt = 5 + 3 * 2;
```

You can add 5 + 3, then multiply the result by 2 (giving you 16). Alternatively, you can multiply 3 * 2 and add 5 to the result (giving you 11). Which is correct?

C has a set of built-in rules for resolving the order of operators. As it turns out, the * operator has a higher precedence than the + operator, so the multiplication will be performed first, yielding a result of 11.

Although it helps to understand the relative precedence of the C operators, it is difficult to keep track of them all. That's why the C gods gave us parentheses! Use parentheses in pairs to define the order in which you want your operators performed. The following statement will leave `myInt` with a value of 16:

```
myInt = ( 5 + 3 ) * 2;
```

The following statement will leave `myInt` with a value of 11:

```
myInt = 5 + ( 3 * 2 );
```

You can use more than one set of parentheses in a statement, as long as they occur in pairs—one left parenthesis associated with each right parenthesis. The following statement will leave `myInt` with a value of 16:

```
myInt = ( ( 5 + 3 ) * 2 );
```

Resolving Operator Precedence

As mentioned previously, C has built-in rules for resolving operator precedence. If you have a question about which operator has a higher precedence, refer to the chart in Figure 5.7. Here's how the chart works.

The higher an operator is in the chart, the higher its precedence. For example, suppose that you are trying to predict the result of this line of code:

```
myInt = 5 * 3 + 7;
```

First, look up the operator * in the chart. Hmmm . . . * seems to be in the chart twice: once with label `pointer` and once with the label `multiply`. You can tell just by looking at this line of code that we want the `multiply` version. The compiler is pretty smart. Just like you, it can tell that this is the `multiply` version of *.

OK, now look up +. Yup, it's in there twice also: once as `unary` and once as `binary`. A `unary` + or – is the sign that appears before a number, as in +147 or

Operators by Precedence	Order
->, ., ++postfix, --postfix	Left to Right
*pointer, &address of, +unary, -unary, !, ~, ++prefix, -prefix, sizeof	Right to Left
Typecast	Right to Left
*multiply, /, %	Left to Right
+binary, -binary	Left to Right
<<left-shift, >>right-shift	Left to Right
>, >=, <, <=,	Left to Right
==, !=	Left to Right
&bitwise-and	Left to Right
^	Left to Right
|	Left to Right
&&	Left to Right
||	Left to Right
?:	Right to Left
=, +=, -=, *=, /=, %=, >>=, <<=, &=, |=, ^=	Right to Left
,	Left to Right

Figure 5.7 The relative precedence of C's built-in operators. The higher its position in the chart, the higher the operator's precedence.

–32768. In our line of code, the + operator has two operands, so clearly `binary +` is the one we want.

Now that you've figured out which operator is which, you can see that the `multiply *` is higher up on the chart than the `binary +` and thus has a higher precedence. This means that the `*` will get evaluated before the `+`, as if the expression were written as:

```
myInt = (5 * 3) + 7;
```

So far, so good. Now consider this line of code:

```
myInt = 27 * 6 % 5;
```

Both of these operators are on the fourth line in the chart. Which one gets evaluated first? If both operators under consideration are on the same line in the chart, the order of evaluation is determined by the entry in the chart's rightmost column. In this case, the operators are evaluated from left to right. In the current example, `%` will get evaluated before `*`, as if the line of code were written:

```
myInt = 27 * (6 % 5);
```

Now look at this line of code:

```
myInt = 27 % 6 * 5;
```

In this case, the `*` will get evaluated before the `%`, as if the line of code were written:

```
myInt = 27 % (6 * 5);
```

Of course, you can avoid this exercise altogether with a judicious sprinkling of parentheses. As you look through the chart, you'll definitely notice some operators that you haven't learned about yet. As you read through the book and encounter new operators, check back on the chart to see where it fits in. In fact, go ahead and dogear the page (pay for the book first, though!) so you can find the chart again later.

Sample Programs

So far in this chapter, we've discussed variables (mostly of type `int`) and operators (mostly mathematical). The program examples on the following pages combine variables and operators into useful C statements. We'll also learn about a powerful part of the Standard Library, the printf() function.

Opening operator.μ

Our next program, operator.μ, provides a testing ground for some of the operators covered in the previous sections. operator.c declares a variable (myInt) and uses a series of statements to change the value of the variable. By including a printf() after each of these statements, operator.c makes it easy to follow the variable, step by step, as its value changes.

Start up CodeWarrior by double-clicking on the project file operator.μ inside the Learn C Projects folder, in the subfolder named 05.01 – operator. The project window for operator.μ should appear (Figure 5.8).

Run operator.μ by selecting **Run** from the **Project** menu. CodeWarrior will first attempt to compile operator.c, turning it into an application named operator. If you haven't mucked around with the source code, things should proceed smoothly, resulting in a clean compile. Once the code compiles, CodeWarrior will run operator, displaying information in the console window.

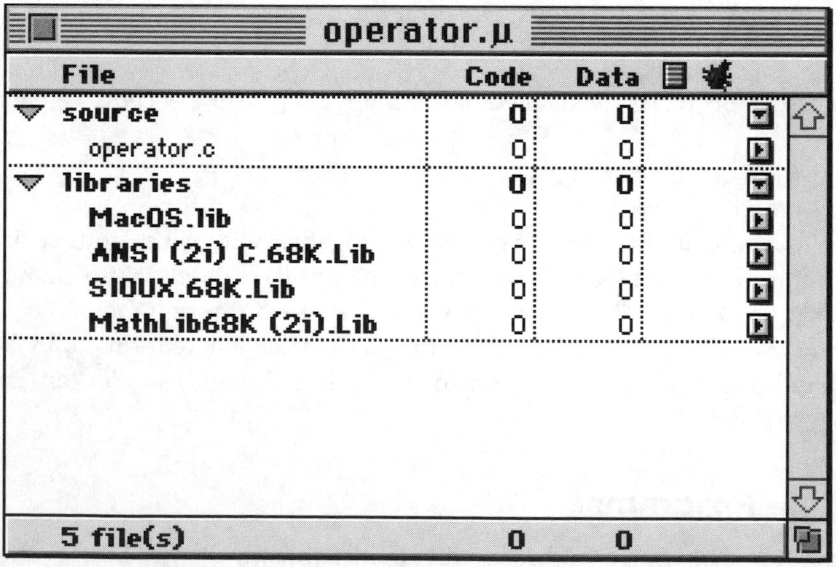

Figure 5.8 The operator.μ project window.

The information displayed by your program is also known as your program's output. Compare your output to that shown in Figure 5.9. They should be the same.

By the Way

In ancient times, programmers used character-based displays to communicate with their computers. These displays were called consoles. A typical console screen supported 24 rows of text, each up to 80 columns wide. When the computer wanted to communicate with you, it displayed some characters on your console. To respond to the computer, you'd type at your keyboard. The characters you typed would also appear on your console.

Programmers love character-based displays because they're simple. To display text on a window-based system (like the Macintosh), you have to worry about things like text font, size, and style. You have to worry about lining all your text up just right.

With a character-based display, you didn't worry about things like that. Typically, you just sent the text out to the display, one line at a time. When you reached the bottom of the screen, the console would scroll the text automatically. So easy!

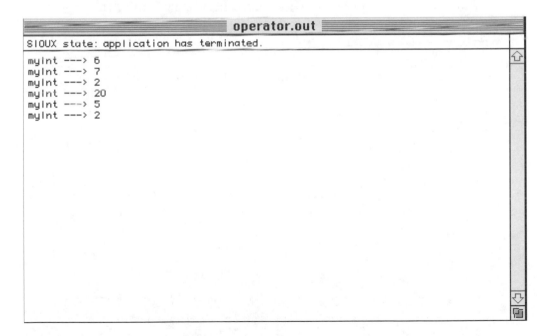

Figure 5.9 The output generated by operator.

61

Modern programming environments, such as CodeWarrior, offer you the best of both worlds. For example, CodeWarrior supports all the elements specific to the Macintosh, such as pull-down menus, scroll bars, windows, and icons. (Once you feel comfortable with C, get a copy of the *Macintosh C Programming Primer*. It will teach you how to add those Mac-specific elements to your programs.)

CodeWarrior also features a standard, scrolling console window. The console window is essentially a 24-line, 80-column display console embedded in a Macintosh window. Since many of the Standard Library routines, such as `printf()`, were designed with this simpler, character-based display in mind, we'll make extensive use of the console window as we learn C.

Stepping Through the Source Code

Before we step through the source code in `operator.c`, you might want to bring the source code up on your screen (double-click on the name `operator.c` in the project window, or select **Open** from the **File** menu). A new window will appear, listing the source code in the file `operator.c`.

The file `operator.c` starts off with a `#include` statement that gives us access to a bunch of Standard Library functions, including `printf()`:

```
#include <stdio.h>
```

Then, `main()` starts out by **defining** an `int` named `myInt`.

```
int   main( void )
{
    int   myInt;
```

By the Way

Note that earlier the term "declaring a variable" was used; now the term "defining" is being used. What's the difference? A variable declaration is any statement that specifies a variable's name and type—for example:

```
int myInt;
```

A variable definition is a declaration that causes memory to be allocated for the variable. Since the previous statement does cause memory to be allocated for `myInt`, it does qualify as a definition. Later in the book, you'll see some declarations that don't qualify as definitions. For now, just remember that a definition causes memory to be allocated.

At this point in the program (after myInt has been declared but before any value has been assigned to it), myInt is said to be **uninitialized**. In computerese, the term **initialization** refers to the process of establishing a variable's value for the first time. A variable that has been declared but that has not had a value assigned to it is said to be uninitialized. You initialize a variable the first time you give it a value.

Since myInt was declared to be of type int and since CodeWarrior is currently set to use 2-byte ints, 2 bytes of memory were reserved for myInt. Since we haven't placed a value in those 2 bytes yet, they could contain any value at all. Some compilers place a value of 0 in a newly allocated variable; some do not. The key is, don't depend on a variable being preset to a specific value. If you want a variable to contain a specific value, assign the value to the variable yourself!

Important

Later in the book, you'll learn about global variables. Global variables are always given an initial value by the compiler. All the variables used in this chapter are local variables, not global variables. Local variables are not guaranteed to be initialized by the compiler.

The next line of code uses the * operator to assign a value of 6 to myInt. Following that, we use printf() to display the value of myInt in the console window:

```
myInt = 3 * 2;
printf( "myInt ---> %d\n", myInt );
```

The code between printf()'s left and right parentheses is known as a parameter list. The **parameters,** or **arguments**, in a parameter list are automatically provided to the function you are calling (in this case, printf()). The receiving function can use the parameters passed to it to determine its next course of action. We'll get into the specifics of parameter passing in Chapter 7. For the moment, let's talk about printf() and the parameters used by this Standard Library function.

The first parameter passed to printf() defines what will be drawn in the console window. The simplest call to printf() uses a quoted text string as its

only parameter. A quoted text string consists of a pair of double-quote characters
(") with zero or more characters between them. For example, this call of
`printf()` will draw the characters `Hello!` in the console window:

```
printf( "Hello!" );
```

Notice that the double-quote characters are not part of the text string.

You can request that `printf()` draw a variable's value in the midst of the
quoted string. In the case of an `int`, do this by embedding the two characters `%d`
within the first parameter and by passing the `int` as a second parameter. Then,
`printf()` will replace the `%d` with the value of the `int`.

In these two lines of code, we first set `myInt` to 6 and use `printf()` to print
the value of `myInt` in the console window:

```
myInt = 3 * 2;
printf( "myInt ---> %d\n", myInt );
```

This code produces the following line of output in the console window:

```
myInt ---> 6
```

The two characters "\n" in the first parameter represent a carriage return and
tell `printf()` to move the cursor to the beginning of the next line before it prints
any more characters.

By the Way

> The `%d` is known as a **format specifier**. The `d` in the format specifier tells
> `printf()` that you are printing an integer variable, such as an `int`. We'll
> cover format specifiers in detail in Chapter 8.

You can place any number of `%` specifications in the first parameter, as long as
you follow the first parameter by the appropriate number of variables. Here's another example:

```
intvar1, var2;

var1 = 5;
var2 = 10;
printf( "var1 = %d\n\nvar2 = %d\n", var1, var2 );
```

The preceding code will draw the following text in the console window:

```
var1 = 5


var2 = 10
```

Notice the blank line between the two lines of output. It was caused by the "\n\n" in the first `printf()` parameter. The first carriage return placed the cursor at the beginning of the next console line (directly under the **v** in **var1**). The second carriage return moved the cursor down one more line, leaving a blank line in its path.

Let's get back to our source code. The next line of `operator.c` increments `myInt` from 6 to 7 and prints the new value in the console window:

```
myInt += 1;
printf( "myInt ---> %d\n", myInt );
```

The next line decrements `myInt` by 5 and prints its new value, 2, in the console window:

```
myInt -= 5;
printf( "myInt ---> %d\n", myInt );
```

Next, `myInt` is multiplied by 10, and its new value, 20, is printed in the console window:

```
myInt *= 10;
printf( "myInt ---> %d\n", myInt );
```

Next, `myInt` is divided by 4, resulting in a new value, 5.

```
myInt /= 4;
printf( "myInt ---> %d\n", myInt );
```

Finally, `myInt` is divided by 2. Since 5 divided by 2 is 2.5 (not a whole number), a truncation is performed, and `myInt` is left with a value of 2:

```
myInt /= 2;
printf( "myInt ---> %d", myInt );

return 0;
}
```

Opening postfix.μ

Our next program demonstrates the difference between postfix and prefix notation (the ++ and -- operators defined earlier in the chapter). In the Finder, go into the **Learn C Projects** folder, then into the **05.02 - postfix** subfolder, and double-click on the project file postfix.μ. CodeWarrior will close the project file operator.μ and open postfix.μ.

Take a look at the source code in the file postfix.c and try to predict the result of the two printf() calls before you run the program. Remember, you can open a source code listing for postfix.c by double-clicking on the name postfix.c in the project window. Careful, this one's tricky.

Once your guesses are locked in, select **Run** from the **Project** menu. How'd you do? Compare your two guesses with the output in Figure 5.10. Let's look at the source code.

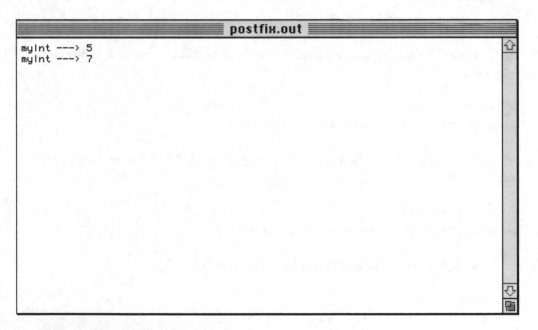

Figure 5.10 The output generated by the program postfix.

Stepping Through the Source Code

The first half of postfix.c is pretty straightforward. The variable myInt is defined to be of type int. Then, myInt is assigned a value of 5. The tricky part comes next:

```
#include <stdio.h>


intmain( void )
{
   int    myInt;

   myInt = 5;
```

The first call to `printf()` has a statement embedded in it. This is another great feature of the C language. Where there's room for a variable, there's room for an entire statement. Sometimes, it's convenient to perform two actions within the same line of code. For example:

```
printf( "myInt ---> %d\n", myInt = myInt * 3 );
```

This line of code first triples the value of `myInt`, then passes the result (the tripled value of `myInt`) on to `printf()`. The same could have been accomplished using two lines of code:

```
myInt = myInt * 3;
printf( "myInt ---> %d\n", myInt );
```

In general, when the compiler encounters an assignment statement where it expects a variable, it first completes the assignment, then passes on the result of the assignment as if it were a variable. Let's see this technique in action.

In `postfix.c`, our friend the postfix operator emerges again. Just prior to the two calls of `printf()`, `myInt` has a value of 5. The first `printf()` increments the value of `myInt` using postfix notation:

```
printf( "myInt ---> %d\n", myInt++ );
```

The use of postfix notation means that the value of `myInt` will be passed on to `printf()` before `myInt` is incremented. This means that the first `printf()` will accord `myInt` a value of 5. However, when the statement is finished, `myInt` will have a value of 6.

The second `printf()` acts in a more rational (and preferable) manner. The prefix notation guarantees that `myInt` will be incremented (from 6 to 7) before its value is passed on to `printf()`:

```
        printf( "myInt ---> %d", ++myInt );

        return 0;
}
```

By the Way

Can you break each of these `printf()` statements into two separate ones? Give it a try, then read on . . .

The first `printf()` looks like this:

```
printf( "myInt ---> %d\n", myInt++ );
```

Here's the two-statement version:

```
printf( "myInt ---> %d\n", myInt );
myInt++;
```

Notice that the statement incrementing `myInt` was placed after the `printf()`. Do you see why? The postfix notation makes this necessary. Run through both versions and verify this for yourself.

The second `printf()` looks like this:

```
printf( "myInt ---> %d", ++myInt );
```

Here's the two-statement version:

```
++myInt;
printf( "myInt ---> %d\n", myInt );
```

This time, the statement incrementing `myInt` came before the `printf()`. This time, it's the prefix notation that makes this necessary. Again, go through both versions and verify this for yourself.

The purpose of demonstrating the complexity of the postfix and prefix operators is twofold. On one hand, it's extremely important that you understand exactly how these operators work from all angles. This will allow you to write code that works and will aid you in making sense of other programmers' code. On the other hand, embedding prefix and postfix operators within function parameters may save you lines of code but, as you can see, may prove a bit confusing.

Opening slasher.μ

The last program in Chapter 5, slasher.μ, demonstrates several backslash combinations. In the Finder, open the Learn C Projects folder; then open the 05.03 – slasher subfolder and double-click on the project file slasher.μ. When CodeWarrior opens the slasher.μ project window, run slasher.μ by selecting **Run** from the **Project** menu. You should see something like the console window shown in Figure 5.11.

Stepping Through the Source Code

slasher.c consists of a series of printf() calls, each of which demonstrates a different backslash combination. The first printf() prints a series of 10 zeros, followed by the characters \r (also known as the **backslash combination** \r):

```
#include <stdio.h>

int main( void )
{
    printf( "0000000000\r" );
```

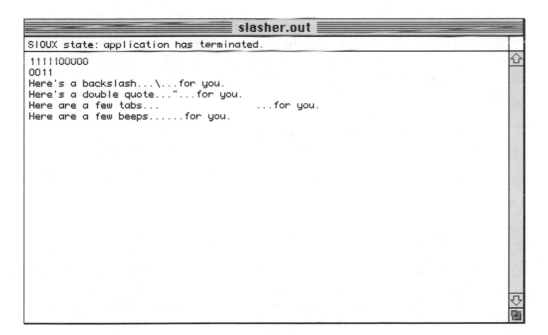

Figure 5.11 The output from slasher.μ.

The \r backslash combination generates a carriage return without a line feed, leaving the cursor at the beginning of the current line (unlike \n, which leaves the cursor at the beginning of the next line down).

The next printf() prints five 1s over the first five 0s, as if someone had printed the text string "1111100000". The \n at the end of this printf() moves the cursor to the beginning of the next line in the console window:

```
printf( "11111\n" );
```

The next printf() demonstrates \b, the backspace backslash combination, which tells printf() to back up one character so that the next character printed replaces the last character printed. This printf() sends out four 0s, backspaces over the last two, then prints two 1s. The result is as if you had printed the string "0011":

```
printf( "0000\b\b11\n" );
```

The \ can also be used to cancel a character's special meaning within a quoted string. For example, the backslash combination \\ generates a single \ character. The difference is, this \ loses its special backslash powers. It doesn't affect the character immediately following it.

The backslash combination \" generates a " character, taking away the special meaning of the ". Without the \ before it, the " character would mark the end of the quoted string. The \ allows you to include a " inside a quoted string.

The backslash combinations \\ and \" are demonstrated in the next two printf() calls:

```
printf( "Here's a backslash...\\...for you.\n" );
printf( "Here's a double quote...\"...for you.\n" );
```

The \t combination generates a single tab character. The console window has a tab stop every eight spaces. Here's a printf() example:

```
printf( "Here's a few tabs...\t\t\t\t...for you.\n" );
```

The Mac offers a host of sound options, unlike most text-based computer consoles, which offer only one: the beep. Although a beep isn't quite as interesting as a clank! or a boing!, it can still serve a useful purpose. The \a backslash combination provides a simple way to make your Mac beep.

```
    printf( "Here are a few beeps...\a\a\a\a...for you." );

    return 0;
}
```

Those are all the sample programs for this chapter. Before we move on, however, I'd like to talk to you about something personal. It's about your coding habits.

Sprucing Up Your Code

You are now in the middle of your C learning curve. You've learned about variables, types, functions, and bytes. You've learned about an important part of the Standard Library, the function `printf()`. It's at this point in the learning process that programmers start developing their coding habits.

Coding habits are the little things programmers do that make their code a little bit different (and hopefully better!) than anyone else's. Before you get too set in your ways, here are a few coding habits you can, and should, add to your arsenal.

Source Code Spacing

You may have noticed the tabs, spaces, and blank lines scattered throughout the sample programs. These are known in C as **white space**. With a few exceptions, white space is ignored by C compilers. Believe it or not, as far as the C compiler goes, the following two programs are equivalent:

```
main()
{
    int myInt;myInt



=
5
;
printf("myInt=",myInt);}
```

```
main()
{
    int myInt;

    myInt = 5;
```

```
        printf( "myInt =", myInt );
}
```

The C compiler doesn't care whether you put 5 statements per line or whether you put 20 carriage returns between your statements and your semicolons. One thing the compiler won't let you do is place white space in the middle of a word, such as a variable or a function name. For example, the following line of code won't compile:

```
my  Int = 5;
```

Instead of a single variable named myInt, the compiler sees two items: one named my and the other named Int. White space can confuse the compiler.

Too little white space can also confuse the compiler. For example, this line of code won't compile:

```
intmyInt;
```

The compiler needs at least one piece of white space to tell where the type ends and where the variable begins. On the other hand, as you've already seen, this line compiles just fine:

```
myInt=5;
```

Since a variable name can't contain the character =, the compiler has no problem telling where the variable ends and where the operator begins.

As long as your code compiles properly, you're free to develop your own style for using white space. Here are a few hints:

- Place a blank line between your variable declarations and the rest of your function's code. Also, use blank lines to group related lines of code.

- Sprinkle single spaces throughout a statement. Here is a line without spaces:

```
printf("myInt=",myInt);
```

Compare that line with this line:

```
printf( "myInt =", myInt );
```

The spaces make the second line easier to read.

- When in doubt, use parentheses. Compare these two lines:

```
myInt=var1+2*var2+4;
```

```
myInt = var1 + (2 * var2) + 4;
```

What a difference parentheses and spaces make!

- Always start variable names with a lowercase letter, using an uppercase letter at the start of each subsequent word in the name. This yields variable names such as `myVar`, `areWeDone`, and `employeeName`.

- Always start function names with an uppercase letter, using an uppercase letter at the start of each subsequent word in the name. This yields function names such as `DoSomeWork()`, `HoldThese()`, and `DealTheCards()`.

These hints are merely suggestions. Use standards that make sense for you and the people with whom you work. The object here is to make your code as readable as possible.

Comment Your Code

One of the most critical elements in the creation of a computer program is clear and comprehensive documentation. When you deliver your award-winning graphics package to your customers, you'll want to have two sets of documentation. One set is for your customers, who'll need a clear set of instructions to guide them through your wonderful new creation.

The other set of documentation consists of the comments you'll weave throughout your code. Comments in source code act as a sort of narrative, guiding a reader through your source code. You'll include comments that describe how your code works, what makes it special, and what to look out for when changing it. Well-commented code includes a comment at the beginning of each function to describe the function, the function parameters, and the function's variables. It's also a good idea to sprinkle individual comments among your source code statements, explaining the role each line plays in your program's algorithm. How do you add a comment to your source code? Take a look . . .

All C compilers recognize the sequence /* as the start of a comment and will ignore all characters until they reach the sequence */ (the end of comment characters). Here's some commented code:

```
int   main( void )
{
    int   numPieces;      /* Number of pieces of pie left */

    numPieces = 8; /*  We started with 8 pieces  */

    numPieces--;/*  Marge had a piece  */
    numPieces--;/*  Lisa had a piece  */
    numPieces -= 2;/*  Bart had two pieces!!  */
    numPieces -= 4;/*  Homer had the rest!!!  */

    printf( "Slices left = %d", numPieces );  /*  How about
                                                  some cake
                                                  instead?  */

    return 0;
}
```

Notice that although most of the comments fit on the same line, the last comment was split among three lines. The preceding code will compile just fine.

Important

Most modern C compilers will also accept the C++ commenting convention. C++ ignores the remainder of a line of code, once it encounters the characters //. For example, this line of code combines both comment styles:

```
printf( "Comments" /* C comment */ );  // C++ comment!!!
```

Use the C++ comment mechanism only if you are sure you won't be porting your code to a C compiler that doesn't understand the C++ mechanism.

Since all the programs in this book are examined in detail, line by line, the comments were left out. This was done to make the examples as simple as possible. In this instance, do as we say, not as we do. Comment your code. No excuses!

What's Next?

This chapter introduced the concepts of variables and operators, tied together in C statements, separated by semicolons. We looked at several examples, each of which made heavy use of the Standard Library function `printf()`. We learned about the console window, quoted strings, and backslash combinations.

Chapter 6 will increase our programming options significantly, introducing C control structures, such as the `for` loop and the `if ... then ... else` statement. Get ready to expand your C programming horizons. See you in Chapter 6.

Exercises

1. Find the error in each of the following code fragments:

   a. `printf( Hello, world );`

   b. `int   myInt   myOtherInt;`

   c. `myInt =+ 3;`

   d. `printf( "myInt = %d" );`

   e. `printf( "myInt = ", myInt );`

   f. `printf( "myInt = %d\", myInt );`

   g. `myInt + 3 = myInt;`

   h.
   ```c
   int main( void )
   {
       int   myInt;
       myInt = 3;
       int   anotherInt;

       anotherInt = myInt;

       return 0;
   }
   ```

2. Compute the value of `myInt` after each code fragment is executed:

   a.
   ```c
   myInt = 5;
   myInt *= (3+4) * 2;
   ```

   b.
   ```c
   myInt = 2;
   myInt *= ( (3*4) / 2 ) - 9;
   ```

```
c.  myInt = 2;
    myInt /= 5;
    myInt--;

d.  myInt = 25;
    myInt /= 3 * 2;

e.  myInt = (3*4*5) / 9;
    myInt -= (3+4) * 2;

f.  myInt = 5;
    printf( "myInt = %d", myInt = 2 );

g.  myInt = 5;
    myInt = (3+4) * 2;

h.  myInt = 1;
    myInt /= (3+4) / 6;
```

Controlling Your Program's Flow

So far, you've learned quite a bit about the C language. You know about functions (especially one named `main()`). You know that functions are made up of statements, each of which is terminated by a semicolon. You know about variables, which have a name and a type. Up to this point, you've dealt with variables of type `int`.

You also know about operators, such as =, +, and +=. You've learned about postfix and prefix notation and the importance of writing clear, easy-to-understand code. You've learned about an important programming tool, the console window. You've learned about the Standard Library, a set of functions supplied as standard equipment with every C programming environment. You've also learned about `printf()`, an invaluable component of the Standard Library.

Finally, you've learned a few housekeeping techniques to keep your code fresh, sparkling, and readable. Comment your code, because your memory isn't perfect, and insert some white space to keep your code from getting too cramped.

Flow Control

One thing you haven't learned about the C language is **flow control**. The programs we've written so far have all consisted of a straightforward series of statements, one right after the other. Every statement is executed in the order it occurred.

Flow control is the ability to define the order in which your program's statements are executed. The C language provides several keywords you can use in your program to control your program's flow. One of these is the keyword `if`.

The `if` Statement

The keyword `if` allows you to choose among several options in your program. In English, you might say something like this:

```
If it's raining outside I'll bring my umbrella; otherwise I
won't.
```

In the previous sentence, you're using "if" to choose between two options. Depending on the weather, you'll do one of two things. You'll bring your umbrella or you won't bring your umbrella. C's `if` statement gives you this same flexibility. Here's an example:

```
int main( void )
{
   int    myInt;

   myInt = 5;

   if ( myInt == 0 )
      printf( "myInt is equal to zero." );
   else
      printf( "myInt is not equal to zero." );

   return 0;
}
```

This program declares `myInt` to be of type `int` and sets the value of `myInt` to 5. Next, we use the `if` statement to test whether `myInt` is equal to 0. If `myInt` is equal to 0 (which we know is not true), we'll print one string. Otherwise, we'll print a different string. As expected, this program prints the string "myInt is not equal to zero".

An `if` statement can come in two ways. The first, known as plain old `if`, fits this pattern:

```
if ( expression )
   statement
```

An `if` statement will always consist of the word `if`, a left parenthesis, an expression, a right parenthesis, and a statement. (We'll define both "expression" and "statement" in a minute.) This first form of `if` executes the statement if the expression in parentheses is true. An English example of the plain `if` might be:

```
If it's raining outside, I'll bring my umbrella.
```

Notice that this statement tells us what will happen only if it's raining outside. No particular action will be taken if it is not raining.

The second form of `if`, known as `if-else`, fits this pattern:

```
if ( expression )
    statement
else
    statement
```

An `if-else` statement will always consist of the word `if`, a left parenthesis, an expression, a right parenthesis, a statement, the word `else`, and a second statement. This form of `if` executes the first statement if the expression is true and executes the second statement if the expression is false. An English example of an `if-else` statement might be:

```
If it's raining outside, I'll bring my umbrella, otherwise I
won't.
```

Notice that this example tells us what will happen if it is raining outside (I'll bring my umbrella) and if it isn't raining outside (I won't bring my umbrella). The example programs presented later in the chapter demonstrate the proper use of both `if` and `if-else`.

Our next step is to define our terms.

Expressions

In C, an **expression** is anything that has a value. For example, a variable is a type of expression, since a variable always has a value. (Even an uninitialized variable has a value—we just don't know what the value is!) The following are all examples of expressions:

- `myInt + 3`
- `( myInt + anotherInt ) * 4`
- `myInt++`

An assignment statement is also an expression. Can you guess the value of an assignment statement? Think back to Chapter 5. Remember when we included an assignment statement as a parameter to `printf()`? The value of an assignment statement is the value of its left side. Check out the following code fragment:

```
myInt - 5;
myInt += 3;
```

Both of these `statements` qualify as expressions. The value of the first expression is 5. The value of the second expression is 8 (because we added 3 to `myInt`'s previous value).

Literals can also be used as expressions. The number 8 has a value. Guess what? Its value is 8. All expressions, no matter what their type, have a numerical value.

By the Way

Technically, there is an exception to this rule. The expression (void)0 has no value. In fact, any value or variable cast to type `void` has no value. Ummm, but, Dave, what's a cast? What is type `void`? We'll get to both of these topics later in the book. For the moment, when you see `void`, think "no value."

True Expressions

Earlier, we defined the `if` statement as follows:

```
if ( expression )
    statement
```

We then said that the statement gets executed if the expression is true. Let's look at C's concept of truth.

Everyone has an intuitive understanding of the difference between true and false. I think we'd all agree that the statement is false:

```
5 equals 3
```

We'd also agree that the following statement is true:

```
5 and 3 are both greater than 0
```

This intuitive grasp of true and false carries over into the C language. In the case of C, however, both true and false have numerical values. Here's how it works.

In C, any expression that has a value of 0 is said to be false. Any expression with a value other than 0 is said to be true. As stated earlier, an `if` statement's statement gets executed if its expression is true. To put this more accurately:

An `if` statement's statement gets executed if (and only if) its expression has a value other than 0.

Here's an example:

```
myInt = 27;

if ( myInt )
    printf( "myInt is not equal to 0" );
```

The `if` statement in this piece of code first tests the value of `myInt`. Since `myInt` is not equal to 0, the `printf()` gets executed.

Comparative Operators

C expressions have a special set of operators, called **comparative operators.** Comparative operators compare their left sides with their right sides and produce a value of either 1 or 0, depending on the relationship of the two sides.

For example, the operator `==` determines whether the expression on the left is equal in value to the expression on the right. In the following expression, `myInt` evaluates to 1 if `myInt` is equal to 5 and to 0 if `myInt` is not equal to 5:

```
myInt == 5
```

Here's an example of the `==` operator at work:

```
if ( myInt == 5 )
    printf( "myInt is equal to 5" );
```

If `myInt` is equal to 5, the expression `myInt == 5` evaluates to 1 and `printf()` gets called. If `myInt` isn't equal to 5, the expression evaluates to 0 and the `printf()` is skipped. Just remember, the key to triggering an `if` statement is an expression that resolves to a value other than 0.

Figure 6.1 shows some of the other comparative operators. You'll see some of these operators in the example programs later in the chapter.

Operator	Resolves to 1 if...
==	left side is equal to right
<=	left side is less than or equal to right
>=	left side is greater than or equal to right
<	left side is less than right
>	left side is greater than right
!=	left side is not equal to right

Figure 6.1 Some comparative operators.

Logical Operators

CodeWarrior provides a pair of constants that really come in handy when dealing with our next set of operators. The constant `true` has a value of 1, and the constant `false` has a value of 0. You can use these constants in your programs to make them a little easier to read. Read on and you'll see why.

By the Way

In addition to `true` and `false`, CodeWarrior also provides the constants `TRUE` and `FALSE` (with values of 1 and 0, respectively). Some people prefer `TRUE` and `FALSE`, others prefer `true` and `false`. Pick a pair and stick with them. We'll work with `true` and `false` throughout the rest of the book.

Our next set of operators, collectively known as **logical operators,** are modeled on the mathematical concept of truth tables. If you don't know much about truth tables (or are just frightened by mathematics in general), don't panic. Everything you need to know is outlined in the next few paragraphs.

The first of the set of logical operators is the `!` operator. The `!` operator turns `true` into `false` and `false` into `true`. Figure 6.2 shows the truth table for the `!` operator. In this table, `T` stands for `true` and `F` stands for `false`. The letter `A` in the table represents an expression. If the expression `A` is `true`, applying the `!` operator to `A` yields the value `false`. If the expression `A` is `false`, applying the `!` operator to `A` yields the value `true`. The `!` operator is commonly referred to as the `NOT` operator; `!A` is pronounced Not A.

Here's a piece of code that demonstrates the `!` operator:

```
int    myFirstInt, mySecondInt;

myFirstInt = false;
mySecondInt = ! myFirstInt;
```

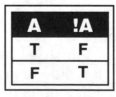

Figure 6.2 The truth table for the ! operator.

First, we declare two ints. We assign the value `false` to the first int, then use the `!` operator to turn the `false` into a `true` and assign it to the second int. This is really important. Take another look at Figure 6.2. The `!` operator converts `true` into `false` and `false` into `true`. What this really means is that `!` converts 1 to 0 and 0 to 1. This really comes in handy when you are working with an if statement's expression, like this one:

```
if ( mySecondInt )
    printf( "mySecondInt must be true" );
```

The previous chunk of code translated mySecondInt from `false` to `true`, which is the same thing as saying that mySecondInt has a value of 1. Either way, mySecondInt will cause the if to fire, and the printf() will get executed.

Take a look at this piece of code:

```
if ( ! mySecondInt )
    printf( "mySecondInt must be false" );
```

This printf() will get executed if mySecondInt is `false`. Do you see why? If mySecondInt is `false`, then `!` mySecondInt must be `true`.

The `!` operator is a **unary** operator. Unary operators operate on a single expression (the expression to the right of the operator). The other two logical operators, `&&` and `||`, are binary operators. Binary operators, such as the `==` operator presented earlier, operate on two expressions, one on the left side and one on the right side of the operator.

The `&&` operator is commonly referred to as the **and** operator. The result of an `&&` operation is `true` if, and only if, both the left side and the right side are `true`. Here's an example:

```
int   hasCar, hasTimeToGiveRide;

hasCar = true;
hasTimeToGiveRide = true;

if ( hasCar && hasTimeToGiveRide )
    printf( "Hop in - I'll give you a ride!\n" );
else
    printf( "I've either got no car, no time, or neither!\n" );
```

83

This example uses two variables. One indicates whether the program has a car, the other whether the program has time to give us a ride to the mall. All philosophical issues aside (Can a program have a car?), the question of the moment is, Which `printf()` will fire? Since both sides of the `&&` were set to `true`, the first `printf()` will be called. If either one (or both) of the variables were set to `false`, the second `printf()` would be called. Another way to think of this is that we'll get a ride to the mall only if our friendly program has a car *and* has time to give us a ride. If either of these is not true, we're not getting a ride. By the way, notice the use here of the second form of if: the `if-else` statement.

The `||` operator is commonly referred to as the `or` operator. The result of a `||` operation is `true` if either the left side or the right side, or both sides, of the `||` are `true`. Put another way, the result of a `||` is `false` if, and only if, both the left side and the right side of the `||` are `false`. Here's an example:

```
int    nothingElseOn, newEpisode;

nothingElseOn = true;
newEpisode = true;

if ( newEpisode || nothingElseOn )
    printf( "Let's watch Star Trek!\n" );
else
    printf( "Something else is on or I've seen this one.\n" );
```

This example uses two variables to decide whether we should watch "Star Trek" (your choice: TOS, TNG, DS9, or VOY). One variable indicates whether anything else is on right now, and the other tells you whether this episode is a rerun. If this is a brand new episode *or* if nothing else is on, we'll watch "Star Trek."

Here's a slight twist on the previous example:

```
int    nothingElseOn, itsARerun;

nothingElseOn = true;
itsARerun = false;

if ( (! itsARerun) || nothingElseOn )
    printf( "Let's watch Star Trek!\n" );
else
    printf( "Something else is on or I've seen this one.\n" );
```

A	B	A && B	A || B
T	T	T	T
T	F	F	T
F	T	F	T
F	F	F	F

Figure 6.3 Truth table for the `&&` and `||` operators.

This time, we've replaced the variable `newEpisode` with its exact opposite, `itsARerun`. Look at the logic that drives the `if` statement. We're combining `itsARerun` with the `!` operator. Before, we cared whether the episode was a `newEpisode`. This time, we are concerned that the episode is not a rerun. See the difference?

Both the `&&` and the `||` operators are summarized in the table in Figure 6.3. If you look in the folder `Learn C Projects`, you'll find a subfolder named `06.01 - truthTester`. The file `truthTester.c` contains the three examples we just went through. Take some time to play with the code. Take turns changing the variables from `true` to `false` and back again. Use this code to get a good feel for the `!`, `&&`, and `||` operators.

By the Way

On most keyboards, you type the character `&` by holding down the shift key and typing a 7. You type the character `|` by holding down the shift key and typing a `\` (backslash). Don't confuse the `|` with the letters l or i or with the `!` character.

Compound Expressions

All of the examples presented so far have consisted of relatively simple expressions. Here's an example that combines several operators:

```
int    myInt;

myInt = 7;

if ( (myInt >= 1) && (myInt <= 10) )
   printf( "myInt is between 1 and 10" );
else
   printf( "myInt is not between 1 and 10" );
```

This example tests whether a variable is in the range between 1 and 10. The key here is the expression:

```
(myInt >= 1) && (myInt <= 10)
```

This expression lies between the `if` statement's parentheses and uses the `&&` operator to combine two smaller expressions. Notice that the two smaller expressions are each surrounded by parentheses to avoid any ambiguity. If we left out the parentheses, the expression might not be interpreted as we intended:

```
myInt >= 1 && myInt <= 10
```

Once again, use parentheses for safe computing.

Statements

At the beginning of the chapter, we defined the `if` statement as:

```
if ( expression )
   statement
```

We've covered expressions pretty thoroughly. Now, we'll turn our attention to the statement.

At this point in the book, you probably have a pretty good intuitive model of the statement. You'd probably agree that this is a statement:

```
myInt = 7;
```

But is this one statement or two?

```
if ( isCold )
   printf( "Put on your sweater!" );
```

The previous code fragment is a statement within another statement. The `printf()` resides within a larger statement, the `if` statement.

The ability to break your code out into individual statements is not a critical skill. Getting your code to compile, however, *is* critical. As we introduce new types of statements, pay attention to the statement syntax. And pay special attention to the examples. Where do the semicolons go? What distinguishes this type of statement from all other types?

As you build up your repertoire of statement types, you'll find yourself using one type of statement within another. That's perfectly acceptable in C. In fact, every time you create an `if` statement, you'll use at least two statements, one within the other. Take a look at this example:

```
if ( myVar >= 1 )
    if ( myVar <= 10 )
        printf( "myVar is between 1 and 10" );
```

This example uses an `if` statement as the statement for another `if` statement. This example calls the `printf()` if both `if` expressions are `true`, that is, if `myVar` is greater than or equal to 1 and less than or equal to 10. You could have accomplished the same result with this piece of code:

```
if ( ( myVar >= 1 ) && ( myVar <= 10 ) )
        printf( "myVar is between 1 and 10" );
```

The second piece of code is a little easier to read. There are times, however, when the method demonstrated in the first piece of code is preferred. Take a look at this example:

```
if ( myVar != 0 )
    if ( ( 1 / myVar ) < 1 )
        printf( "myVar is in range" );
```

One thing you don't want to do in C is divide a number by 0. Any number divided by 0 is infinity, and infinity is a foreign concept to the C language. If your program ever tries to divide a number by 0, your program is likely to crash. The first expression in this example tests to make sure that `myVar` is not equal to 0. If `myVar` is equal to 0, the second expression won't even be evaluated! The sole purpose of the first `if` is to make sure that the second `if` never tries to divide by 0. Make sure that you understand this point. Imagine what would happen if we wrote the code this way:

```
if ( (myVar != 0) && ((1 / myVar) < 1) )
      printf( "myVar is in range" );
```

As it turns out, if the left half of the && operator evaluates to false, the right half of the expression will never be evaluated, and the entire expression will evaluate to false. Why? Because if the left operand is false, it doesn't matter what the right operand is; true or false, the expression will evaluate to false. Be aware of this as you construct your expressions.

The Curly Braces

Earlier in the book, you learned about the curly braces ({ }) that surround the body of every function. These braces also play an important role in statement construction. Just as parentheses can be used to group terms of an expression together, curly braces can be used to group multiple statements together. Here's an example:

```
onYourBack = TRUE;

if ( onYourBack )
{
   printf( "Flipping over" );
   onYourBack = FALSE;
}
```

In the example, if onYourBack is true, both of the statements in curly braces will be executed. A pair of curly braces can be used to combine any number of statements into a single superstatement, also known as a **block**. You can use this technique anywhere a statement is called for.

Curly braces can be used to organize your code, much as you'd use parentheses to ensure that an expression is evaluated properly. This concept is especially appropriate when dealing with nested statements. Consider this code, for example:

```
if ( myInt >= 0 )
   if ( myInt <= 10 )
      printf( "myInt is between 0 and 10.\n" );
else
   printf( "myInt is negative.\n" ); /* <---Error!!! */
```

Do you see the problem with this code? Which if does the else belong to? As written (and as formatted), the else looks as though it belongs to the first if.

That is, if `myInt` is greater than or equal to 0, the second `if` is executed; otherwise, the second `printf()` is executed. Is this right?

Nope. As it turns out, an `else` belongs to the `if` closest to it (the second `if`, in this case). Here's a slight rewrite:

```
if ( myInt >= 0 )
   if ( myInt <= 10 )
      printf( "myInt is between 0 and 10.\n" );
   else
      printf( "myInt is not between 0 and 10.\n" );
```

One point here is that formatting is nice, but it won't fool the compiler. More important, this example shows how easy it is to make a mistake. Check out this version of the code:

```
if ( myInt >= 0 )
{
   if ( myInt <= 10 )
      printf( "myInt is between 0 and 10.\n" );
}
else
   printf( "myInt is negative.\n" );
```

Do you see how the curly braces help? In a sense, they act to hide the second `if` inside the first `if` statement. There is no chance for the `else` to connect to the hidden `if`.

No one I know ever got fired for using too many parentheses or too many curly braces.

Where to Place the Semicolon

So far, the statements we've seen fall into two categories. Function calls, such as calls to `printf()`, and assignment statements are called **simple statements**. Always place a semicolon at the end of a simple statement, even if it is broken over several lines, like this:

```
printf( "%d%d%d%d", var1,
                var2,
                var3,
                var4 );
```

Statements made up of several parts—including, possibly, other statements—are called **compound statements**. Compound statements obey some pretty strict rules of syntax. The `if` statement, for example, always looks like this:

```
if ( expression )
    statement
```

Notice there are no semicolons in this definition. The statement part of the `if` can be a simple statement or a compound statement. If the statement is simple, follow the semicolon rules for simple statements by placing a semicolon at the end of the statement. If the statement is compound, follow the semicolon rules for that particular type of statement.

Notice that using "curlies" to build a superstatement, or block, out of smaller statements does not require the addition of a semicolon.

The Loneliest Statement

Guess what? A single semicolon qualifies as a statement, albeit a somewhat lonely one. For example:

```
if ( bored )
    ;
```

This code fragment is a legitimate (and thoroughly useless) `if` statement. If `bored` is `true`, the semicolon statement gets executed. The semicolon by itself doesn't do anything but fill the bill where a statement was needed. There are times where the semicolon by itself is exactly what you need.

The `while` Statement

The `if` statement uses the value of an expression to decide whether to execute or to skip over a statement. If the statement is executed, it is executed just once. Another type of statement, the `while` statement, repeatedly executes a statement as long as a specified expression is `true`. The `while` statement follows this pattern:

```
while ( expression )
    statement
```

The `while` statement is also known as the `while` **loop**, because once the statement is executed, the `while` loops back to reevaluate the expression. Here's an example of the `while` loop in action:

```
int    i;

i=0;

while ( ++i < 3 )
    printf( "Looping: %d\n", i );

printf( "We are past the while loop." );
```

This example starts by declaring a variable, i, to be of type int; i is then initialized to 0. Next comes the while loop. The first thing the while loop does is evaluate its expression. The while loop's expression is:

```
++i < 3
```

Before this expression is evaluated, i has a value of 0. The prefix notation used in the expression (++i) increments the value of i to 1 before the remainder of the expression is evaluated. The evaluation of the expression results in true, since 1 is less than 3. Since the expression is true, the while loop's statement, a single printf( ), is executed. Here's the output after the first pass through the loop:

```
Looping: 1
```

Next, the while loops back and reevaluates its expression. Once again, the prefix notation increments i, this time to a value of 2. Since 2 is less than 3, the expression evaluates to true, and the printf( ) is executed again. Here's the output after the second pass through the loop:

```
Looping: 1
Looping: 2
```

Once the second printf( ) completes, it's back to the top of the loop to reevaluate the expression. Will this never end? Once again, i is incremented, this time to a value of 3. Aha! This time, the expression eval-uates to false, since 3 is not less than 3. Once the expression evaluates to false, the while loop ends. Control passes to the next statement, the second printf( ) in our example:

```
printf( "We are past the while loop." );
```

The while loop was driven by three factors: initialization, modification, and termination. Initialization is any code that affects the loop but occurs before the loop is entered. In our example, the critical initialization occurred when the variable i was set to 0.

By the Way

> In a loop, you'll frequently use a variable that changes value each time through the loop. In our example, the variable i was incremented by 1 each time through the loop. The first time through the loop, i had a value of 1. The second time, i had a value of 2. Variables that maintain a value based on the number of times through a loop are known as **counters**.
>
> Traditionally, programmers have given counter variables simple names, such as i, j, or k (it's an old FORTRAN convention). In the interest of clarity, some programmers use such names as `counter` or `loopCounter`. The nice thing about names like i, j, and k is that they don't get in the way; they don't take up a lot of space on the line. On the other hand, your goal should be to make your code as readable as possible, so it would seem that a name like `counter` would be better than the uninformative i, j, or k.
>
> Once again, pick a style you are comfortable with and stick with it!

Within the loop, modification is any code that changes the value of the loop's expression. In our example, the modification occurred within the expression itself when the counter, i, was incremented.

Termination is any condition that causes the loop to end. In our example, termination occurs when the expression has a value of `false`. This occurs when the counter, i, has a value that is not less than 3. Take a look at this example:

```
int    i;

i=1;

while ( i < 3 )
{
    printf( "Looping: %d\n", i );
    i++;
}

printf( "We are past the while loop." );
```

This example produces the same results as the previous example. This time, however, the initialization and modification conditions have changed slightly. In this example, i starts with a value of 1 instead of 0. In the previous example, the ++ operator was used to increment i at the very *top of the loop*. This example modifies i at the *bottom of the loop*.

Both of these examples show different ways to accomplish the same end. The phrase "There's more than one way to eat an Oreo" sums up the situation perfectly. There will always be more than one solution to any programming problem. Don't be afraid to do things your own way. Just make sure that your code works properly and is easy to read.

The `for` Statement

Nestled inside the C toolbox, right next to the `while` statement, is the `for` statement. The `for` statement is similar to the `while` statement, following the basic model of initialization, modification, and termination. Here's the pattern for a `for` statement:

```
for ( expression1 ; expression2 ; expression3 )
    statement
```

The first expression represents the `for` statement's initialization. Typically, this expression consists of an assignment statement, setting the initial value of a counter variable. This first expression is evaluated once, at the beginning of the loop.

The second expression is identical in function to the expression in a `while` statement, providing the termination condition for the loop. This expression is evaluated each time through the loop, before the statement is executed.

Finally, the third expression provides the modification portion of the `for` statement. This expression is evaluated at the bottom of the loop, immediately following execution of the statement.

Important

All three of these expressions are optional and may be left out entirely. For example, here's a `for` loop that leaves out all three expressions:

```
for ( ; ; )
    DoSomethingForever();
```

Since this loop has no terminating expression, it is known as an **infinite loop**. Infinite loops are generally considered bad form and should be avoided like the plague!

The for loop can also be described in terms of a while loop:

```
expression1;
while ( expression2 )
{
    statement
    expression3;
}
```

By the Way

Since you can always rewrite a for loop as a while loop, why introduce the for loop at all? Sometimes, a programming idea fits more naturally into the pattern of a for statement. If the for loop makes the code more readable, why not use it? As you write more and more code, you'll develop a sense for when to use the while and when to use the for.

Here's an example of a for loop:

```
int    i;

for ( i = 1; i < 3; i++ )
    printf( "Looping: %d\n", i );

printf( "We are past the for loop." );
```

This example is identical in functionality to the while loops presented earlier. Note the three expressions on the first line of the for loop. Before the loop is entered, the first expression is evaluated (remember, assignment statements make great expressions):

```
i = 1
```

Once the expression is evaluated, i has a value of 1. We are now ready to enter the loop. At the top of each pass through the loop, the second expression is evaluated:

```
i < 3
```

If the expression evaluates to true, the loop continues. Since i is less than 3, we can proceed. Next, the statement is executed:

```
printf( "Looping: %d\n", i );
```

Here's the first line of output:

```
Looping: 1
```

Having reached the bottom of the loop, the `for` evaluates its third expression:

```
i++
```

This changes the value of `i` to 2. Back to the top of the loop. Evaluate the termination expression:

```
i < 3
```

Since `i` is still less than 3, the loop continues. Once again, the `printf()` does its thing. The console window looks like this:

```
Looping: 1
Looping: 2
```

Next, the `for` evaluates `expression3`:

```
I++
```

The value of `i` is incremented to 3. Back to the top of the loop. Evaluate the termination expression:

```
i < 3
```

Lo and behold! Since `i` is no longer less than 3, the loop ends, and the second `printf()` in our example is executed:

```
printf( "We are past the for loop." );
```

As was the case with `while`, `for` can take full advantage of a pair of curly braces:

```
for ( i = 0; i < 10; i++ )
{
```

```
        DoThis();
        DoThat();
        DanceALittleJig();
}
```

In addition, both `while` and `for` can take advantage of the loneliest statement, the lone semicolon:

```
for ( i = 0; i < 1000; i++ )
    ;
```

This example does nothing 1000 times. But the example does take some time to execute. The initialization expression is evaluated once, and the modification and termination expressions are each evaluated 1000 times. Here's a `while` version of the loneliest loop:

```
i = 0;

while ( i++ < 1000 )
    ;
```

By the Way

> Some compilers will eliminate this loop and just set `i` to its terminating value (the value it would have if the loop executed normally). This is known as **code optimization**. The nice thing about code optimization is that it can make your code run faster and more efficiently. However, an optimization pass on your code can sometimes have unwanted side effects, such as eliminating the `while` loop just discussed. It's a good idea to get to know your compiler's optimization capabilities and tendencies. Read your manual!

loopTester.μ

Interestingly, there is an important difference between the `for` and `while` loops you just saw. Take a minute to look back and try to predict the value of `i` the first time through each loop and after each loop terminates. Were the results the same for the while and for loops? Hmmm. . . . You might want to take another look. Here's a sample program that should clarify the difference between these two loops. Look in the folder `Learn C Projects`, inside the subfolder named `06.02 - loopTester`, and open the project `loopTester.μ`. The file `loopTester.c` implements a `while` loop and two slightly different `for` loops. Run the project. Your output should look like that shown in Figure 6.4.

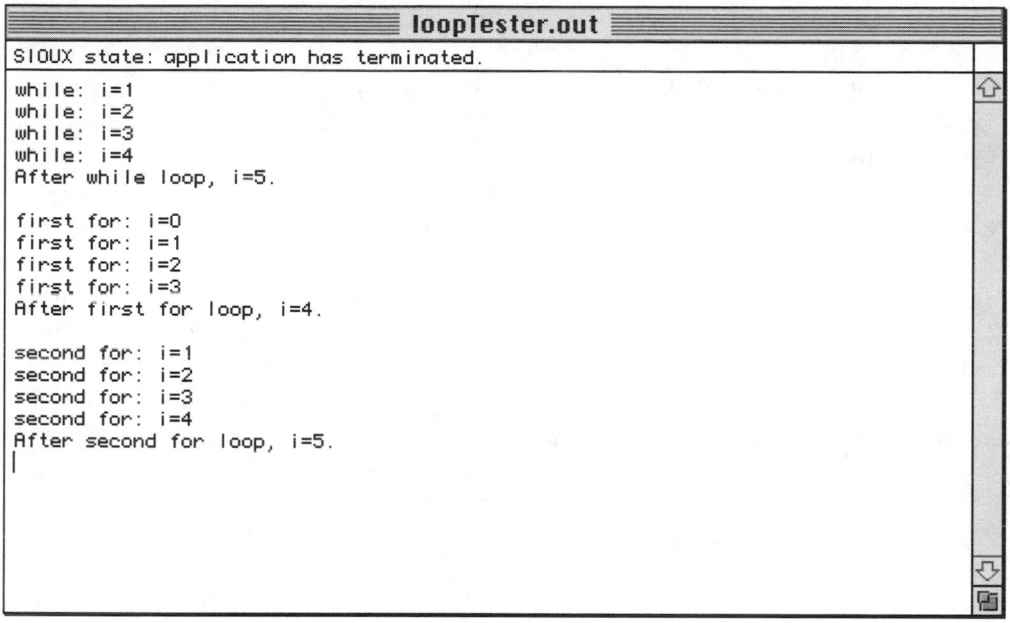

```
═══════════════ loopTester.out ═══════════════
SIOUX state: application has terminated.
while: i=1
while: i=2
while: i=3
while: i=4
After while loop, i=5.

first for: i=0
first for: i=1
first for: i=2
first for: i=3
After first for loop, i=4.

second for: i=1
second for: i=2
second for: i=3
second for: i=4
After second for loop, i=5.
```

Figure 6.4 The output from loopTester.μ, showing the output from three different loops.

The loopTester program starts off with the standard #include. The main() function defines a counter variable, i; sets i to 0; and then enters a while loop:

```
while ( i++ < 4 )
    printf( "while: i=%d\n", i );
```

The loop executes four times, resulting in this output:

```
while: i=1
while: i=2
while: i=3
while: i=4
```

Do you see why? If not, go through the loop yourself, calculating the value for i each time through the loop. Remember, since we are using postfix notation (i++), i gets incremented *after* the test is made to see whether it is less than 4. The test and the increment happen at the top of the loop, before the loop is entered.

Once the loop completes, we print the value of i again:

```
printf( "After while loop, i=%d.\n\n", i );
```

Here's the result:

```
After while loop, i=5.
```

Here's how we got that value. The last time through the loop (with i equal to 4), we go back to the top of the while loop, test to see whether i is less than 4 (it no longer is), and then do the increment of i, bumping it from 4 to 5.

OK, one loop down, two to go. This next loop looks as if it should accomplish the same thing. The difference is, we don't do the increment of i until the bottom of the loop, until we've been through the loop once already.

```
for ( i = 0; i < 4; i++ )
    printf( "first for: i=%d\n", i );
```

As you can see by the output, i ranges from 0 to 3 instead of from 1 to 4.

```
first for: i=0
first for: i=1
first for: i=2
first for: i=3
```

After we drop out of the for loop, we once again print the value of i:

```
printf( "After first for loop, i=%d.\n\n", i );
```

Here's the result:

```
After first for loop, i=4.
```

As you can see, the while loop ranged i from 1 to 4, leaving i with a value of 5 at the end of the loop. The for loop ranged i from 0 to 3, leaving i with a value of 4 at the end of the loop. So how do we fix the for loop so that it works the same way as the while loop? Take a look:

```
for ( i = 1; i <= 4; i++ )
    printf( "second for: i=%d\n", i );
```

This `for` loop started `i` at 1 instead of 0 and it tests to see whether `i` is *less than or equal to* 4 instead of just less than 4. We could also have used the terminating expression i < 5 instead. Either one will work. As proof, here's the output from this loop:

```
second for: i=1
second for: i=2
second for: i=3
second for: i=4
```

Once again, we print the value of `i` at the end of the loop:

```
printf( "After second for loop, i=%d.\n", i );

    return 0;
}
```

Here's the last piece of output:

```
After second for loop, i=5.
```

This second `for` loop is the functional equivalent of the `while` loop. Take some time to play with this code. You might try to modify the `while` loop to match the first `for` loop.

The `while` and `for` statements are by far the most common types of C loops. For completeness, however, we'll cover the remaining loop, a little-used gem called the `do` statement.

The do Statement

The do statement is a `while` statement that evaluates its expression at the bottom of its loop instead of at the top. Here's the pattern a do statement must match:

```
do
    statement
while ( expression ) ;
```

Here's a sample:

```
i = 1;

do
{
    printf( "%d\n", i );
    i++;
}
while ( i < 3 );

printf( "We are past the do loop." );
```

The first time through the loop, i has a value of 1. The `printf()` prints a 1 in the console window, then the value of i is bumped to 2. It's not until this point that the expression (i < 3) is evaluated. Since 2 is less than 3, a second pass through the loop occurs.

During this second pass, the `printf()` prints a 2 in the console window; then the value of i is bumped to 3. Once again, the expression (i < 3) is evaluated. Since 3 is not less than 3, we drop out of the loop to the second `printf()`.

The important thing to remember about do loops is this: Since the expression is not evaluated until the bottom of the loop, the body of the loop (the statement) is always executed at least once. Since `for` and `while` loops both check their expressions at the top of the loop, it's possible for either to drop out of the loop before the body of the loop is executed.

Let's move on to a completely different type of statement, known as the `switch`.

The `switch` Statement

The `switch` statement uses the value of an expression to determine which of a series of statements to execute. Here's an example that should make this concept a little clearer:

```
switch ( theYear )
{
    case 1066:
        printf( "Battle of Hastings" );
        break;
    case 1492:
        printf( "Columbus sailed the ocean blue" );
        break;
```

```
    case 1776:
       printf( "Declaration of Independence\n" );
       printf( "A very important document!!!" );
       break;
    default:
       printf( "Don't know what happened during this year" );
}
```

The switch is constructed of a series of cases, each based on a specific value of theYear. If theYear has a value of 1066, execution continues with the statement following that case's colon, in this case, the line:

```
printf( "Battle of Hastings" );
```

Execution continues, line after line, until either the bottom of the switch (the right-curly brace) or a break statement is reached. In this case, the next line is a break statement.

The break statement comes in handy when you are working with switch statements and loops. The break tells the computer to jump immediately to the next statement after the end of the loop or switch.

Continuing with the example, if theYear has a value of 1492, the switch jumps to the lines:

```
printf( "Columbus sailed the ocean blue" );
break;
```

A value of 1776 jumps to the lines:

```
printf( "Declaration of Independence\n" );
printf( "A very important document!!!" );
break;
```

Notice that this case has two statements before the break. There is no limit to the number of statements a case can have: One is OK; 653 is OK. You can even have a case with no statements at all.

The original example also contains a default case. If the switch can't find a case that matches the value of its expression, the switch looks for a case labeled default. If the default is present, its statements are executed. If no default is present, the switch completes without executing any of its statements.

Here's the pattern the switch tries to match:

```
switch ( expression )
{
   case constant:
      statements
   case constant:
      statements
   default:
      statements
}
```

Why would you want a case with no statements? Here's an example:

```
switch ( myVar )
{
      case 1:
      case 2:
         DoSomething();
         break;
      case 3:
         DoSomethingElse();
}
```

In this example, if myVar has a value of 1 or 2, the function DoSomething() is called. If myVar has a value of 3, the function DoSomethingElse() is called. If myVar has any other value, nothing happens. Use a case with no statements when you want two different cases to execute the same statements.

Think about what happens with this example:

```
switch ( myVar )
{
      case 1:
         DoSometimes();
      case 2:
         DoFrequently();
      default:
         DoAlways();
}
```

If `myVar` is 1, all three functions will get called. If `myVar` is 2, `DoFrequently()` and `DoAlways()` will get called. If `myVar` has any other value, `DoAlways()` gets called by itself. This is a good example of a `switch` without `break`s.

At the heart of each `switch` is its expression. Most `switch`es are based on single variables, but, as we mentioned earlier, assignment statements make perfectly acceptable expressions.

Each `case` is based on a **constant**. Numbers (such as 47 or –12,932) are valid constants. Variables, such as `myVar`, are not. As you'll see later, single-byte characters (such as 'a' or '\n') are also valid constants. Multiple-byte character strings (like "Gummy-bear") are not.

If your `switch` uses a `default` `case`, make sure that you use it as shown in the pattern described. Don't include the word `case` before the word `default`.

break Statements in Other Loops

The `break` statement has other uses besides the `switch` statement. Here's an example of a `break` used in a `while` loop:

```
i=1;

while ( i <= 9 )
{
   PlayAnInning( i );
   if ( ItIsRaining() )
      break;
   i++;
}
```

This sample tries to play nine innings of baseball. As long as the function `ItIsRaining()` returns with a value of `false`, the game continues uninterrupted. If `ItsRaining()` returns a value of `true`, the `break` statement is executed, and the program drops out of the loop, interrupting the game.

The `break` statement allows you to construct loops that depend on multiple factors. The termination of the loop depends on the value of the expression found at the top of the loop, as well as on any outside factors that might trigger an unexpected `break`.

Sample Programs

isOdd.c

This program combines `for` and `if` statements to tell you whether the numbers 1 through 20 are odd or even and whether they are an even multiple of 3. The program also introduces a brand new operator: the `%` operator. Go into the `Learn C Projects` folder, then into the `06.03 - isOdd` subfolder, and open the project `isOdd.`μ.

Run `isOdd.`μ by selecting **Run** from the **Project** menu. You should see something like the console window shown in Figure 6.5. You should see a line for each number from 1 through 20. Each of the numbers will be described as either odd or even. Each of the multiples of 3 will have additional text describing them as such. Here's how the program works.

Stepping Through the Source Code

This program starts off with the usual `#include` and the beginning of `main()`, which begins by declaring a counter variable named `i`.

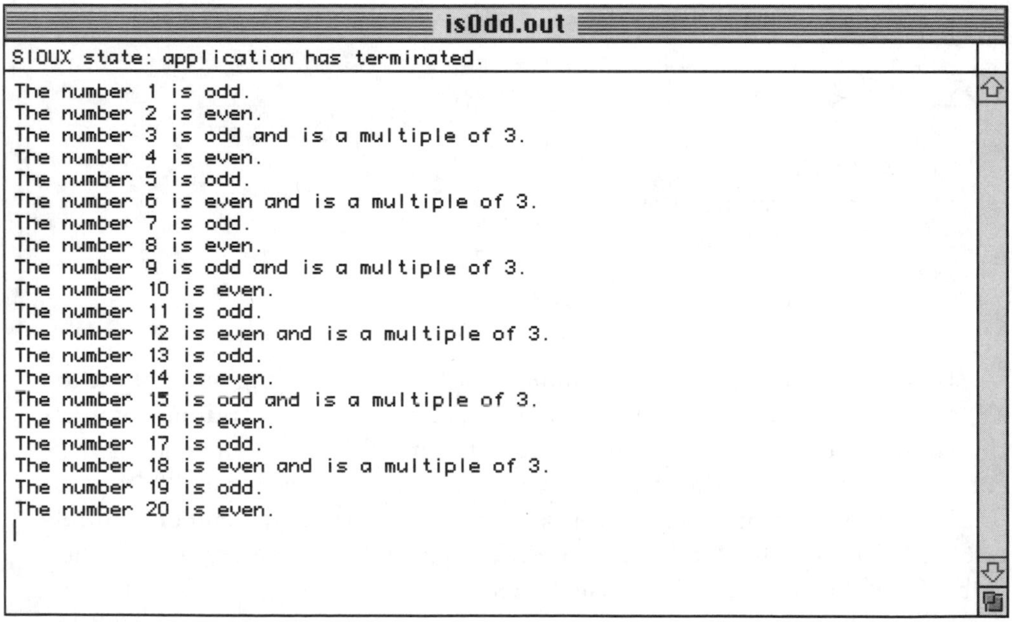

```
================= isOdd.out =================
SIOUX state: application has terminated.
The number 1 is odd.
The number 2 is even.
The number 3 is odd and is a multiple of 3.
The number 4 is even.
The number 5 is odd.
The number 6 is even and is a multiple of 3.
The number 7 is odd.
The number 8 is even.
The number 9 is odd and is a multiple of 3.
The number 10 is even.
The number 11 is odd.
The number 12 is even and is a multiple of 3.
The number 13 is odd.
The number 14 is even.
The number 15 is odd and is a multiple of 3.
The number 16 is even.
The number 17 is odd.
The number 18 is even and is a multiple of 3.
The number 19 is odd.
The number 20 is even.
```

Figure 6.5 Running `isOdd.`μ.

```
int main( void )
{
    inti;
```

Our goal here is to step through each of the numbers from 1 to 20. For each number, we want to check to see whether the number is odd or even. We also want to check whether the number is evenly divisible by 3. Once we've analyzed a number, we'll use `printf()` to print a description of the number in the console window.

By the Way

> The scheme that defines the way a program works is called the program's algorithm. It's a good idea to try to work out the details of your program's algorithm before writing even one line of source code.

As you might expect, the next step is to set up a `for` loop, using `i` as a counter initialized to 1. The loop will keep running as long as the value of `i` is less than or equal to 20. This is the same as saying that the loop will exit as soon as the value of `i` is found to be greater than 20. Every time the loop reaches the bottom, the third expression, `i++`, will be evaluated, incrementing the value of `i` by 1. This is a classic `for` loop.

```
for ( i = 1; i <= 20; i++ )
{
```

Now we're inside the `for` loop. Our goal is to print a single line for each number, that is, one line each time through the `for` loop. If you check back to Figure 6.4, you'll notice that each line starts with the phrase:

```
The number x is
```

In that phrase, `x` is the number being described. That's the purpose of this first `printf()`:

```
printf( "The number %d is ", i );
```

Notice that this `printf()` wasn't part of an `if` statement. We want this `printf()` to print its message every time through the loop. The next sequence of `printf()` statements are a different story altogether.

105

The next chunk of code determines whether i is even or odd, then uses printf() to print the appropriate word in the console window. Because the last printf() didn't end with a newline character ('\n'), the word "even" or "odd" will appear in the console window on the *same line* as, and immediately following:

```
The number x is
```

This next chunk of code introduces a brand new operator—%—a binary operator that returns the remainder when the left operand is divided by the right operand. For example, i % 2 divides 2 into i and returns the remainder. If i is even, this remainder will be 0. If i is odd, this remainder will be 1.

```
if ( (i % 2) == 0 )
    printf( "even" );
else
    printf( "odd" );
```

In the expression i % 3, the remainder will be 0 if i is evenly divisible by 3 and either 1 or 2 otherwise.

```
if ( (i % 3) == 0 )
    printf( " and is a multiple of 3" );
```

If i is evenly divisible by 3, we'll add the following phrase to the end of the current line:

```
" and is a multiple of 3"
```

Finally, we add a period "." and a newline "\n" to the end of the current line, placing us at the beginning of the next line of the console window:

```
printf( ".\n" );
```

The loop ends with a curly brace, and main() ends with our normal return and a righ-curly brace.

```
    }

    return 0;
}
```

nextPrime.π

Our next program focuses on the mathematical concept of **prime numbers**. A prime number is any number whose only factors are 1 and itself. For example, 6 is not a prime number, because its factors are 1, 2, 3, and 6. The number 5 is prime because its factors are limited to 1 and 5. The number 12 isn't prime, because its factors are 1, 2, 3, 4, 6, and 12.

Our next program will find the next prime number greater than a specified number. For example, if we set our starting point to 14, the program would find the next prime, 17. We have the program set up to check for the next prime after 19. Know what that is?

Go into the folder Learn C Projects, into the subfolder 06.04 - nextPrime, and open the project nextPrime.μ. Run nextPrime.μ by selecting **Run** from the **Project** menu. You should see something like the console window shown in Figure 6.6. As you can see, the next prime number after 19 is (drum roll, please . . .) 23. Here's how the program works.

Stepping Through the Source Code

This program starts off with two #includes instead of the usual one. The new #include, <math.h>, gives us access to a series of math functions, most notably

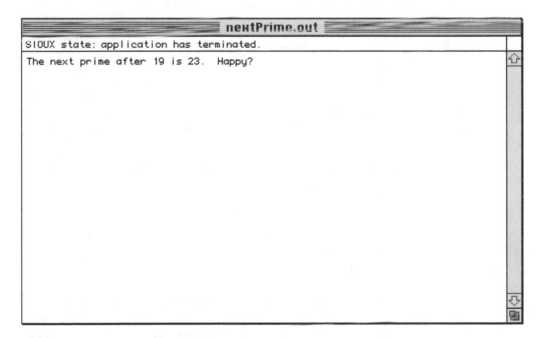

Figure 6.6 Running nextPrime.μ.

the function sqrt(). This function takes a single parameter and returns the square root of that parameter. You'll see how this works in a minute.

```
#include <stdio.h>
#include <math.h>


int    main( void )
{
```

We're going to need a boatload of variables. They're all defined as ints:

```
int    startingPoint, candidate, last, i;
int    isPrime;
```

The first variable, startingPoint, is the number we want to start off with. We'll find the next prime after startingPoint; candidate is the current candidate we are considering. Is candidate the lowest prime number greater than startingPoint? By the time we are done, it will be!

```
startingPoint = 19;
```

Since 2 is the lowest prime number, if startingPoint is less than 2, we know that the next prime is 2. By setting candidate to 2, our work is done:

```
if ( startingPoint < 2 )
{
    candidate = 2;
}
```

If startingPoint is 2, the next prime is 3, and we'll set candidate accordingly:

```
else if ( startingPoint == 2 )
{
    candidate = 3;
}
```

If we got this far, we know that startingPoint is greater than 2. Since 2 is the only even prime number and since we've already checked for startingPoint being equal to 2, we can now limit our search to odd numbers only. We'll start candidate at startingPoint, then make sure that candidate is odd. If it isn't, we'll decrement `candidate`. Why decrement instead of increment? If you peek ahead a few lines, you'll see that we're about to enter a do loop and that we bump `candidate` to the next odd number at the *top* of the loop. By decrementing `candidate` now, we're preparing for the bump at the top of the loop, which will take `candidate` to the next odd number greater than `startingPoint`.

```
else
{
    candidate = startingPoint;

    if (candidate % 2 == 0)
        candidate--;
```

This loop will continue stepping through consecutive odd numbers until we find a prime number. We'll start `isPrime` off as `true`, then check the current `candidate` to see whether we can find a factor. If we do find a factor, we'll set `isPrime` to `false`, forcing us to repeat the loop.

```
do
{
    isPrime = true;
    candidate += 2;
```

Now we'll check to see whether `candidate` is prime. This means verifying that `candidate` has no factors other than 1 and `candidate`. To do this, we'll check the numbers from 3 to the square root of `candidate` to see whether any of them divides evenly into `candidate`. If not, we know we've got ourselves a prime!

```
last = sqrt( candidate );
```

By the Way

So why don't we check from 2 up to `candidate` –1? Why start with 3? Since `candidate` will never be even, we know that 2 will never be a factor. For the same reason, we know that no even number will ever be a factor.

Why stop at the square root of `candidate`? Good question! To help understand this approach, consider the factors of 12, other than 1 and 12. They are 2, 3, 4, and 6. The square root of 12 is approximately 3.46. Notice how this fits nicely in the middle of the list of factors. Each of the factors less than the square root will have a matching factor greater than the square root. In this case, 2 matches with 6 (2*6=12) and 3 matches with 4 (3*4=12). This will always be true. If we don't find a factor by the time we hit the square root, there won't be a factor, and the candidate is prime.

Take a look at the top of the `for` loop. We start `i` at 3. Each time we hit the top of the loop (including the first time through the loop), we'll check to make sure that we haven't passed the square root of `candidate` and that `isPrime` is still `true`. If `isPrime` is `false`, we can stop searching for a factor, since we've just found one! Finally, each time we complete the loop, we bump `i` to the next odd number.

```
for ( i = 3; (i <= last) && isPrime; i += 2 )
{
```

Each time through the loop, we'll check to see whether `i` divides evenly into `candidate`. If so, we know that it is a factor, and we can set `isPrime` to `false`:

```
if ( (candidate % i) == 0 )
        isPrime = false;
    }
} while ( ! isPrime );
}
```

Once we drop out of the do loop, we use `printf()` to print both the starting point and the first prime number greater than the starting point:

```
printf( "The next prime after %d is %d.  Happy?\n",
        startingPoint, candidate );

return 0;
}
```

If you are interested in prime numbers, play around with this program. See if you can modify the code to print all the prime numbers from 1 to 100. How about the first 100 prime numbers?

What's Next?

Congratulations! You've made it through some tough concepts. You've learned about the C statements that allow you to control your program's flow. You've learned about C expressions and the concept of `true` and `false`. You've also learned about the logical operators based on the values `true` and `false`. You've learned about the `if`, `if-else`, `for`, `while`, `do`, `switch`, and `break` statements. In short, you've learned a lot!

Our next chapter introduces the concept of **pointers**, also known as variable addresses. From now on, you'll use pointers in almost every C program you write. Pointers allow you to implement complex data structures, opening up a world of programming possibilities.

Chapter 7 also discusses function parameters in detail. As usual, plenty of code fragments and sample applications will be presented to keep you busy. See you there.

Exercises

1. What's wrong with each of the following code fragments:

   a.
   ```
   if i
       i++;
   ```

   b.
   ```
   for( i=0; i<20; i++ )
       i--;
   ```

   c.
   ```
   while ( )
       i++;
   ```

   d.
   ```
   do ( i++ )
       until ( i == 20 );
   ```

   e.
   ```
   switch ( i )
   {
       case "hello":
       case "goodbye":
           printf( "Greetings." );
           break;
       case default:
           printf( "Boring." );
   }
   ```

   f.
   ```
   if    ( i < 20 )
       if    ( i == 20 )
           printf( "Lonely..." );
   ```

   g.
   ```
   while ( done = TRUE )
       done = ! done;
   ```

   h.
   ```
   for( i=0; i<20; i*20 )
       printf( "Modification..." );
   ```

2. Modify nextPrime.c to compute the prime numbers from 1 to 100.

3. Modify nextPrime.c to compute the first 100 prime numbers.

Pointers and Parameters

You've come a long way. You've mastered variable basics, operators, and statements. You're about to add some powerful, new concepts to your programming toolbox.

For starters, we'll introduce the concept of pointers. In programming, pointers are references to other things. When someone calls your name to get your attention, they're using your name as a pointer. Your name is one way people refer to you.

What Is a Pointer?

Your name and address can combine to serve as a pointer, telling the mail carrier where to deliver the new Sears catalog. Your address distinguishes your house from all the other houses in your neighborhood, and your name distinguishes you from the rest of the people living in your house.

A pointer to a variable is really the address of the variable in memory. If you pass the value of a variable to a function, the function can make use of the variable's value but can't *change* the variable's value. If you pass the address of the variable to the function, the function can also change the value of the variable.

When you declare a variable in C, memory is allocated to the variable. This memory has an address. C pointers are special variables, specifically designed to hold one of these addresses. Later in the chapter, you'll learn how to create a pointer, how to make it point to a specific variable, and how to use the pointer to change the variable's value.

Why Use Pointers?

Pointers can be extremely useful, allowing you to access your data in ways that ordinary variables just don't allow. Here's a real-world example of "pointer flexibility."

When you go to the library in search of a specific title, you probably start your search in a card catalog. Card catalogs contain thousands of index cards, one for every book in the library. Each index card contains information about a specific book: the author's name, the book's title, and the copyright date, for example.

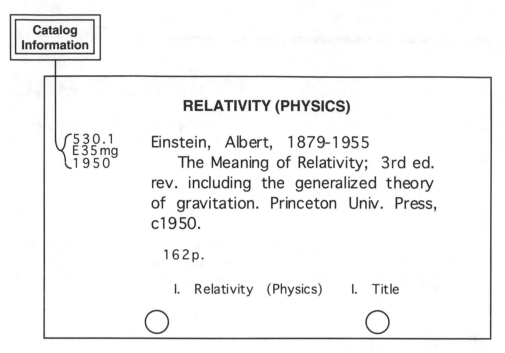

Figure 7.1 Catalog card for a rather famous book. Note the catalog information on the left side of the card.

Most libraries have three card catalogs. Each lists all the books, sorted alphabetically by subject, by author, or by title. In the subject card catalog, a book can be listed more than once. For example, a book about Thomas Jefferson might be listed under "Presidents, U.S.," "Architects," or even under "Inventors" (Jefferson was quite an inventor).

Figure 7.1 shows a catalog card for Albert Einstein's famous book on relativity, called *The Meaning of Relativity*. The card was listed in the subject catalog under the subject "RELATIVITY (PHYSICS)." Take a minute to look the card over. Pay special attention to the catalog information located on the left side of the card. The catalog number for this book is 530.1. This number tells you exactly where to find the book among all the other books on the shelves. The books are ordered numerically, so you'll find this book , between 530 and 531 on the shelves.

Important

In this example, the library bookshelves are like your computer's memory, with the books acting as data. The catalog number is the address of your data (a book) in memory (on the shelf).

As you might have guessed, the catalog number acts as a pointer. The card catalogs use these pointers to rearrange all the books in the library, without moving a single book. Think about it. In the subject card catalog, all the books are arranged by subject. Physically, the book arrangements have nothing to do with subject. Physically, the books are arranged numerically, by catalog number. By adding a layer of pointers between you and the books, the librarians achieve an extra layer of flexibility.

In the same way, the author and title card catalogs use a layer of pointers to arrange all the books by author and by title. With these pointers, all the books in the library can be arranged in four different ways without ever leaving the shelves. The books are arranged physically (sorted by catalog number) and logically (sorted in one catalog by author, in another by subject, and in another by title). Without the support of a layer of pointers, these logical book arrangements would be impossible.

By the Way

> Adding a layer of pointers is also known as "adding a level of indirection." The number of levels of indirection is the number of pointers you have to use to get to your library book (or to your data).

Checking Out of the Library

So far, we've talked about pointers in terms of library catalog numbers. The use of pointers in your C programs is not much different from this model. Each card catalog number points out the location of a book on the library shelf. In the same way, each pointer in your program will point out the location of a piece of data in computer memory.

If you wrote a program to keep track of your compact disc collection, you might maintain a list of pointers, each one of which might point to a block of data describing a single CD. Each block of data might contain such information as the name of the artist, the name of the album, the year of release, and a category (jazz, rock, blues). If you got more ambitious, you could create several pointer lists. One list might sort your CDs alphabetically by artist name. Another might sort them chronologically by year of release. Yet another list might sort your CDs by musical category. You get the picture.

There's a lot you can do with pointers. By mastering the techniques presented in these next few chapters, you'll be able to create programs that take full advantage of pointers.

Our goal for this chapter is to master pointer basics. We'll talk about C pointers and C pointer operations. You'll learn how to create a pointer and how to make the pointer point to a variable. You'll also learn how to use a pointer to change the value of the variable the pointer points to.

Pointer Basics

Pointers are variable addresses. Instead of an address such as:

```
1313 Mockingbird Lane
Raven Heights, California  90263
```

a variable's address refers to a memory location within your computer. As we discussed in Chapter 3, your computer's memory consists of a sequence of bytes. A 1-megabyte computer has exactly 2^{20} (or 1,048,576) bytes of memory, also known as **random-access memory**, or **RAM**. An 8-megabyte computer has exactly $8 \times 2^{20} = 2^{23}$ = 8,388,608 bytes of RAM. Every one of those bytes has its own unique address. The first byte has an address of 0. The next byte has an address of 1. Computer addresses always start with 0 and continue up, one at a time, until they reach the highest address. Figure 7.2 shows the addressing scheme for an 8-megabyte computer. Notice that the addresses run from 0 (the lowest address) all the way up to 8,388,607 (the highest address).

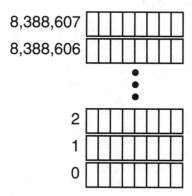

Figure 7.2 Addressing scheme for 8 megabytes of bytes.

Variable Addresses

When you run a program, one of the first things the computer does is allocate memory for your program's variables. For example, suppose that you declare an int in your code, like this:

```
int     myVar;
```

The compiler reserves memory for the exclusive use of `myVar`.

Important

> The amount of memory allocated for an `int` depends on your development environment. For example, CodeWarrior allows you to select either 2- or 4-byte `int`s. Since all of the projects in this book were built using 2-byte `int`s, the figures showing `int` memory allocation also show 2-byte `int`s. Don't be fooled! If your development environment is set to use 4-byte `int`s, 4 bytes will be allocated for each `int`.

Each of `myVar`'s bytes has a specific address. Figure 7.3 shows an 8-megabyte computer with 2 bytes allocated to the variable `myVar`. In this picture, the 2 bytes allocated to `myVar` have the addresses 508 and 509.

By convention, a variable's address is said to be the address of its first byte (the first byte is the one with the lowest-numbered address). If a variable uses memory locations 508 and 509 (as `myVar` does), its address is 508 and its length is 2 bytes.

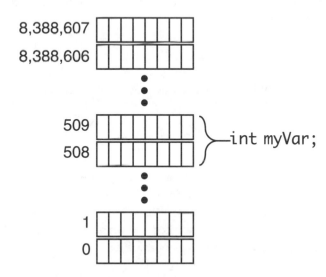

Figure 7.3 The 2 bytes allocated for the `int` named `myVar`.

Important

> When more than 1 byte is allocated to a variable, the bytes will always be consecutive (next to each other in memory). The 2 bytes allocated to an `int` might have such addresses as 508 and 509 or 64,000 and 64,001. You will never see an `int` whose byte addresses are 508 and 695. A variable's bytes are like family—they stick together!

As we showed earlier, a variable's address is a lot like the catalog number on a library catalog card. Both act as pointers: one to a book on the library shelf and the other to a variable. From now on, when we use the term pointer with respect to a variable, we are referring to the variable's address.

Now that you understand what a pointer is, your next goal is to learn how to use pointers in your programs. The next few sections will teach you some valuable pointer-programming skills. You'll learn how to create a pointer to a variable. You'll also learn how to use that pointer to access the variable it points to.

The C language provides you with a few key tools to help you. These tools come in the form of two special operators: `&` and `*`.

The `&` Operator

The `&` operator (also called the "address of" operator) pairs with a variable name to produce the variable's address. For example, the following expression refers to `myVar`'s address in memory:

```
&myVar
```

If `myVar` owned memory locations 508 and 509 (as in Figure 7.3), the expression would have a value of 508:

```
&myVar
```

The expression `&myVar` is a pointer to the variable `myVar`.

As you start programming with pointers, you'll find yourself using the `&` operator frequently. An expression like `&myVar` is a common way to represent a pointer. Another way to represent a pointer is with a **pointer variable**, a variable specifically designed to hold the address of another variable.

Declaring a Pointer Variable

C supports a special notation for declaring pointer variables. The following line declares a variable called myPointer:

```
int    *myPointer;
```

Notice that the * is not part of the variable's name. Instead, it tells the compiler that the associated variable is a pointer, specifically designed to hold the address of an int. If there were a data type called bluto, you could declare a variable designed to point to a bluto like this:

```
bluto *blutoPointer;
```

For now, we'll limit ourselves to pointers that point to ints. Look at this code:

```
int    *myPointer, myVar;
myPointer = &myVar;
```

The assignment statement puts myVar's address in the variable myPointer. If myVar's address is 508, this code will leave myPointer with a value of 508. Note that this code has absolutely no effect on the value of myVar.

There will be times in your coding when you have a pointer to a variable but not the variable itself. This happens a lot. You can use the pointer to manipulate the value of the variable it points to. Observe:

```
int    *myPointer, myVar;

myPointer = &myVar;
*myPointer = 27;
```

As before, the first assignment statement places myVar's address in the variable myPointer. The second assignment introduces the * operator. The * operator (called the **star** operator) converts a pointer variable to the item the pointer points to.

By the Way

The * that appears in the declaration statement isn't really an operator. It's there only to designate the variable myPointer as a pointer.

119

If myPointer points to myVar, as is the case in our example, *myPointer refers to the variable myVar. In this case, the next two lines say the same thing:

```
*myPointer = 27;

myVar = 27;
```

Confused? These memory pictures should help. Figure 7.4 joins our program in progress, just after the variables myVar and myPointer were declared:

```
int    *myPointer, myVar;
```

Notice that 2 bytes were allocated for the variable myVar and that 4 bytes were allocated for myPointer. Why? Because myVar is an int and myPointer is a

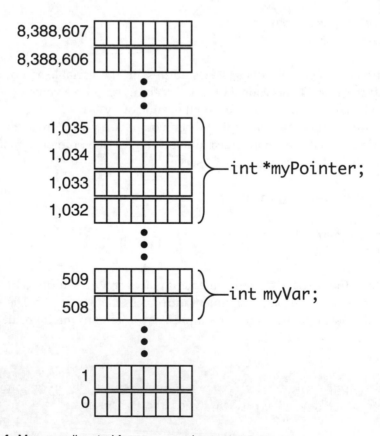

Figure 7.4 Memory allocated for myVar and myPointer.

pointer, designed to hold a 4-byte address; 4 bytes equal 32 bits. Since memory addresses start at 0 and can never be negative, 4-byte memory addresses range from 0 up to $2^{32} - 1 = 4,294,967,295$. That means that a 32-bit computer can address a maximum of 4 gigabytes (4096 megabytes) of memory. That's a lot of RAM!

Important

> Older computers (such as the Apple IIe, for example) represented an address using 2 bytes (16-bits) of memory, yielding a range of addresses from 0 to $2^{16} - 1 = 65,535$. Imagine having to fit your operating system, as well as all your applications, in a mere 64K of RAM (1K = 1024 bytes).
>
> When the Mac first appeared, it came with 128K of RAM and used 24-bit memory addresses, yielding a range of addresses from 0 to $2^{24} - 1 = 16,777,215$ (also known as 16 megabytes). In those days, no one could imagine a computer that included 16 entire megabytes of memory!
>
> Of course, these days we are much smarter. We absolutely know for a fact that we'll never exceed the need for 32-bit addresses. I mean, there's no way that a computer could ever make use of 4 gigabytes of RAM, right? Hmmm. . . . Better not count on that. In fact, if you are a betting person, I'd wager that someday we'll see 8-byte addresses. For now, it's OK to think of addresses as all being 4 bytes in length. Just remember that that number is strictly implementation dependent!

Once memory is allocated for `myVar` and `myPointer`, we move on to the statement:

```
myPointer = &myVar;
```

The 4-byte address of the variable `myVar` is written to the 4 bytes allocated to `myPointer`. In our example, `myVar`'s address is 508. Figure 7.5 shows the value 508 stored in `myPointer`'s 4 bytes. Now `myPointer` is said to "point to" `myVar`.

OK, we're almost there. The next line of our example writes the value 27 to the location pointed to by `myPointer`:

```
*myPointer = 27;
```

Without the * operator, the computer would place the value 27 in the memory allocated to `myPointer`. The * operator **dereferences** `myPointer`. Dereferencing a pointer turns the pointer into the variable it points to. Figure 7.6 shows the end results.

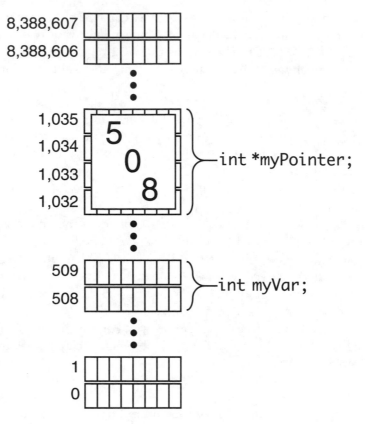

Figure 7.5 The address of myVar is assigned to myPointer.

If the concept of pointers seems alien to you, don't worry. You are not alone. Programming with pointers is one of the most difficult topics you'll ever take on. Just keep reading, and follow each of the examples line by line. By the end of the chapter, you'll be a pointer expert!

Function Parameters

One of the most important uses of pointers (and perhaps the easiest to understand) lies in the implementation of **function parameters.** In this section, we'll focus on parameters and, at the same time, have a chance to see pointers in action.

What Are Function Parameters?

A function parameter is your chance to share a variable between a calling function and the called function.

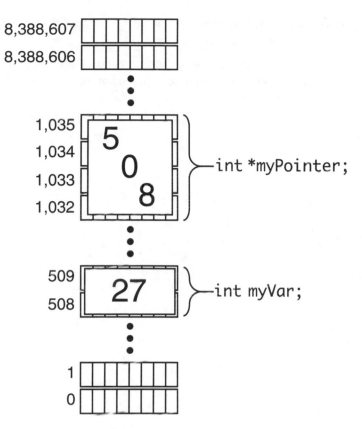

Figure 7.6 Finally, the value 27 is assigned to *myPointer.

Suppose that you wanted to write a function called AddTwo() that took two numbers, added them, and returned their sum. How would you get the two original numbers into AddTwo()? How would you get the sum of the two numbers back to the function that called AddTwo()?

As you might have guessed, the answer to both questions lies in the use of parameters. Before you can learn how to use parameters, however, you'll have to first understand the concept of **variable scope**.

Variable Scope

In C, every variable is said to have a scope, or range. A variable's scope defines where in the program you have access to a variable. In other words, if a variable is declared inside one function, can another function refer to that same variable?

C defines variable scope as follows:

- A variable declared inside a function is local to that function and may be referenced only inside that function.

This statement is important. It means that you can't declare a variable inside one function, then refer to that same value inside another function. Here's an example that will never compile:

```
int    main( void )
{
    int    numDots;

    numDots = 500;

    DrawDots();

    return 0;
}

void  DrawDots( void )
{
    int    i;

    for ( i = 1; i <= numDots; i++ )
        printf( "." );
}
```

The error in this code occurs when the function `DrawDots()` tries to reference the variable `numDots`. According to the rules of scope, `DrawDots()` doesn't even know about the variable `numDots`. If you tried to compile this program, the compiler would complain that `DrawDots()` tried to use the variable `numDots` without declaring it.

The problem you are faced with is getting the value of `numDots` to the function `DrawDots()` so `DrawDots()` knows how many "dots" to draw. The answer to this problem is function parameters.

By the Way

DrawDots() is another example of the value of writing functions. We've taken the code needed to perform a specific function (in this case, draw some dots) and embedded it in a function. Now, instead of having to duplicate the code inside DrawDots() every time we want to draw some dots in our program, all we'd need is a single line of code: a call to the function DrawDots().

How Function Parameters Work

Function parameters are just like variables. Instead of being declared at the beginning of a function, function parameters are declared between the parentheses on the function's title line, like this:

```
void DrawDots( int numDots )
{
    /* function's body goes here */
}
```

When you call a function, you just match up the parameters, making sure that you pass the function what it expects. To call the version of `DrawDots()` we just defined, make sure that you place an `int` between the parentheses. The call to `DrawDots()` inside `main()` passes the value 30 into the function `DrawDots()`:

```
int main( void )
{
    DrawDots( 30 );

    return 0;
}
```

When `DrawDots()` starts executing, it sets its parameter to the passed-in value. In this case, `DrawDots()` has one parameter, an `int` named `numDots`. When the call executes, the function `DrawDots()` sets its parameter, `numDots`, to a value of 30:

```
DrawDots( 30 );
```

To make things a little clearer, here's a revised version of our example:

```
int    main( void )
{
    DrawDots( 30 );

    return 0;
}

void  DrawDots( int numDots )
{
```

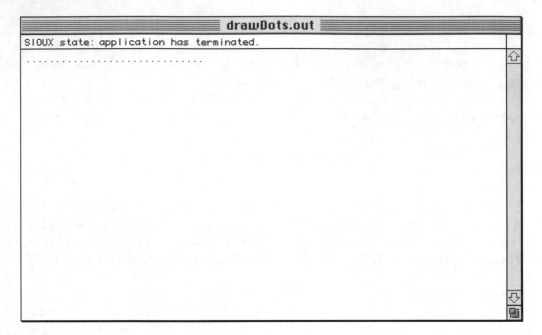

Figure 7.7 The program `drawDots` in action.

```
int    i;

for ( i = 1; i <= numDots; i++ )
   printf( "." );
}
```

This version of `main()` calls `DrawDots()`, passing as a parameter the constant 30. `DrawDots()` receives the value 30 in its `int` parameter, `numDots`. This means that the function `DrawDots()` starts execution with a variable named `numDots` having a value of 30.

Inside `DrawDots()`, the `for` loop behaves as you might expect, drawing 30 periods in the console window. Figure 7.7 shows this program in action. You can run this example yourself. The project file, `drawDots.µ`, is located in the `Learn C Projects` folder in a subfolder named `07.01 - drawDots`.

Parameters Are Temporary

When you pass a value from a calling function to a called function, you are creating a temporary variable inside the called function. Once the called function exits (returns to the calling function), that variable ceases to exist.

In our example, we passed a value of 30 into `DrawDots()` as a parameter. The value came to rest in the parameter variable named `numDots`. Once `DrawDots()` exited, `numDots` ceased to exist.

- Remember, a variable declared inside a function can be referenced only by that function.

It is perfectly acceptable for two functions to use the same variable names for completely different purposes. It's fairly standard, for example, to use a variable name like `i` as a counter in a `for` loop. What happens when, in the middle of just such a `for` loop, you call a function that also uses a variable named `i`? Here's an example:

```
int    main( void )
{
    int    i;

    for ( i=1; i<=10; i++ )
    {
        DrawDots( 30 );
        printf( "\n" );
    }

    return 0;
}

void   DrawDots( int numDots )
{
    int    i;

    for ( i = 1; i <= numDots; i++ )
        printf( "." );
}
```

This code prints a series of 10 rows of dots, with 30 dots in each row. After each call to `DrawDots()`, a carriage return (`"\n"`) is printed, moving the cursor in position to begin the next row of dots.

Notice that both `main()` and `DrawDots()` feature a variable named `i`. In `main()`, the variable `i` is used as a counter, tracking the number of rows of dots printed. `DrawDots()` also uses `i` as a counter, tracking the number of dots in the row it is printing. Won't the copy of `i` in `DrawDots()` mess up the copy of `i` in `main()`? No!

When `main()` starts executing, memory gets allocated for its copy of `i`. When `main()` calls `DrawDots()`, additional memory gets allocated for the copy of `i` in `DrawDots()`. When `DrawDots()` exits, the memory for its copy of `i` is **deallocated**, freed up so it can be used again for some other **variable.** A variable declared within a specific function is known as a **local variable.** `DrawDots()` has a single local variable, the variable `i`.

What Do Parameters Have to Do with Pointers?

OK. Now we're getting to the crux of the whole matter. What does all this have to do with pointers? To answer this question, you have to understand the two different methods of parameter passing.

Parameters are passed from function to function either by value or by address. Passing a parameter by value passes only the value of a variable or a literal on to the called function. Take a look at this code:

```
int    main( void )
{
    int    numDots;

    numDots = 30;

    DrawDots( numDots );

    return 0;
}

void  DrawDots( int numDots )
{
    int    i;

    for ( i = 1; i <= numDots; i++ )
        printf( "." );
}
```

Here's what happens when `main()` calls `DrawDots()`. On the calling side, the expression passed as a parameter to `DrawDots()` is resolved to a single value. In this case, the expression is simply the variable `numDots`. The value of the expression is the value of `numDots`, which is 30.

On the receiving side, when `DrawDots()` gets called, memory is allocated for its parameters, as well as for its local variables. This means that memory is allocated for its copy of numDots, as well as for its copy of i. The value that DrawDots() receives from main() (in this case, 30) is copied into the memory allocated to its copy of numDots.

It is important to understand that whatever main() passes as a parameter to DrawDots() is *copied* into its local copy of the parameter. Think of this copy of numDots as just another local variable that will disappear when DrawDots() exits. DrawDots() can do whatever it likes to its copy of the parameter. Since it is just a local copy, any changes will have absolutely no effect on the copy of the parameter in main().

Since passing parameters by value is a one-way operation, there's no way to get data back from the called function. Why would you ever want to? Several reasons. You might write a function that takes an employee number as a parameter. You might want that function to return the employee's salary in another parameter. How about a function that turns yards into meters? You could pass the number of yards as a value parameter, but how would you get back the number of meters?

Passing a parameter by address (instead of by value) solves this problem. If you pass the address of a variable, the receiving function can use the * operator to change the value of the original variable. Here's an example:

```
int    main( void )
{
    int    square;

    SquareIt( 5, &square );

    printf( "5 squared is %d.\n", square );

    return 0;
}


void  SquareIt( int  number, int    *squarePtr )
{
    *squarePtr = number * number;
}
```

In this example, main() calls the function SquareIt(), which takes two parameters. As in the previous example, both parameters are declared between the parentheses on the function's title line. Notice that a comma separates the parameter declarations.

The first of the two SquareIt() parameters is an int. The second parameter is a pointer to an int. SquareIt() squares the value passed in the first parameter, using the pointer in the second parameter to return the squared value.

By the Way

> If it's been 10 or more years since your last math class, squaring a number is the same as multiplying the number by itself. The square of 4 is 16, and the square of 5 is 25.

Here's how main() calls SquareIt():

```
SquareIt( 5, &square );
```

Here's the function prototype of SquareIt():

```
void SquareIt( int   number, int     *squarePtr );
```

When SquareIt() gets called, memory is allocated for an int (number) and for a pointer to an int (squarePtr).

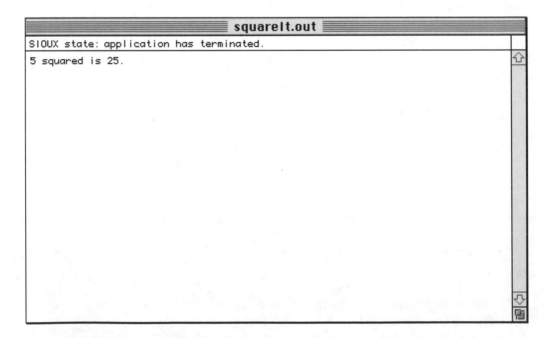

Figure 7.8 squareIt in action.

Once the local memory is allocated, the value 5 is copied into the local parameter `number`, and the address of `square` is copied into `squarePtr`. (Remember, the `&` operator produces the address of a variable.)

Inside the function `SquareIt()`, any reference to `*squarePtr` is just like a reference to `square`. The following assignment statement assigns the value 25 (since number has a value of 5) to the variable pointed to by `squarePtr`:

```
*squarePtr = number * number;
```

This has the effect of assigning the value 25 to `square`. When `SquareIt()` returns control to `main()`, the value of `square` has been changed, as evidenced by the screen shot in Figure 7.8. If you'd like to give this code a try, you'll find it in the `Learn C Projects` folder, inside the `07.02 - squareIt` subfolder.

We'll see lots more pointer-wielding examples throughout the rest of the book.

Global Variables and Function Returns

The combination of pointers and parameters gives us one way to share variables between different functions. This section demonstrates two more techniques for doing the same.

Global variables are variables that are accessible from inside every function in your program. By declaring a global variable, two separate functions can access the same variable without passing parameters. We'll show you how to declare a global variable, then talk about when and when not to use global variables in your programs.

Another topic we'll discuss later in the chapter is a property common to all functions. All functions written in C have the ability to **return** a value to the function that calls them. You set this return value inside the function. You can use a function's return value in place of a parameter, use it to pass "additional information" to the calling function, or not use it at all. We'll show you how to add a return value to your functions.

Global Variables

Earlier in the chapter, you learned how to use parameters to share variables between two functions. Passing parameters between functions is great. You can call a function and pass it some data to work on; when the function's done, it can pass you back the results.

Global variables provide an alternative to parameters. Global variables are just like regular variables, with one exception. Global variables are immune to C's scope rules. They can be referenced inside each of your program's functions. One function might initialize the global variable, another might change its value, and another function might print the value of the global variable in the console window.

As you design your programs, you'll have to make some basic decisions about data sharing between functions. If you'll be sharing a variable among a number of functions, you might want to consider making the variable a global. Globals are especially useful when you want to share a variable between two functions that are several calls apart.

Several calls apart? At times, you'll find yourself passing a parameter to a function not because that function needs the parameter but because the function calls another function that needs the parameter. Look at this code:

```c
#include <stdio.h>

void PassAlong( int myVar );
void PrintMyVar( int myVar );

int main( void )
{
    int    myVar;

    myVar = 10;

    PassAlong( myVar );

    return 0;
}

void PassAlong( int myVar )
{
    PrintMyVar( myVar );
}

void PrintMyVar( int myVar )
{
    printf( "myVar = %d", myVar );
}
```

Notice that `main()` passes `myVar` to the function `PassAlong()`. `PassAlong()` doesn't make use of `myVar` but instead just passes `myVar` along to the function `PrintMyVar()`. `PrintMyVar()` prints `myVar`, then returns.

If myVar were a global, you could have avoided some parameter passing. In that case, main() and PrintMyVar() could have shared myVar without the use of parameters. When should you use parameters? When should you use globals? There's no easy answer. As you write more code, you'll develop your own coding style and, with it, your own sense of when to use globals versus parameters. For the moment, let's take a look at the proper way to add globals to your programs.

Adding Globals to Your Programs

Adding globals to your programs is easy. Just declare a variable at the beginning of your source code, before the start of any of your functions. Here's the example we showed you earlier, using globals in place of parameters:

```c
#include <stdio.h>

void PassAlong( void );
void PrintMyVar( void );

int    gMyVar;

int main( void )
{
    gMyVar = 10;

    PassAlong();

    return 0;
}

void PassAlong( void )
{
    PrintMyVar();
}

void PrintMyVar( void )
{
    printf( "gMyVar = %d", gMyVar );
}
```

This example starts with a variable declaration, right at the top of the program. Because gMyVar was declared at the top of the program, gMyVar becomes a global variable, accessible to each of the program's functions. Notice that none of the functions in this version use parameters. As a reminder, when a function is declared without parameters, use the keyword void in place of a parameter list.

Important

> Did you notice that funny g at the beginning of the global's name? Get used to it. In general, Macintosh C programmers start each global variable with the letter g (for global). Doing this will distinguish your local variables from your global variables and will make your code much easier to read.

When to Use Globals

In general, you should try to minimize your use of globals. On the one hand, global variables make programming easier, because you can access a global anywhere. With parameters, you have to pass the parameter from function to function, until it gets to where it will be used.

On the other hand, globals are expensive, memorywise. Since the memory available to your program is finite, you should try to be memory conscious whenever possible. What makes global variables expensive where memory is concerned? Whenever a function is called, memory for the function's variables is allocated on a temporary basis. When the function exits, the memory allocated to the function is freed up (put back into the pool of available memory). Global variables, on the other hand, are around for the life of your program. Memory for each global is allocated when the program first starts running and isn't freed up until the program exits.

Try to minimize your use of globals, but don't be a miser. If using a global will make your life easier, go ahead and use it.

Function Returns

Before we get to our source code examples, there's one more subject to cover. In addition to passing a parameter and using a global variable, there's one more way to share data between two functions. Every function returns a value to the function that called it. You can use this return value to pass data back from a called function.

So far, all of our examples have ignored **function return values**. The return value comes into play only when you call a function in an expression, like this:

```
int    main( void )
{
```

```
    int    sum;

    sum = AddTheseNumbers( 5, 6 );

    printf( "The sum is %d.", sum );

    return 0;
}

int   AddTheseNumbers( int num1, int num2 )
{
    return( num1 + num2 );
}
```

There are a few things worth noting in this example. First, take a look at the function specifier for AddTheseNumbers(). So far in this book, every single function other than main() has been declared by using the keyword void. AddTheseNumbers(), like main(), starts with the keyword int. This keyword tells you the type returned by this function. A function declared with the void keyword doesn't return a value. A function declared with the int keyword returns a value of type int.

A function returns a value by using the return keyword, followed by an expression that represents the value you want returned. For example, take a look at this line of code from AddTheseNumbers():

```
    return( num1 + num2 );
```

This line of code adds the two variables num1 and num2, then returns the sum. To understand what that means, take a look at this line of code, which calls AddTheseNumbers() from main():

```
    sum = AddTheseNumbers( 5, 6 );
```

This line of code first calls AddTheseNumbers(), passing in values of 5 and 6 as parameters. AddTheseNumbers() adds these numbers and returns the value 11, which is then assigned to the variable sum.

When you use a function inside an expression, the computer makes the function call, then substitutes the function's return value for the function when it evaluates the rest of the expression.

There are several ways to use `return`. To exit a function immediately, without establishing a return value, you could use this statement:

```
return;
```

You could also use this statement:

```
return();
```

The parentheses in a `return` statement are optional. You'd use the plain `return`, without an expression, to return from a function of type `void`. You might use this immediate `return` in case of an error, like this:

```
if ( OutOfMemory() )
    return;
```

What you'll want to remember about this form of `return` is that it does not establish the return value of the function. This works fine if your function is declared `void`:

```
void  MyVoidFunction( int myParam );
```

But it won't cut it if your function is declared to return a value:

```
int    AddTheseNumbers( int num1, int num2 )
```

By the Way

> If you forget to specify a return value, some compilers will say nothing, some will print warnings, and others will report errors.

`AddTheseNumbers()` is declared to return a value of type `int`. Here are two versions of the `AddTheseNumbers()` return statement:

```
return( num1 + num2 );
```

```
return num1 + num2;
```

Notice that the second version did not include any parentheses. Since `return` is a keyword and not a function call, either of these forms is fine.

You can find a version of this program on your hard drive. Look in the folder `Learn C Projects`, in the subfolder `07.03 – addThese`. Figure 7.9 shows the output of this program.

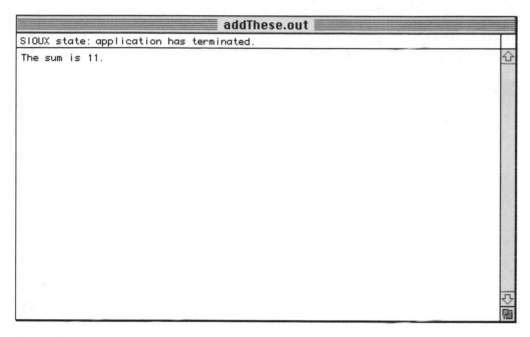

Figure 7.9 addThese in action.

Danger! Avoid Uninitialized Return Values!

Before we leave the topic of function return values, there's one pitfall worth mentioning. If you're going to use a function in an expression, make sure that the function provides a return value. For example, this code will produce unpredictable results:

```
int    main( void )
{
   int    sum;

   sum = AddTheseNumbers( 5, 6 );

   printf( "The sum is %d.", sum );

   return 0;
}


int    AddTheseNumbers( int num1, int num2 )
{
   return;   /* Yikes! We forgot to
             set the return value */
}
```

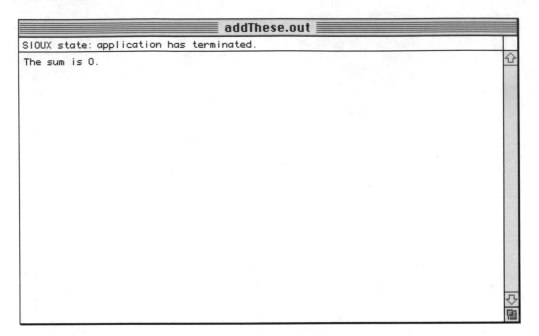

Figure 7.10 Yikes! The sum of 5 + 6 is not equal to 0. Someone forgot to set the return value.

When `AddTheseNumbers()` returns, what will its value be? No one knows! Figure 7.10 shows one possibility. As you can see, the computer used 0 as the return value for `AddTheseNumbers()`. Don't forget to set a return value if you intend to use a function in an expression.

To Return or Not to Return

Should you use a return value or a passed-by-address parameter? Which is correct? This is basically a question of style. Either solution will get the job done, so feel free to use whichever works best for you. Just remember that a function can have only one return value but an unlimited number of parameters. If you need to get more than one piece of data back to the calling function, your best bet is to use parameters.

The function `AddTheseNumbers()` was a natural fit for the `return` statement. It took in a pair of numbers (the input parameters) and needed to return the sum of those numbers. Since it needed to return only a single value, the `return` statement worked perfectly.

Another nice thing about using the `return` statement is that it frequently allows us to avoid declaring an extra variable. In `addThese`, we declared `sum` to receive the value returned by `AddTheseNumbers()`. Since all we did with `sum` was print its value, we could have accomplished the same thing with this version of `main()`:

```
int   main( void )
{
    printf( "The sum is %d.", AddTheseNumbers( 5, 6 ) );

    return 0;
}
```

See the difference? We included the call to `AddTheseNumbers()` in the `printf()`, bypassing `sum` entirely. When `AddTheseNumbers()` returns its `int`, that value is passed on to `printf()`.

More Sample Programs

Are you ready for some more code? The next few sample programs use pointers, function parameters, global variables, and function returns. Crank up the stereo, break out the pizza, and fire up your Mac. Let's code!

listPrimes.μ

Our next sample program is an updated version of `nextPrime`, the Chapter 6 program that found the next prime number following a specified number. The example we presented reported that the next prime number after 19 was 23.

This version of the program, called `listPrimes.μ`, uses a function named `IsItPrime()` and lists all the prime numbers between 1 and 50. Open up the project `listPrimes.μ`. You'll find the program in the `Learn C Projects` folder, inside the subfolder named `07.04 - listPrimes`. Run `listPrimes` and then compare your results with the console window shown in Figure 7.11.

Stepping Through the Source Code

The `listPrimes.c` source code consists of two functions: `main()` and `IsItPrime()`. `IsItPrime()` takes a single parameter, an `int` named `candidate`, which is passed by value. `IsItPrime()` returns a value of `true` if `candidate` is a prime number and a value of `false` otherwise.

```
┌──────────────────────────────────────────────────────────┐
│                    listPrimes.out                        │
├──────────────────────────────────────────────────────────┤
│ SIOUX state: application has terminated.                 │
│ 2 is a prime number.                                     │
│ 3 is a prime number.                                     │
│ 5 is a prime number.                                     │
│ 7 is a prime number.                                     │
│ 11 is a prime number.                                    │
│ 13 is a prime number.                                    │
│ 17 is a prime number.                                    │
│ 19 is a prime number.                                    │
│ 23 is a prime number.                                    │
│ 29 is a prime number.                                    │
│ 31 is a prime number.                                    │
│ 37 is a prime number.                                    │
│ 41 is a prime number.                                    │
│ 43 is a prime number.                                    │
│ 47 is a prime number.                                    │
└──────────────────────────────────────────────────────────┘
```

Figure 7.11 listPrimes in action.

The program starts off with two #includes: stdio.h gives us access to the function prototype of printf(), and math.h gives us access to the function prototype for sqrt():

```
#include <stdio.h>
#include <math.h>
```

Next comes the function prototype for IsItPrime(). The compiler will use this function prototype to make sure that all calls to IsItPrime() pass the right number of parameters (in this case, 1) and that the parameters are of the correct type (in this case, a single int).

```
/**********************/
/* Function Prototypes */
/**********************/
int    IsItPrime( int candidate );
```

The main() function defines a single variable, an int named i. We'll use i as a counter to step through the integers from 1 to 50. We'll pass each number to IsItPrime(). If the result is true, we'll report the number as prime:

```
int    main( void )
{
   int    i;

   for ( i = 1; i <= 50; i++ )
   {
      if ( IsItPrime( i ) )
          printf( "%d is a prime number.\n", i );
   }

   return 0;
}
```

By the Way

As usual, main() ends with a return statement. By convention, returning a value of 0 tells the outside world that everything ran just hunky-dory. If something goes wrong (if we ran out of memory, perhaps), the same convention calls for us to return a negative number from main(). Some operating systems will make use of this return value, and others won't. It doesn't cost you anything to follow the convention, so go ahead and follow it.

IsItPrime() first checks to see whether the number passed in is less than 2. If it is, IsItPrime() returns false, since 2 is the first prime number:

```
int    IsItPrime( int candidate )
{
   int    i, last;

   if ( candidate < 2 )
      return false;
```

If candidate has a value of 2 or greater, we'll step through all the numbers between 2 and the square root of candidate, looking for a factor. If this algorithm is new to you, go back to the previous chapter and check out the program nextPrime. If we find a factor, we know that the number isn't prime, and we'll return false:

```
      else
      {
         last = sqrt( candidate );

         for ( i = 2; i <= last; i++ )
         {
            if ( (candidate % i) == 0 )
               return false;
         }
      }
```

If we get through the loop without finding a factor, we know that `candidate` is prime, and we return `true`:

```
      return true;
   }
```

By the Way

> If `candidate` is equal to 2, `last` will be equal to 1.414, which will get truncated to 1, since `last` is an `int`. If `last` is 1, the `for` loop won't even get through one iteration and will fall through to the statement:
>
> ```
> return true;
> ```
>
> The same thing happens if `candidate` is 3. Since 2 and 3 are both prime, this works just fine. On the other hand, this little example shows you how careful you have to be to check your code, to make sure it works in all cases.

Consider the function name `IsItPrime()`. In C, when you name a function in the form of a `true` or `false` question, it is good form to return a value of `true` or `false`. The question this function answers is, Is the candidate prime? It is critical that `IsItPrime()` return `true` if the candidate was prime and `false` otherwise. When `main()` calls `IsItPrime()`, `main()` is asking the question, Is the candidate prime? In the case of the `if` statement, `main()` is saying, If `i` is prime, do the `printf()`:

```
if ( IsItPrime( i ) )
   printf( ... );
```

Make sure that your function return values make sense!

power.μ

Our next program combines a global variable, a pointer parameter, and some value parameters. At the heart of the program is a function, called `DoPower()`, that takes three parameters. `DoPower()` takes a base and an exponent, raises the base to the exponent power, and returns the result in a parameter. Raising a base to an exponent power is the same as multiplying the base by itself, an exponent number of times.

For example, raising 2 to the fifth power (written as 2^5) is the same as saying 2*2*2*2*2, which is equal to 32. In the expression 2^5, 2 is the base and 5 is the exponent. The function `DoPower()` takes a base and an exponent as parameters and raises the base to the exponent power. `DoPower()` uses a third parameter to return the result to the calling function.

The program also uses a global variable, an `int` named `gPrintTraceInfo`, which demonstrates one of the most important uses of a global variable. Every function in the program checks the value of the global `gPrintTraceInfo`. If `gPrintTraceInfo` is `true`, each function prints a message when the function is entered and another message when the function exits. In this way, you can **trace** the execution of the program. By reading each `printf()`, you can see when a function is entered and when it leaves.

If `gPrintTraceInfo` is set to `true`, the extra function-tracing information will be printed in the console window. If `gPrintTraceInfo` is set to `false`, the extra information will not be printed. As you'll see in a moment, by simply changing the value of a global, you can dramatically change the way your program runs.

Running power.μ

You'll find `power.μ` in the `Learn C Projects` folder, in the `07.05 – power` subfolder. Run `power.μ` and compare your results with the console window shown in Figure 7.12. This output was produced by three consecutive calls to the function `DoPower()`. The three calls calculated the result of the expressions 2^5, 3^4, and 5^3. Here's how the program works.

Stepping Through the Source Code

The program starts with a standard `#include` and the function prototype for `DoPower()`. Notice that `DoPower()` is declared to be of type `void`, telling you that `DoPower()` doesn't return a value. As you read through the code, think about how you might rewrite `DoPower()` to return its result by using the `return` statement instead of in a parameter.

```
power.out
SIOUX state: application has terminated.
2 to the 5th = 32.
3 to the 4th = 81.
5 to the 3rd = 125.
```

Figure 7.12 power output, with gPrintTraceInfo set to false.

```
#include <stdio.h>


/**********************/
/* Function Prototypes */
/**********************/
void   DoPower( int *resultPtr, int base, int exponent );
```

Next comes the declaration of our global, gPrintTraceInfo. Once again, notice that the global starts with a g:

```
/***********/
/* Globals */
/***********/
int        gPrintTraceInfo;
```

Next, main() starts off by setting gPrintTraceInfo to false. We then check to see whether tracing is turned on. If so, we'll print a message telling us we've entered main():

```
int    main( void )
{
   int    power;

   gPrintTraceInfo = false;

   if ( gPrintTraceInfo )
      printf( "---> Starting main()...\n" );
```

Here are our three calls to DoPower(), each of which is followed by a printf() reporting our results. If DoPower() returned its results in a return statement, we could have eliminated the variable power and embedded the call to DoPower() inside the printf() in place of power.

```
DoPower( &power, 2, 5 );
printf( "2 to the 5th = %d.\n", power );

DoPower( &power, 3, 4 );
printf( "3 to the 4th = %d.\n", power );

DoPower( &power, 5, 3 );
printf( "5 to the 3rd = %d.\n", power );
```

If tracing is turned on, we'll print a message saying that we are leaving main():

```
   if ( gPrintTraceInfo )
      printf( "---> Leaving main()...\n" );

   return 0;
}
```

The function DoPower() takes three parameters. We'll use resultPtr, a pointer to an int, to pass back the function results. The value parameters base and exponent represent the —guess what?—base and exponent.

```
void  DoPower( int *resultPtr, int base, int exponent )
{
    int    i;
```

Once again, check the value of gPrintTraceInfo. If it's true, print a message telling us that we're at the beginning of DoPower(). Notice the tab character (represented by the characters \t) at the beginning of the printf() quoted string. You'll see what this was for when we set gPrintTraceInfo to true.

```
if ( gPrintTraceInfo )
    printf( "\t---> Starting DoPower()...\n" );
```

The following three lines calculate base raised to the exponent power, accumulating the results in the memory pointed to by resultPtr. When main() called DoPower(), it passed &power as its first parameter. This means that resultPtr contains the address of (points to) the variable power. Changing *resultPtr is exactly the same as changing power. When DoPower() returns to main(), the value of power will have been changed; power was passed by address (also called by reference) instead of by value.

```
*resultPtr = 1;
for ( i = 1; i <= exponent; i++ )
    *resultPtr *= base;
```

Finally, if gPrintTraceInfo is true, print a message telling us that we're leaving DoPower():

```
if ( gPrintTraceInfo )
    printf( "\t---> Leaving DoPower()...\n" );
}
```

Figure 7.13 shows the console window when power is run with gPrintTraceInfo set to true. See the trace information? Find the lines printed when you enter and exit DoPower(). The leading tab characters help distinguish these lines.

This tracing information was turned on and off by a single global variable. As you start writing your own programs, you'll want to develop your own set of tricks for global variables. For example, programmers who write programs that can run in color or black and white usually create a global called something like gIsColor. They set gIsColor to true or false, once they establish whether they are running in a color or a black-and-white environment. In this way, a function buried

```
power.out
SIOUX state: application has terminated.
---> Starting main()...
   ---> Starting DoPower()...
   ---> Leaving DoPower()...
2 to the 5th = 32.
   ---> Starting DoPower()...
   ---> Leaving DoPower()...
3 to the 4th = 81.
   ---> Starting DoPower()...
   ---> Leaving DoPower()...
5 to the 3rd = 125.
---> Leaving main()...
```

Figure 7.13 power output, with `gPrintTraceInfo` set to `true`.

deep inside the program doesn't have to figure out whether it's running in color or in black and white. All it has to do is check the value of `gIsColor`.

What's Next?

Wow! You really are becoming a C programmer. In this chapter alone, you covered pointers, function parameters (both by value and by address), global variables, and function return values.

You're starting to develop a sense of just how powerful and sophisticated the C language really is. You've built an excellent foundation. Now you're ready to take off.

Chapter 8 introduces the concept of data types. Throughout the book, you've been working with a single data type, the `int`. Chapter 8 introduces the concepts of arrays, strings, pointer arithmetic, and typed function return values. Let's go.

Exercises

1. Predict the result of each of the following code fragments:

```
a.  int main( void )
    {
        int    num, i;
```

```
            num = 5;

            for ( i = 0; i < 20; i++ )
               AddOne( &num );

            printf( "Final value is %d.", num );

            return 0;
        }

        void  AddOne( int     *myVar )
        {
            (*myVar) ++;
        }
```

b.
```
    int    gNumber;

    int    main( void )
    {
        int    i;
        gNumber = 2;

        for ( i = 1; i <= 2; i++ )
           gNumber *= MultiplyIt( gNumber );

        printf( "Final value is %d.", gNumber );
    }



    int    MultiplyIt( intmyVar )
    {
        return( myVar * gNumber );
    }
```

c.
```
    int    gNumber;

    int    main( void )
    {
        int    i;
```

```
    gNumber = 1;

    for ( i = 1; i <= 10; i++ )
        gNumber = DoubleIt( gNumber );

    printf( "Final value is %d.", gNumber );
}




int   DoubleIt( int   myVar )
{
    return 2 * myVar;
}
```

2. Modify power.c. Delete the first parameter of the function DoPower(), modifying the routine to return its result as a function return value instead.

3. Modify listPrimes.c. Instead of printing prime numbers, print only nonprime numbers. In addition, print one message for nonprimes that are multiples of 3 and a different message for nonprimes that are not multiples of 3.

Variable Data Types

OK, now we're cooking! You may now consider yourself a C Programmer, First Class. At this point, you've mastered all the basic elements of C programming. You know that C programs are made up of functions, one—and only one!—of which is named `main()`. Each of these functions uses keywords (such as `if`, `for`, and `while`), operators (such as `=`, `++`, and `*=`), and variables to manipulate the program's data.

Sometimes, you'll use a global variable to share data between functions. At other times, you'll use a parameter to share a variable between a calling and a called function. Sometimes, these parameters are passed by value; sometimes, pointers are used to pass a parameter by address. Some functions return values. Others, declared with the `void` keyword, don't return a value.

In this chapter, we'll focus on **variable types**. Each of the variables in the previous example programs has been declared as an `int`. As you'll soon see, there are many other data types out there.

Other Data Types

So far, the focus has been on `int`s, which are extremely useful when it comes to working with numbers. You can add two `int`s. You can check whether an `int` is even, odd, or prime. You can do a lot with `int`s, as long as you limit yourself to whole numbers.

By the Way

> Just as a reminder, 527, 33, and –2 are all whole numbers, whereas 35.7, 92.1, and –1.2345 are not whole numbers.

What do you do if you want to work with nonwhole numbers, such as 3.14159 and –98.6? Check out this slice of code:

```
int myNum;

myNum = 3.5;
printf( "myNum = %d", myNum );
```

Since `myNum` is an `int`, the number 3.5 will be truncated before it is assigned to `myNum`. When this code ends, `myNum` will be left with a value of 3 and not 3.5 as intended. Do not despair. There are several special C data types created especially for working with nonwhole, or floating-point numbers.

By the Way

> The term floating point refers to the decimal point found in all floating-point numbers.

Floating-Point Data Types

The three floating-point data types are `float`, `double`, and `long double`. These types differ in the number of bytes allocated to each and, therefore, the range of values each can hold. The relative sizes of these three types are completely implementation dependent. Here's a program you can run to tell you the size of these three types in your development environment and to show you various ways to use `printf()` to print floating-point numbers.

floatSizer

Look inside the `Learn C Projects` folder, inside the subfolder named `08.01 - floatSizer`, and open the project named `floatSizer.μ`. Figure 8.1 shows the results when I ran `floatSizer` on my Macintosh using the 68000 version of CodeWarrior. The first three lines of output tell you the size, in bytes, of the types `float`, `double`, and `long double`, respectively. If you run the same program using THINK C, you'll find that a `float` is still 4 bytes long but that a `double` and a `long double` are 12 bytes each. If you compiled this program into native code using the Power Macintosh version of CodeWarrior, you'll find that a `float` is 4 bytes long but that a `double` and a `long double` are each 8 bytes long. The point here is this: Never assume that you know the size of a type. As you'll see when we go through the source code, C gives you everything you need to check the size of a specific type in your development environment. If you need to be sure of a type's size, write a program and check the size for yourself.

```
                    floatSizer.out
SIOUX state: application has terminated.

sizeof( float ) = 4
sizeof( double ) = 10
sizeof( long double ) = 10

myFloat = 12345.678711
myDouble = 12345.678901
myLongDouble = 12345.678901

myFloat =       12345.6787109375000000
myDouble =      12345.6789012345678900
myLongDouble =      12345.6789012345678900

myFloat =       12345.7
myFloat = 12345.68
myFloat = 12345.6787109375000
myFloat = 12345.678710938

myFloat = 1.234568e+04

myFloat = 100000
myFloat = 1e+06
```

Figure 8.1 The output from `floatSizer`.

Stepping Through the Source Code

The code starts with the standard #include:

```
#include <stdio.h>
```

Then main() defines three variables: float, a double, and a long double:

```
int    main( void )
{
    float          myFloat;
    double         myDouble;
    long double    myLongDouble;
```

Next, we'll assign a value to each of the three variables. Notice that we've assigned the same number to each:

```
    myFloat = 12345.67890123456789;
    myDouble = 12345.67890123456789;
    myLongDouble = 12345.67890123456789;
```

Now comes the fun part. We'll start by using C's `sizeof` operator to print the size of each of the three floating-point types. Even though `sizeof` doesn't look like the other operators we've seen (+, *, <<, and so on), it is indeed an operator. Stranger yet, `sizeof` requires a pair of parentheses surrounding a single parameter, much like a function. The parameter is either a type or a variable; `sizeof()` returns the size, in bytes, of its parameter.

By the Way

> Like `return`, `sizeof` doesn't always *require* a pair of parentheses. If the `sizeof` operand is a type, the parentheses are required. If the `sizeof` operand is a variable, the parentheses are optional. Rather than trying to remember this rule, avoid confusion and always use parentheses with `sizeof`.

Did you notice the `(int)` to the left of each `sizeof`? This is known as a **typecast**. A typecast tells the compiler to convert a value of one type to a specified type. In this case, we are taking the type returned by `sizeof` and converting it to an `int`. Why do this? The reason is that `sizeof` returns a value of type `size_t` (weird type name, eh?), and `printf()` doesn't have a format specifier that corresponds to a `size_t`. By converting the `size_t` to an `int`, we can use the format specifier `%d` to print the value returned by `sizeof`. Notice the extra `\n` at the end of the third `printf()`, which gives us a blank line between the first three lines of output and the next line of output:

```
printf( "sizeof( float ) = %d\n", (int)sizeof( float ) );
printf( "sizeof( double ) = %d\n", (int)sizeof( double ) );
printf( "sizeof( long double ) = %d\n\n", (int)sizeof( long double ) );
```

Important

> If the concept of typecasting is confusing to you, have no fear. We'll get into typecasting in Chapter 11. Until then, you can use this method whenever you want to print the value returned by `sizeof`. Alternatively, you might declare a variable of type `int`, assign the value returned by `sizeof` to the `int`, and then print the `int`:
>
> ```
> int       myInt;
>
> myInt = sizeof( float );
> printf( "sizeof( float ) = %d\n", myInt );
> ```
>
> Use whichever method works for you.

The rest of this program is dedicated to various and sundry ways you can print your floating-point numbers. So far, all of our programs have printed `int`s using the format specifier `%d`. The Standard Library has a set of format specifiers for all of C's built-in data types, including several for printing floating-point numbers.

First, we'll use the format specifer `%f` to print our three floating-point numbers in their natural, decimal format:

```
printf( "myFloat = %f\n", myFloat );
printf( "myDouble = %f\n", myDouble );
printf( "myLongDouble = %f\n\n", myLongDouble );
```

Here's the result:

```
myFloat = 12345.678711
myDouble = 12345.678901
myLongDouble = 12345.678901
```

As a reminder, all three of these numbers were assigned the value:

```
12345.67890123456789
```

Hmmm . . . none of the numbers we printed matches this number. And the first number we printed is different from the second and third numbers. What gives? There are several problems here. As we've already seen, this development environment uses 4 bytes for a `float` and 10 bytes each for a `double` and a `long double`. This means that the number:

```
12345.67890123456789
```

can be represented more accurately using a `double` or a `long double` than it can be using a `float`. In addition, we are printing using the default precision of the `%f` format specifier. In this case, we are printing only six places past the decimal point. Although this might be plenty of precision for most applications, we'd like to see how accurate we can get.

We then use **format specifier modifiers** to more closely specify the output produced by each `printf()`. By using `%25.16f` instead of `%f`, we tell `printf()` to print the floating-point number with an accuracy of 16 places past the decimal and to add spaces if necessary so the number takes up at least 25 character positions:

```
printf( "myFloat = %25.16f\n", myFloat );
printf( "myDouble = %25.16f\n", myDouble );
printf( "myLongDouble = %25.16f\n\n", myLongDouble );
```

Here's the result:

```
myFloat =      12345.6787109375000000
myDouble =     12345.6789012345678900
myLongDouble =     12345.6789012345678900
```

As requested, `printf()` printed each of these numbers to 16 places past the decimal place (count the digits yourself), padding each result with zeros as needed. Since adding the 16 digits to the right of the decimal, plus 1 space for the decimal, plus 5 for the 5 digits to the left of the decimal equals 22 (16+1+5=22) and we asked `printf()` to use 25 character positions, `printf()` added 3 spaces to the left of the number.

By the Way

We originally asked `printf()` to print a `float` with a value of:

```
12345.67890123456789
```

The best approximation of this number we were able to represent by a `float` is:

```
12345.6787109375000000
```

Where did this approximation come from? The answer has to do with the way your computer stores floating-point numbers.

The fractional part of a number (the number to the right of the decimal) is represented in binary just like an integer. Instead of the sum of powers of 2, the fractional part is represented as the sum of powers of ½. For example, the number 0.75 is equal to ½ + ¼. In binary, that's 11.

The problem with this representation is that it's impossible to represent some numbers with complete accuracy. If you need a higher degree of accuracy, use `double` or a `long double` instead of `float`. Unless you cannot afford the extra memory that the larger data types require, you are probably better off using a `double` or a `long double` in your programs instead of a `float` for all your floating-point calculations.

The next portion of code shows you the result of using different modifer values to print the same `float`:

```
printf( "myFloat = %10.1f\n", myFloat );
printf( "myFloat = %.2f\n", myFloat );
printf( "myFloat = %.12f\n", myFloat );
printf( "myFloat = %.9f\n\n", myFloat );
```

Here's the output produced by each `printf()`:

```
myFloat =    12345.7
myFloat = 12345.68
myFloat = 12345.678710937500
myFloat = 12345.678710938
```

The specifier `%10.1f` told `printf()` to print 1 digit past the decimal and to use 10 character positions for the entire number. The specifier `%.2f` told `printf()` to print 2 digits past the decimal and to use as many character positions as necessary to print the entire number. Notice that `printf()` rounds off the result for you and doesn't simply cut off the number after the specified number of places.

The specifier `%.12f` told `printf()` to print 12 digits past the decimal, and the specifier `%.9f` told `printf()` to print 9 digits past the decimal. Again, notice the rounding that takes place.

By the Way

Unless you need to exactly control the total number of characters used to print a number, you'll probably leave off the first modifier and just specify the number of digits past the decimal you want printed, using specifiers such as `%.2f` and `%.9f`.

If you do use a two-part modifier, such as `%3.2f`, `printf()` will never cut off numbers to the left of the decimal. For example, the output `myFloat = 255.54` will be produced by the following code:

```
myFloat = 255.543;
printf( "myFloat = %3.2f", myFLoat );
```

Even though you told `printf()` to use three character positions to print the number, `printf()` was smart enough to not lose the numbers to the left of the decimal.

The next `printf()` uses the specifier `%e`, asking `printf()` to print the
`float` using **scientific,** or **exponential, notation:**

```
printf( "myFloat = %e\n\n", myFloat );
```

Here's the corresponding output:

```
myFloat = 1.234568e+04
```

The result, `1.234568e+04` is equal to 1.234568 times 10 to the fourth power, or
`1.234568*10⁴`, or 1.234568 * 10000 == 12,345.68.

The next two `printf()` calls use the specifier `%g`, letting `printf()` decide
whether decimal or scientific notation will be the most efficient way to represent
this number. The first `%g` deals with a `myFloat` value of 100,000:

```
myFloat = 100000;
printf( "myFloat = %g\n", myFloat );
```

Here's the output:

```
myFloat = 100000
```

Next, the value of `myFloat` is changed to 1,000,000, and `%g` is used once again:

```
myFloat = 1000000;
printf( "myFloat = %g\n", myFloat );

return 0;
}
```

Here's the result of this last `printf()`. As you can see, this time `printf()` decided to represent the number using exponential notation:

```
myFloat = 1e+06
```

The lesson here is: Use `float` if you want to work with floating-point numbers. Use `double` or `long double` for extra accuracy, but beware the extra cost in memory usage. Use `int` for maximum speed, if you want to work exclusively with whole numbers, or if you want to truncate a result.

The Integer Types

So far, you've learned about four types: three floating-point types (`float`, `double`, and `long double`) and one integer type (`int`). In this section, we'll introduce the remaining integer types: `char`, `short`, and `long`. As was the case with the three floating-point types, the size of each of the four integer types is implementation dependent. Our next program, `intSizer` proves that point. You'll find `intSizer`, in the `Learn C Projects` folder, in the `08.02 - intSizer` subfolder.

Important

Although these forms are rarely used, a `short` is also known as a `short int`, and a `long` is also known as a `long int`. As an example, these declarations are perfectly legal:

```
short int    myShort;
long int     myLong;
```

Although the preceding declarations are just fine, you are more likely to encounter declarations like these:

```
short        myShort;
long         myLong;
```

As always, choose your favorite style and be consistent.

The `intSizer` program contains one `printf()` for each integer type:

```
printf( "sizeof( char ) = %d\n", (int)sizeof( char ) );
printf( "sizeof( short ) = %d\n", (int)sizeof( short ) );
printf( "sizeof( int ) = %d\n", (int)sizeof( int ) );
printf( "sizeof( long ) = %d\n", (int)sizeof( long ) );
```

Like their `floatSizer` counterparts, these `printf()` calls use `sizeof` to determine the size of a `char`, a `short`, an `int`, and a `long`. When `intSizer` was compiled using the 68000 version of CodeWarrior, here's what came back:

```
sizeof( char ) = 1
sizeof( short ) = 2
sizeof( int ) = 2
sizeof( long ) = 4
```

Here's the result when `intSizer` was compiled with the PowerPC native version of CodeWarrior:

```
sizeof( char ) = 1
sizeof( short ) = 2
sizeof( int ) = 4
sizeof( long ) = 4
```

As you can see, an `int` is 2 bytes in the 68000 version of CodeWarrior and 4 bytes in the PowerPC version of CodeWarrior. Again, the point to remember is: There are *no* guarantees. Don't assume that you know the size of a type. Write a program and check for yourself.

Warning

> The 68000 version of CodeWarrior uses 2-byte `ints` by default but does allow you to specify 4-byte `ints` and 8-byte `doubles`. Select **Preferences...** from the **Edit** menu, then click on the `Processor` icon. Be warned, however. The libraries `ANSI(2i) C.68K.Lib` and `MathLib68K(2i).Lib` were built specifically to work with 2-byte `ints` and will not work properly with 4-byte `ints`. You'll need to replace these libraries with `ANSI(4i)C.68K.Lib` and `MathLib68K(4i).Lib`, something you may not be able to do with CodeWarrior Lite.

Type Value Ranges

All the integer types can be either `signed` or `unsigned`. This obviously affects the range of values handled by that type. For example, a `signed` 1-byte `char` can store a value from –128 to 127, and an `unsigned` 1-byte `char` can store a value from 0 to 255. If this clouds your mind with pain, now might be a good time to go back and review Chapter 5.

A `signed` 2-byte `short` or `int` can store values ranging from –32768 to 32767. An `unsigned` 2-byte `short` or `int` can store values ranging from 0 to 65535.

A `signed` 4-byte `long` or `int` can store values ranging from –2,147,483,648 to 2,147,483,647. An `unsigned` 4-byte `long` or `int` can store values ranging from 0 to 4,294,967,295.

A 4-byte `float` can range in value from –3.4e+38 to 3.4e+38. An 8-byte `double` or `long double` can range in value from –1.7e+308 to 1.7e+308.

Memory Efficiency Versus Safety

Each time you declare one of your program's variables, you'll have a decision to make. What's the best type for this variable? In general, it's a good policy not to waste memory. Why use a `long` when a `short` will do just fine? Why use a `double` when a `float` will do the trick?

There is a danger in being *too* concerned with memory efficiency, however. For example, suppose that a customer asked you to write a program designed to print the numbers 1 through 100, one number per line. Sounds pretty straightforward. Just create a `for` loop and embed a `printf()` in the loop. In the interests of memory efficiency, you might use a `char` to act as the loop's counter. After all, if you declare your counter as an `unsigned char`, it can hold values ranging from 0 to 255. That should be plenty, right?

```
unsigned char   counter;

for ( counter=1; counter<=100; counter++ )
   printf( "%d\n", counter );
```

This program works just fine. But suppose that your customer then asks you to extend the program to count from 1 to 1000 instead of just to 100. You happily change the 100 to 1000 like so:

```
unsigned char   counter;

for ( counter=1; counter<=1000; counter++ )
   printf( "%d\n", counter );
```

What do you think will happen when you run the program? To find out, open the `Learn C Projects` folder, open the `08.03 - typeOverflow` subfolder, and open and run the project `typeOverflow.`μ.

Keep an eye on the numbers as they scroll by on the screen. When the number 255 appears, a funny thing happens. The next number will be 0, then 1, 2, and so on. If you leave the program running for a while, it will climb back up to 255, then jump to 0 and climb back up again. This will continue forever. Type command-period (⌘.) to halt the program, then quit.

Warning

> If you can't get the program to quit, hold down the command (⌘) and option keys and press the Escape key. When the dialog box appears, click on the **Force quit** button. You can use this trick to quit almost any program, but be aware that you'll lose any unsaved changes.

The problem with this program occurs when the `for` loop increments `counter` when it has a value of 255. Since an `unsigned char` can hold a maximum value of 255, incrementing it gives it a value of 0 again. Since `counter` can never get higher than 255, the `for` loop never exits.

Just for kicks, edit the code and change the `unsigned char` to a `signed char`. What do you think will happen? Try it!

The real solution here is to use a `short`, `int`, or `long` instead of a `char`. Don't be stingy. Unless there is a real reason to worry about memory usage, err on the side of extravagence. Err on the side of safety!

Working with Characters

With its minimal range, you might think that a `char` isn't good for much. Actually, the C deities created the `char` for a good reason. It is the perfect size to hold a single alphabetic character. In C, an alphabetic character is a single character placed between a pair of single quotes ('). Here's a test to see whether a `char` variable contains the letter 'a':

```
char  c;

c = 'a';

if ( c == 'a' )
    printf( "The variable c holds the character 'a'." );
```

As you can see, the character 'a' is used in both an assignment statement and an `if` statement, just as if it were a number or a variable.

The ASCII Character Set

In C, a `signed char` takes up a single byte and can hold a value from -128 to 127. How can a `char` hold a numerical value, as well as a character value, such as 'a' or '+'? The answer lies with the **ASCII character set**. The ASCII (American Standard Code for Information Interchange) character set of 128 standard characters features the 26 lowercase letters, the 26 uppercase letters, the 10 numerical digits, and an assortment of other exciting characters, such as } and =. Each of these characters corresponds exactly to a value between 0 and 127. The ASCII character set ignores the values between –128 and –1.

For example, the character 'a' has an ASCII value of 97. When a C compiler sees the character 'a' in a piece of source code, it substitutes the value 97. Each of the values from 0 to 127 is interchangeable with a character from the ASCII character set.

Warning

> Although we use the ASCII character set throughout this book, you should know that there are other character sets out there. Another commonly used character set is the EBCDIC character set. Each EBCDIC character, like an ASCII character, has a value between 0 and 127 and, therefore, fits nicely inside a `char`.
>
> Some foreign alphabets have more characters than can be represented by a single byte. To accommodate these multibyte characters, ISO C features **wide-character** and **wide-string data types.**
>
> Although we won't get into EBCDIC and multibyte character sets in this book, you should keep these things in mind as you write your own code. Read up on the multibyte extensions introduced as part of the ISO C standard. There's an excellent writeup in Harbison and Steele's *C: A Reference Manual* (see the bibliography at the back of this book).
>
> Learn how to **localize** your programs, how to isolate the portions of your programs that depend on human language from the rest of your source code. Read about the Script Manager, the Macintosh system software that simplifies the process of translating your program's human-language features from one language to another. There's a nice write-up (called "Worldwide Compatibility") in the *Macintosh Human Interface Guidelines,*.

ascii.µ

Here's a program that will make the ASCII character set easier to understand. Go into the `Learn C Projects` folder, then into the `08.04 – ascii` subfolder, and open the project `ascii.µ`.

Before we step through the project source code, let's take it for a spin. Select **Run** from the **Project** menu. A console window similar to the one in Figure 8.2 should appear. The first line of output shows the characters corresponding to the ASCII values from 32 to 47. Why start with 32? As it turns out, the ASCII characters between 0 and 31 are nonprintable characters, such as the backspace (ASCII 8) or the carriage return (ASCII 13). A table of the nonprintable ASCII characters is presented later on.

163

Notice that ASCII character 32 is a space, or ' '. ASCII character 33 is '!'. ASCII character 47 is '/'. This presents some inter-esting coding possibilities. For example, this code is perfectly legitimate:

```
int    sumOfChars;

sumOfChars = '!' + '/';
```

What a strange piece of code! Although you will probably never do anything like this, try to predict the value of the variable sumOfChars after the assignment statement. And the answer is . . .

The character '!' has a value of 33, and the character '/' has a value of 47. Therefore, sumOfChars will be left with a value of 80 following the assignment statement. C allows you to represent any number between 0 and 127 in two differ-ent ways: as an ASCII character or as a number. Let's get back to the console win-dow in Figure 8.2.

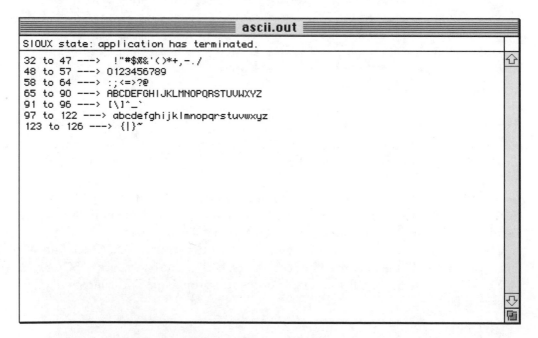

Figure 8.2 The printable ASCII characters.

The second line of output shows the ASCII characters from 48 through 57. As you can see, these 10 characters represent the digits 0 through 9. Here's a little piece of code that converts an ASCII digit to its numerical counterpart:

```
char   digit;
int    convertedDigit;

digit = '3';

convertedDigit = digit - '0';
```

This code starts with a `char` named `digit`, initialized to hold the ASCII character `'3'`, which has a numerical value of 51. The next line of code subtracts the ASCII character `'0'` from `digit`. Since the character `'0'` has a numerical value of 48, and `digit` started with a numerical value of 51, `convertedDigit` ends up with a value of 51 – 48, or 3. Isn't that interesting?

Warning

Subtracting `'0'` from any ASCII digit yields that digit's numerical counterpart. Although this is a great trick if you know you're working with ASCII, your code will fail if the digits of the current character set are not represented in the same way as they are in ASCII. For example, if you were on a machine that used a character set in which the digits were sequenced from 1 to 9, followed by 0, this trick wouldn't work.

The next line of the console window shown in Figure 8.2 shows the ASCII characters with values ranging from 58 to 64. The following line is pretty interesting. It shows the range of ASCII characters from 65 to 90. Notice anything familiar about these characters? They represent the complete uppercase alphabet.

The next line in Figure 8.2 lists ASCII characters with values from 91 through 96. The next line lists the ASCII characters with values ranging from 97 through 122. These 26 characters represent the complete lowercase alphabet.

Warning

Adding 32 to an uppercase ASCII character yields its lowercase equivalent. Likewise, subtracting 32 from a lowercase ASCII character yields its uppercase equivalent.

Guess what? You never want to take advantage of this information! Instead, use the Standard Library routines `tolower()` and `toupper()` to do the conversions for you.

As a general rule, try not to make assumptions about the order of characters in the current character set. Use Standard Library functions rather than working directly with character values. Although it is tempting to do these kinds of conversions yourself, by going through the Standard Library, you know that your program will work across single-byte character sets.

The final line in Figure 8.2 lists the ASCII characters from 123 to 126. As it turns out, the ASCII character with a value of 127 is another nonprintable character. Figure 8.3 lists these "unprintables." The left-hand column shows the ASCII code; the right-hand column shows the keyboard equivalent for that code, along with any appropriate comments. The characters with comments by them are probably the only unprintables you'll ever use.

Stepping Through the Source Code

Before we move on to our next topic, let's take a look at the `ascii.c` source code that generated the ASCII character listing in Figure 8.2. This code begins with the usual #include, followed by a function prototype of the function `PrintChars()`. `PrintChars()` takes two parameters, which define a range of chars to print.

```
#include <stdio.h>


/**********************/
/* Function Prototypes */
/**********************/
void  PrintChars( char low, char high );
```

The `main()` function calls `PrintChars()` seven times in an attempt to functionally organize the ASCII characters:

```
int    main( void )
{
    PrintChars( 32, 47 );
    PrintChars( 48, 57 );
    PrintChars( 58, 64 );
    PrintChars( 65, 90 );
```

```
    PrintChars( 91, 96 );
    PrintChars( 97, 122 );
    PrintChars( 123, 126 );

    return 0;
}
```

ASCII Unprintables	
0	Used to terminate text strings (Explained later in chapter)
1	Control-A
2	Control-B
3	Control-C
4	Control-D (End of file mark, see Chapter 10)
5	Control-E
6	Control-F
7	Control-G (Beep character - Try it!)
8	Control-H (Backspace)
9	Control-I (Tab)
10	Control-J (Line feed)
11	Control-K (Vertical feed)
12	Control-L (Form feed)
13	Control-M (Carriage return, no line feed)
14	Control-N
15	Control-O
16	Control-P
17	Control-Q
18	Control-R
19	Control-S
20	Control-T
21	Control-U
22	Control-V
23	Control-W
24	Control-X
25	Control-Y
26	Control-Z
27	Control-[(Escape character)
28	Control-l
29	Control-]
30	Control-^
31	Control-_
127	del

Figure 8.3 The ASCII unprintables.

PrintChars() declares a local variable, c, to act as a counter as we step through a range of chars:

```
void  PrintChars( char low, char high )
{
   char  c;
```

We'll use low and high to print a label for the current line, showing the range of ASCII characters to follow. Notice that we use %d to print the integer version of these chars; %d can handle any integer types no bigger than an int:

```
   printf( "%d to %d ---> ", low, high );
```

Next, a for loop is used to step through each of the ASCII characters, from low to high, using printf() to print each of the characters consecutively on the same line. The printf() bears closer inspection. Notice the use of %c (instead of our usual %d) to tell printf() to print a single ASCII character:

```
   for ( c = low; c <= high; c++ )
      printf( "%c", c );
```

Once the line is printed, a single new line is printed, moving the cursor to the beginning of the next line in the console window. Thus ends PrintChars():

```
   printf( "\n" );
}
```

The char data type is extremely useful to C programmers. The next two topics—arrays and text strings—will show you why. As you read through these two topics, keep the concept of ASCII characters in the back of your mind. As you reach the end of the section on text strings, you'll see an important relationship develop among the three topics.

Arrays

An **array** turns a single variable into a list of variables; for example:

```
int    myNumber [ 3 ];
```

This declaration creates three separate `int` variables, referred to in your program as `myNumber[ 0 ]`, `myNumber[ 1 ]`, and `myNumber[ 2 ]`. Each of these variables is known as an **array element**. The number enclosed in brackets ([ ]) is called an **index**.

```
char   myChar[ 20 ];
```

In this declaration, the name of the array is `myChar`. This declaration will create an array of type `char` with a **dimension** of 20. The dimension of an array is the array's number of elements. The array elements will have **indices** that run from 0 to 19.

Important

> In C, array indices always run from 0 to one less than the array's dimension.

This slice of code first declares an array of 100 `int`s, then assigns each `int` a value of 0:

```
int    myNumber[ 100 ], i;

for ( i=0; i<100; i++ )
   myNumber[ i ] = 0;
```

You could have accomplished the same thing by declaring 100 individual `int`s, then initializing each individual `int`. Here's what that code might look like:

```
int    myNumber0, myNumber1, ......., myNumber99;

myNumber0 = 0;
myNumber1 = 0;
      .
      .
      .
myNumber99 = 0;
```

It would take 100 lines of code just to initialize these variables! By using an array, we've accomplished the same thing in just a few lines of code. Look at this code fragment:

```
sum = 0;
for ( i=0; i<100; i++ )
   sum += myNumber[ i ];

printf( "The sum of the 100 numbers is %d.", sum );
```

This code adds the value of all 100 elements of the array `myNumber`.

Important

> In this example, the `for` loop is used to **step through** an array, performing some operation on each of the array's elements. You'll use this technique frequently in your own C programs.

Why Use Arrays?

Programmers would be lost without arrays. Arrays allow you to keep lists of things. For example, if you need to maintain a list of 50 employee numbers, declare an array of 50 `int`s. You can declare an array using any C type. For example, the following code declares an array of 50 floating-point numbers:

```
float salaries[ 50 ];
```

This might be useful for maintaining a list of employee salaries.

Use an array when you want to maintain a list of related data. Here's an example.

dice.μ

Look in the `Learn C Projects` folder, inside the `08.05 - dice` subfolder, and open the project `dice.μ`. This program simulates the rolling of a pair of dice. After each roll, the program adds the two dice, keeping track of the total. It rolls the dice 1000 times, then reports on the results. Give it a try!

Run `dice` by selecting **Run** from the **Project** menu. A console window should appear, similar to the one in Figure 8.4. Take a look at the output—it's pretty interesting. The first column lists all the possible totals of two dice. Since the lowest-possible roll of a pair of six-sided dice is 1 and 1, the first entry in the column is 2. The column counts all the way up to 12, the highest-possible roll (achieved by a roll of 6 and 6).

The number in parentheses is the total number of rolls (out of 1000 rolls) that matched that row's number. For example, the first row describes the dice rolls that total 2. In this run, the total is 28. Finally, the program prints an x for every 10 of

```
┌──────────────────────────────────────────────────────┐
│                      dice.out                          │
├──────────────────────────────────────────────────────┤
│ SIOUX state: application has terminated.          ┌─┐ │
│   2 ( 28):   xx                                   │⇧│ │
│   3 ( 63):   xxxxxx                               └─┘ │
│   4 ( 77):   xxxxxxx                                   │
│   5 (110):   xxxxxxxxxxx                               │
│   6 (146):   xxxxxxxxxxxxxx                            │
│   7 (160):   xxxxxxxxxxxxxxxx                          │
│   8 (132):   xxxxxxxxxxxxx                             │
│   9 (116):   xxxxxxxxxxx                               │
│  10 ( 82):   xxxxxxxx                                  │
│  11 ( 60):   xxxxxx                                    │
│  12 ( 26):   xx                                        │
│                                                        │
│                                                        │
│                                                        │
│                                                   ┌─┐ │
│                                                   │⇩│ │
│                                                   └─┘ │
└──────────────────────────────────────────────────────┘
```

Figure 8.4 `dice` in action. Your mileage may vary!

these rolls. For the total 28, for example, the program prints two **x**'s at the end of the 2s row. Since 160 7s were rolled, 16 **x**'s were printed at the end of the 7s row.

By the Way

Recognize the curve depicted by the **x**'s in Figure 8.4? The curve represents a "normal" probability distribution, also known as a bell curve. According to the curve, you are about six times more likely to roll a 7 as you are to roll a 12. Want to know why? Check out a book on probability and statistics.

Let's take a look at the source code that makes this possible.

Stepping Through the Source Code

The source code starts off with three #includes: <stdlib.h> gives us access to the routines rand() and srand(), <time.h> gives us access to clock(), and <stdio.h> gives us access to printf().

```
#include <stdlib.h>
#include <time.h>
#include <stdio.h>
```

Following are the function prototypes for `RollOne()`, `PrintRolls()`, and `PrintX()`. You'll see how these routines work as we step through the code.

```
/**********************/
/* Function Prototypes */
/**********************/
int    RollOne( void );
void   PrintRolls( int    rolls[] );
void   PrintX( int howMany );
```

`main()` declares an array of 13 `int`s named `rolls`, which will keep track of the 11 possible types of dice rolls. For example, `rolls[2]` will keep track of the total number of 2s, `rolls[3]` will keep track of the total number of 3s, and so on, up until `rolls[12]`, which will keep track of the total number of 12s rolled. Since there is no way to roll a 0 or a 1 with a pair of dice, `rolls[0]` and `rolls[1]` will go unused.

```
int    main( void )
{
    int        rolls[ 13 ], twoDice, i;
```

By the Way

We could have rewritten the program using an array of 11 `int`s, thereby saving 2 `int`s worth of memory. If we did that, `rolls[0]` would track the number of 2s rolled, `rolls[1]` would track the number of 3s rolled, and so on. This would have made the program a little more difficult to read, since `rolls[i]` would be referring to the number of (`i+2`)'s rolled.

In general, it is OK to sacrifice memory to make your program easier to read, as long as program performance isn't compromised.

The function `srand()`, part of the Standard Library, initializes a random-number generator, using a seed provided by another Standard Library function, `clock()`. Once the random-number generator is initialized, another function, `rand()`, will return an `int` with a random value.

```
    srand( clock() );
```

Why random numbers? Sometimes, you want to add an element of unpredictability to your program. For example, in our program, we want to roll a pair of dice again and again. The program would be pretty boring if it rolled the same numbers over and over. By using a random-number generator, we can generate a random number between 1 and 6, thus simulating the roll of a single die!

The next step is for `main()` to initialize each of the elements of the array `rolls` to 0:

```
for ( i=0; i<=12; i++ )
    rolls[ i ] = 0;
```

This is appropriate, since no rolls of any kind have taken place yet.

The next `for` loop rolls the dice 1000 times. As you'll see, the function `RollOne()` returns a random number between 1 and 6, simulating the roll of a single die. By calling it twice and storing the sum of the two rolls in the variable `twoDice`, we've simulated the roll of two dice:

```
for ( i=1; i <= 1000; i++ )
{
    twoDice = RollOne() + RollOne();
```

The next line is pretty tricky, so hang on. At this point, the variable `twoDice` holds a value between 2 and 12, the total of two individual dice rolls. We'll use that value to specify which `int` to increment. If `twoDice` is 12 (if we rolled a pair of 6s), we'll increment `rolls[12]`. Get it? If not, go back and read through this again. If you still feel stymied (and it's OK if you do), find a C buddy to help you through this. It is important that you get this concept. Be patient.

```
    ++ rolls[ twoDice ];
}
```

Once we're finished with our 1000 rolls, we'll pass `rolls` as a parameter to `PrintRolls()`:

```
PrintRolls( rolls );

return 0;
}
```

Notice that we used the array name without the brackets (`rolls` instead of `rolls[ ]`). The name of an array is a pointer to the first element of the array. If you have access to this pointer, you have access to the entire array. You'll see how this works when we look at `PrintRolls()`.

Important

Just remember that passing the name of an array as a parameter is exactly the same as passing a pointer to the first element of the array. To prove this, edit `dice.c` and change `PrintRolls( rolls );` to:

```
PrintRolls( &( rolls[0] ) );
```

The two lines of code are equivalent! The second form passes the address of the first array element. If you think back to Chapter 7, we used the `&` operator to pass a parameter by reference instead of by value. By passing the address of the first array element, you give `PrintRolls()` the ability to both access and modify all of the array elements. This is an important concept!

`RollOne()` first calls `rand()` to generate a random number ranging from 0 to 32,767 (in fact, the upper bound is defined by the constant `RAND_MAX`, which is guaranteed to be at least 32,767). Next, the `%` operator is used to return the remainder when the random number is divided by 6. This yields a random number ranging from 0 to 5. Finally, 1 is added to this number, converting it to a number between 1 and 6, and that number is returned:

```
int    RollOne( void )
{
    return (rand() % 6) + 1;
}
```

`PrintRolls()` starts off by declaring a single parameter, an array pointer named `rolls`. Notice that `rolls` was declared using square brackets, telling the compiler that `rolls` is a pointer to the first element of an array (in this case, to an array of `int`s).

```
void  PrintRolls( int rolls[] )
{
    int       i;
```

`PrintRolls()` could also have declared its parameter using this notation:

```
void   PrintRolls( int *rolls )
```

Instead, it used this notation:

```
void   PrintRolls( int rolls[] )
```

Both of these notations describe a pointer to an `int`, and both can be used to access the elements of an array. You'll learn more about the close relationship between pointers and arrays as you make your way through the rest of the book.

For now, remember this convention. If you are declaring a parameter that will point to an array, use the square-bracket form. Otherwise, use the normal pointer form.

Let's get back to our program. We had just started looking at `PrintRolls()`. The `for` loop steps through the `rolls` array, one `int` at a time, starting with `rolls[2]` and making its way to `rolls[12]`. For each element, `PrintRolls()` first prints the roll number and then, in parentheses, the number of times (out of 1000) that roll occurred. Next, `PrintX()` is called to print a single x for every 10 rolls that occurred. Finally, a carriage return is printed, preparing the console window for the next roll.

```
for ( i=2; i<=12; i++ )
{
   printf( "%2d (%3d):  ", i, rolls[ i ] );
   PrintX( rolls[ i ] / 10 );
   printf( "\n" );
}
}
```

`PrintX` is pretty straightforward. It uses a `for` loop to print the number of x's specified by the parameter `howMany`:

```
void  PrintX( int howMany )
{
```

```
   int    i;

   for ( i=1; i<=howMany; i++ )
      printf( "x" );
}
```

Danger, Will Robinson!!!

Before we move on, there is one danger worth discussing at this point. See if you can spot the potential hazard in this piece of code:

```
int    myInts[ 3 ];

for ( i=0; i<20; i++ )
   myInts[ i ] = 0;
```

Yikes! The array `myInts` consists of exactly three array elements, yet the `for` loop tries to initialize 20 elements. This is called **exceeding the bounds** of your array. Because C is such an informal language, it will let you "get away" with this kind of source code. In other words, CodeWarrior will compile this code without complaint. Your problems will start as soon as the program tries to initialize the fourth array element, which was never allocated.

What will happen? The safest thing to say is that the results will be unpredictable. The problem is, the program is trying to assign a value of 0 to a block of memory that it doesn't necessarily own. Anything could happen. The program would most likely crash, which means that it stops behaving in a rational manner. I've seen some cases where the computer actually leaps off the desk, hops across the floor, and jumps face first into the trash can.

Well, OK, not really. But odd things will happen if you don't keep your array references in bounds.

Warning

As you code, be aware of the limitations of your variables. For example, a `char` is limited to values from –128 to 127. Don't try to assign a value such as 536 to a `char`. Don't reference `myArray[ 27 ]` if you declared `myArray` with only 10 elements. Be careful!

Text Strings

The first C program in this book made use of a text string:

```
printf( "Hello, world!" );
```

This section will teach you how to use such text strings in your own programs. It will teach you how these strings are stored in memory and how to create your own strings from scratch.

A Text String in Memory

The text string "Hello, world!" exists in memory as a sequence of 14 bytes (Figure 8.5). The first 13 bytes consist of the 13 ASCII characters in the text string. Note that the seventh byte contains a space (on an ASCII-centric computer, that translates to a value of 32).

The final byte (byte 14) has a value of 0, not to be confused with the ASCII character '0'. The 0 is what makes this string a C string. Every C string ends with a byte having a value of 0. The 0 identifies the end of the string.

When you use a quoted string like "Hello, world!" in your code, the compiler creates the string for you. This type of string is called a **string constant**. When you use a string constant in your code, the detail work is done for you automatically. In the following example, the 14 bytes needed to represent the string in memory are allocated automatically:

```
printf( "Hello, world!" );
```

The 0 is placed in the fourteenth byte, automatically. You don't have to worry about these details when you use a string constant.

String constants are great, but they are not always appropriate. For example, suppose that you want to read in somebody's name, then pass the name on to printf() to display in the console window. Since you won't be able to predict the name that will be typed in, you can't predefine the name as a string constant. Here's an example.

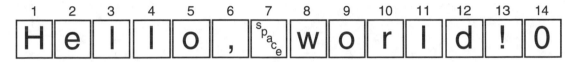

Figure 8.5 The "Hello, World!" text string.

name.μ

Look in the Learn C Projects folder, inside the 08.06 – name subfolder, and open the project name.μ. The program will ask you to type your first name on the keyboard. Once you've typed your first name, the program will use your name to create a custom welcome message. Then, name will tell you how many characters long your name is. How useful!

To run name, select **Run** from the **Project** menu. A console window will appear, prompting you for your first name, like this:

```
Type your first name, please:
```

Type your first name, then enter a carriage return. When I did, I saw the output shown in Figure 8.6. Let's take a look at the source code that generated this output.

Stepping Through the Source Code

At the heart of name.c is a new Standard Library function called scanf(). This function uses the same format specifiers as printf() to read text in from the keyboard. This code will read in an int:

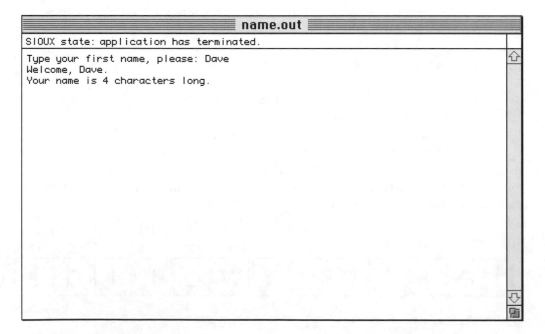

Figure 8.6 name prompts you to type in your name, then tells you how long your name is.

```
int    myInt;

scanf( "%d", &myInt );
```

The %d tells scanf() to read in an int. Notice the use of the & before the variable myInt. This passes the address of myInt to scanf(), allowing scanf() to change the value of myInt. To read in a float, use code like:

```
float myFloat;

scanf( "%f", &myFloat );
```

The program name.c starts off with a pair of #includes: <string.h> gives us access to the Standard Library function strlen(), and <stdio.h>, well, you know what we get from <stdio.h> —printf(), right? Right.

```
#include <string.h>
#include <stdio.h>
```

To read in a text string, you have to first declare a variable to place the text characters in. The program uses an array of characters for this purpose:

```
int    main( void )
{
    char   name[ 50 ];
```

The array name is big enough to hold a 49-byte text string. When you allocate space for a text string, remember to save 1 byte for the 0 that terminates the string.

The program starts by printing a **prompt**. A prompt is a text string that lets the user know that the program is waiting for input, as in the following:

```
    printf( "Type your first name, please: " );
```

Before we get to the scanf() call, it helps to understand how the computer handles input from the keyboard. When the computer starts running your program, it automatically creates a big array of chars for the sole purpose of storing keyboard input to your program. This array is known as your program's **input buffer**. Every time you enter a carriage return, all the characters typed since the previous carriage return are appended to the current input buffer.

When your program starts, the input buffer is empty. If you type 123 abcd from your keyboard, followed by a carriage return, the input buffer will look like

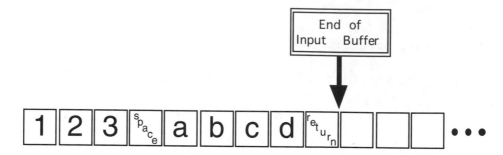

Figure 8.7 A snapshot of the input buffer.

Figure 8.7. The computer keeps track of the current end of the input buffer. The space character between the '123' and the 'abcd' has an ASCII value of 32. Notice that the carriage return was placed in the input buffer.

By the Way

> The ASCII value of the character used to indicate a carriage return is implementation dependent. In most development environments, an ASCII 10 indicates a carriage return. On some (most notably, MPW), an ASCII 13 indicates a carriage return. Use '\n' and you'll always be safe.

Given the input buffer shown in Figure 8.7, suppose that your program called scanf(), like this:

```
scanf( "%d", &myInt );
```

Starting at the beginning of the input buffer, scanf() reads a character at a time until it reaches one of the nonprintables, such as a carriage return, tab, space, or 0, until it reaches the end of the buffer or a character that conflicts with the format specifier (if %d was used and the letter 'a' was encountered, for example).

After the scanf(), the input buffer looks like Figure 8.8. Notice that the characters passed on to scanf() were removed from the input buffer and that the rest of the characters slid over to the beginning of the buffer. In fact, scanf() took the characters '1', '2', and '3' and converted them to the integer 123, placing 123 in the variable myInt.

If you then typed the line:

```
3.5 Dave
```

followed by a carriage return, the input buffer would look like Figure 8.9. At this point, the input buffer contains two carriage returns. To the input buffer, a carriage

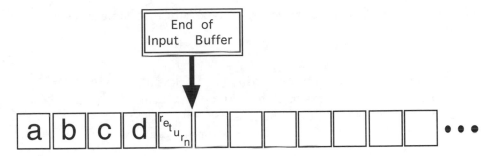

Figure 8.8 A second snapshot of the input buffer.

return is just like any other character. To a function like `scanf()`, the carriage return is white space.

> If you forgot what white space is, now would be a good time to turn back to Chapter 5, where white space was first described.

By the Way

Before we started our discussion on the input buffer, `main()` had just called `printf()` to prompt for the user's first name:

```
printf( "Type your first name, please: " );
```

Next, we called `scanf()` to read the first name from the input buffer:

```
scanf( "%s", name );
```

Since the program just started, the input buffer is empty; `scanf()` will wait until characters appear in the input buffer, which will happen as soon as you type

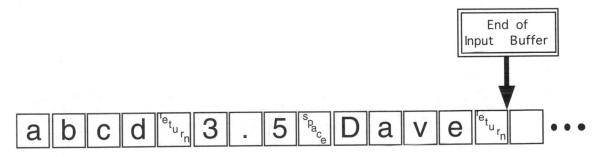

Figure 8.9 A third snapshot of the input buffer.

some characters and enter a carriage return. Type your first name and enter a carriage return.

By the Way

> Note that `scanf()` will ignore white-space characters in the input buffer. For example, if you type a few spaces and tabs and then enter a carriage return, `scanf()` will still sit there, waiting for some real input. Try it!

Once you type in your name, `scanf()` will copy the characters, a byte at a time, into the array of `chars` pointed to by `name`. Remember, because `name` was declared as an array, `name` points to the first of the 50 bytes allocated for the array.

If you type in the name `Dave`, `scanf()` will place the four characters `'D'`, `'a'`, `'v'`, and `'e'` into the first four of the 50 bytes allocated for the array. Next, `scanf()` will set the fifth byte to a value of 0 to terminate the string properly (Figure 8.10). Since the string is properly terminated by the 0 in `name[4]`, we don't really care about the value of the bytes `name[5]` through `name[49]`.

Next, we pass `name` on to `printf()`, asking it to print the name as part of a welcoming message. The `%s` tells `printf()` that `name` points to the first byte of a zero-terminated string. Stepping through memory, one byte at a time, `printf()` starts with the byte that `name` points to and prints each byte in turn until it reaches a byte with a value of 0, marking the end of the string.

```
printf( "Welcome, %s.\n", name );
```

Warning

> If `name[4]` didn't contain a 0, the string wouldn't be properly terminated. Passing a nonterminated string to `printf()` is a sure way to confuse `printf()`, which will step through memory one byte at a time, printing a byte and looking for a 0. It will keep printing bytes until it happens to encounter a byte set to 0. Remember, C strings must be terminated!

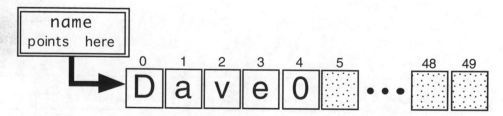

Figure 8.10 The array `name` after the string "`Dave`" is copied to it. Notice that `name[4]` has a value of 0.

The next line of the program calls another Standard Library function, called `strlen()`, which takes a pointer as a parameter and returns the length, in bytes, of the string pointed to by the parameter. This function depends on the string being terminated with a 0. Just like `sizeof()`, `strlen()` returns a value of type `size_t`. We'll use a typecast to convert the value to an `int`, then print it using `%d`. Again, we'll cover typecasting later in the book.

```
printf( "Your name is %d characters long.", (int)strlen( name ) );

return 0;
}
```

Our last program for this chapter demonstrates a few more character-handling techniques, a new Standard Library function, and an invaluable programmer's tool, the `#define`.

#define

The `#define` (pronounced pound-define) tells the compiler to substitute one piece of text for another throughout your source code. The following statement, for example, tells the compiler to substitute 6 every time it finds the text `kMaxPlayers` in the source code.

```
#define kMaxPlayers    6
```

The text `kMaxPlayers` is known as a **macro**. As the C compiler goes through your code, it enters each `#define` into a list, known as a **dictionary**, performing all the `#define` substitutions as it goes.

Important

It's important to note that the compiler never modifies your source code. The dictionary it creates as it goes through your code is separate from your source code, and the substitutions it performs are made as the source code is translated into machine code.

Here's an example of a `#define` in action:

```
#define kMaxArraySize    100

int    main( void )
```

```
{
   char  myArray[ kMaxArraySize ];
   int      i;

   for ( i=0; i<kMaxArraySize; i++ )
      myArray[ i ] = 0;

   return 0;
}
```

The #define at the beginning of this example substitutes 100 for kMaxArraySize everywhere it finds it in the source code file. In this example, the substitution will be done twice. Although your source code is not modified, here's the effect of this #define:

```
int   main( void )
{
   char  myArray[ 100 ];
   int       i;

   for ( i=0; i<100; i++ )
      myArray[ i ] = 0;

   return 0;
}
```

Warning

> Note that a #define must appear in the source code file before it is used. In other words, this code won't compile:
>
> ```
> int   main( void )
> {
>     char  myArray[ kMaxArraySize ];
>     int       i;
>
> #define kMaxArraySize 100
>
>     for ( i=0; i<kMaxArraySize; i++ )
> ```

```
        myArray[ i ] = 0;

    return 0;
}
```

Having a #define in the middle of your code is just fine. The problem here is that the declaration of myArray uses a #define that hasn't occurred yet!

If you use #defines effectively, you'll build more flexible code. In the previous example, you can change the size of the array by modifying a single line of code, the #define. If your program is designed correctly, you should be able to change the line to:

```
#define kMaxArraySize    200
```

You can then recompile your code, and your program should still work properly. A good sign that you are using #defines properly is an absence of constants in your code. In the example, the constant 100 was replaced by kMaxArraySize. You can also use the **Preprocess** command from the **Project** menu to get a preview of the result of all your #define substitutions.

Important

Most Macintosh programmers use the same naming convention for #defines as they use for global variables. Instead of starting the name with a g (as in gMyGlobal), a #define constant starts with a k (as in kMyConstant).

UNIX programmers tend to name their #define constants using all uppercase letters, sprinkled with underscores (_) to act as word dividers (as in MAX_ARRAY_SIZE).

As you'll see in our next program, you can put practically anything, even source code, into a #define. Take a look:

```
#define kPrintReturn          printf( "\n" );
```

Although not particularly recommended, this #define will work just fine:

```
printf( "\n" );
```

It will substitute that statement for every occurrence of the text `kPrintReturn` in your source code. You can also base one `#define` on a previous `#define`:

```
#define kSideLength      5
#define kArea       kSideLength * kSideLength
```

Interestingly, you could have reversed the order of these two `#defines`, and your code would still have compiled. As long as both entries are in the dictionary, their order of occurrence in the dictionary is not important.

What is important is that `#define` appear in the source code before any source code that refers to it. If this seems confusing, don't sweat it. It won't be on the test.

FunctionLike #define Macros

You can create a `#define` macro that takes one or more arguments. Here's an example:

```
#define kSquare( a )    ((a) * (a))
```

This macro takes a single argument. The argument can be any C expression; for example:

```
myInt = kSquare( myInt + 1 );
```

If you called the macro like that, the compiler would use its first pass to turn the line into this:

```
myInt = (( myInt + 1 ) * ( myInt + 1 ));
```

Notice the usefulness of the parentheses in the macro. Suppose, however, the macro were defined like this:

```
#define kSquare( a )    a * a
```

The compiler would have produced:

```
myInt = myInt + 1 * myInt + 1;
```

But that is not what we wanted. The only multiplication that gets performed by this statement is `1 * myInt`, because the `*` operator has a higher precedence than the `+` operator.

Be sure that you pay strict attention to your use of white space in your `#define` macros. For example, there's a world of difference between these two macros:

```
#define kSquare( a )     ((a) * (a))

#define kSquare ( a )     ((a) * (a))
```

(Note the space between `kSquare` and `( a )`.) The second form of the macro creates a `#define` constant named `kSquare`, which is defined as:

```
( a ) ((a) * (a))
```

This won't even compile (see the error message in Figure 8.11), because the compiler doesn't know what `a` is.

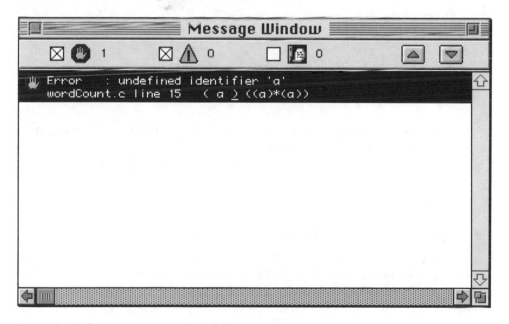

Figure 8.11 An error generated by adding one space to a macro.

187

Here's another interesting macro side effect. Suppose that you wanted to call this macro:

```
#define kSquare( a )    ((a) * (a))
```

But instead, you called it like this:

```
mySquare = kSquare( myInt++ );
```

The preprocessor pass expands this macro call to:

```
mySquare = ((myInt++) * (myInt++));
```

Do you see the problems here? First, `myInt` will get incremented twice by this macro call (probably not what was intended). Second, the first `myInt++` will get executed before the multiply happens, yielding a final result of `myInt*(myInt+1)`, definitely not what you wanted! The point here: Be careful when you pass an expression as a parameter to a macro.

A Sample Program: wordCount

Look in the `Learn C Projects` folder, inside the `08.07 - wordCount` subfolder, and open the project `wordCount.µ`. This program will ask you to type in a line of text and will count the number of words in the text you type.

To run `wordCount`, select **Run** from the **Project** menu. The program will then prompt you to type in a line of text:

```
Type a line of text, please:
```

Type in a line of text, at least a few words long. End your line by entering a carriage return. When you do, `wordCount` will report its results. The program will ignore any white space, so feel free to sprinkle your input with tabs, spaces, and the like. My output is shown in Figure 8.12. Let's take a look at the source code that generated this output.

Stepping Through the Source Code

The program begins with the usual `#include` and then adds a new one—`<ctype.h>`—which includes the prototype of the function `isspace()`. This function takes a `char` as input and returns `true` if the `char` is a tab (`'\t'`), hard carriage return (a return without a line feed: `'\r'`), newline (a return with a line feed: `'\n'`), vertical tab (`'\v'`), form feed (`'\f'`), or space (`' '`). Otherwise, it returns `false`.

```
┌═══════════════════════ wordCount.out ═══════════════════════┐
│ SIOUX state: application has terminated.                    │⇧│
│ Type a line of text, please:                                │ │
│ I   find delight    in the     gruesome and    grim!!!      │ │
│                                                             │ │
│ ---- This line has 8 words ----                             │ │
│ I   find delight    in the     gruesome and    grim!!!      │ │
│                                                             │ │
│                                                             │ │
│                                                             │ │
│                                                             │ │
│                                                             │ │
│                                                             │ │
│                                                             │ │
│                                                             │⇩│
│                                                             │▣│
└─────────────────────────────────────────────────────────────┘
```

Figure 8.12 wordCount, doing its job.

```
#include <stdio.h>
#include <ctype.h>
```

By the Way

> Older C environments may include a variant of isspace() called iswhite().

Next, we define a pair of constants: kMaxLineLength specifies the largest line this program can handle (200 bytes should be plenty); kZeroByte has a value of 0 and is used to mark the end of the line of input. More of this in a bit.

```
#define kMaxLineLength          200
#define kZeroByte               0
```

Here are the function prototypes for the two functions ReadLine() and CountWords(). ReadLine() reads in a line of text, and CountWords() takes a line of text and returns the number of words in the line:

```
/**********************/
/* Function Prototypes */
/**********************/
void  ReadLine( char *line );
int      CountWords( char *line );
```

The main() function starts by defining an array of chars that will hold the line of input we type and an int that will hold the result of our call to CountWords():

```
/***********************************************> main <*/
int   main( void )
{
    char      line[ kMaxLineLength ];
    int       numWords;
```

By the Way

> Notice that we've added a comment line that appears immediately before each of the wordCount functions. As your programs get larger and larger, a comment like this makes it easier to spot the beginning of a function and makes your code a little easier to read.

Once we type the prompt, we'll pass line to ReadLine(). Remember that line is a pointer to the first byte of the array of chars. When ReadLine() returns, line contains a line of text, terminated by a zero byte, making line a legitimate, 0-terminated C string. We'll pass that string on to CountWords():

```
printf( "Type a line of text, please:\n" );

ReadLine( line );
numWords = CountWords( line );
```

We then print a message telling us how many words we just counted:

```
printf( "\n---- This line has %d word", numWords );

if ( numWords != 1 )
    printf( "s" );
```

```
    printf( " ----\n%s\n", line );

    return 0;
}
```

This last bit of code shows attention to detail, something very important in a good program. Notice that the first `printf()` ended with the characters `"word"`. If the program found either no words or more than one word, we want to say either of the following:

```
This line has 0 words.
```

```
This line has 2 words.
```

If the program found exactly one word, the sentence should read:

```
This line has 1 word.
```

The last `if` statement makes sure that the `"s"` gets added if needed.

In `main()`, we defined an array of `char`s to hold the line of characters we type in. When `main()` called `ReadLine()`, it passed the name of the array as a parameter to `ReadLine()`:

```
char      line[ kMaxLineLength ];
ReadLine( line );
```

As we said earlier, the name of an array also acts as a pointer to the first element of the array. In this case, `line` is equivalent to `&(line[0])`. `ReadLine()` now has a pointer to the first byte of the `line` array in `main()`.

```
/***********************************************> ReadLine <*/
void  ReadLine( char *line )
{
```

This `while` loop calls `getchar()` to read one character at a time from the input buffer; `getchar()` returns the next character in the input buffer. Or, if there's an error, it returns the constant `EOF`. You'll learn more about `EOF` in Chapter 10.

By the Way

> As was the case with `scanf()`, when a character is read from the input buffer, the character is removed, and the rest of the characters in the buffer move over to take the place of the removed character.

The first time through the loop, `line` points to the first byte of the `line` array in `main()`. At this point, the expression `*line` is equivalent to the expression `line[0]`. The first time through the loop, we're getting the first character from the input buffer and copying it into `line[0]`.

The `while` loop continues as long as the character we just read in is not `'\n'` (as long as we have not yet retrieved the return character from the input buffer):

```
while ( (*line = getchar()) != '\n' )
    line++;
```

Each time through the loop, we'll increment the local copy of the pointer `line` in `ReadLine()` to point to the next byte in the `line` array of `main()`. The next time through the loop, we'll read a character into the second byte of the array, then the third byte, and so on, until read in a `'\n'` and drop out of the loop.

Important

> This technique is known as **pointer arithmetic**. When you increment a pointer that points into an array, the value of the pointer is incremented just enough to point to the next element of the array. For example, if `line` were an array of 4-byte `floats` instead of `chars`, the following line of code would increment `line` by 4 instead of by 1:
>
> ```
> line++;
> ```
>
> In both cases, `line` would start off pointing to `line[0]`; then, after the statement `line++`, `line` would point to `line[1]`.
>
> Take a look at this code:
>
> ```
> char    charPtr;
> float   floatPtr;
> double    doublePtr;
>
> charPtr++;
> ```

```
floatPtr++;
doublePtr++;
```

In the last three statements, `charPtr` gets incremented by 1 byte, `floatPtr` gets incremented by 4 bytes, and `doublePtr` gets incremented by 8 bytes (assuming 1-byte `chars`, 4-byte `floats`, and 8-byte `doubles`).

This is an extremely important concept to understand. If this seems fuzzy to you, go back and reread this section, then write some code to make sure that you truly understand how pointers work, especially as they relate to arrays.

Once we drop out of the loop, we'll place a 0 in the next position of the array. This turns the line into a 0-terminated string we can print using `printf()`:

```
    *line = kZeroByte;
}
```

`CountWords()` also takes a pointer to the first byte of the `main()` function's `line` array as a parameter. `CountWords()` will step through the array, looking for nonwhite space characters. When one is encountered, `CountWords()` sets `inWord` to `true` and increments `numWords`, then keeps stepping through the array looking for a white-space character, which marks the end of the current word. Once the white space is found, `inWord` is set to `false`:

```
/********************************************> CountWords <*/
int     CountWords( char *line )
{
    int        numWords, inWord;

    numWords = 0;
    inWord = false;
```

This process continues until the zero byte marking the end of the line is encountered:

```
    while ( *line != kZeroByte )
    {
        if ( ! isspace( *line ) )
```

```
    {
        if ( ! inWord )
        {
            numWords++;
            inWord = true;
        }
    }
    else
        inWord = false;

    line++;
    }
```

Once we drop out of the loop, we'll return the number of words in the line:

```
return numWords;
}
```

What's Next?

Congratulations! You've made it through one of the longest chapters in the book. You've mastered several new data types, including floats and chars. You've learned how to use arrays, especially in conjunction with chars. You've also learned about C's text-substitution mechanism, the #define.

Chapter 9 will teach you how to combine C's data types to create your own customized data types, called structs. So go grab some lunch, lean back, prop up your legs, and turn the page.

Exercises

1. What's wrong with each of the following code fragments:

```
a.  char  c;
    int   i;

    i=0;
    for ( c=0; c<=255; c++ )
        i += c;
```

b.
```
float    myFloat;

myFloat = 5.125;
printf( "The value of myFloat is %d.\n", f );
```

c.
```
char   c;

c = "a";

printf( "c holds the character %c.", c );
```

d.
```
char   c[ 5 ];

c = "Hello, world!";
```

e.
```
char   c[ kMaxArraySize ]

#define kMaxArraySize    20

int    i;

for ( i=0; i<kMaxArraySize; i++ )
   c[ i ] = 0;
```

f.
```
#define kMaxArraySize    200

char   c[ kMaxArraySize ];

c[ kMaxArraySize ] = 0;
```

g.
```
#define kMaxArraySize    200

char   c[ kMaxArraySize ], *cPtr;
int        i;

cPtr = c;
for ( i=0; i<kMaxArraySize; i++ )
   cPtr++ = 0;
```

h. #define kMaxArraySize   200

    char   c[kMaxArraySize];
    int   i;

    for (i=0; i<kMaxArraySize; i++)
    {
       *c = 0;
       c++;
    }

i. #define kMaxArraySize   200;

2. Rewrite `dice.c`, showing the possible rolls using three dice instead of two.

3. Rewrite `wordCount.`π, printing each of the words, one per line.

Designing Your Own Data Structures

In Chapter 8, we introduced several new data types, such as `float`, `char`, and `short`. We discussed the range of each type and introduced the format specification characters necessary to print each type using `printf()`. Next, we introduced the concept of arrays, focusing on the relationship between `char` arrays and text strings. Along the way, we discovered the `#define`, C's mechanism for text substitution.

This chapter will show you how to use existing C types as building blocks to design your own customized data structures. Sometimes, your programs will want to bundle certain data together. For example, suppose that you were writing a program to organize your compact disc collection. Imagine the type of information you'd like to access for each CD. At the least, you'd want to keep track of the artist's name and the name of the CD. You might also want to rate each CD's listenability on a scale of 1 to 10.

In the next few sections, we'll look at two approaches to a basic CD tracking program. Each approach will center on a different set of data structures. One approach (Model A) will use arrays, and the other (Model B) will use a set of custom-designed data structures.

Using Arrays (Model A)

One way to model your CD collection is to use a separate array for each CD's attributes:

```
#define kMaxCDs                300
#define kMaxArtistLength       50
#define kMaxTitleLength        50

char   rating[ kMaxCDs ];
char   artist[ kMaxCDs ][ kMaxArtistLength + 1 ];
char   title[ kMaxCDs ][ kMaxTitleLength + 1 ];
```

This code fragment uses three #defines: kMaxCDs defines the maximum number of CDs this program will track, kMaxArtistLength defines the maximum length of a CD artist's name, and kMaxTitleLength defines the maximum length of a CD's title.

The array rating has of 300 chars, one char for each CD. Each char in this array will hold a number from 1 to 10, the rating we've assigned to a particular CD. For example, this line of code assigns a value of 8 to CD 37:

```
rating[ 37 ] = 8; /* A pretty good CD */
```

The arrays artist and title are known as **multidimensional arrays**. A normal array, such as rating, is declared using a single dimension:

```
float     myArray[ 5 ];
```

This statement declares a normal, or one-dimensional, array containing five floats:

```
myArray[ 0 ]
myArray[ 1 ]
myArray[ 2 ]
myArray[ 3 ]
myArray[ 4 ]
```

The following statement, however, differs from a normal array:

```
float     myArray[ 3 ][ 5 ];
```

This statement declares a two-dimensional array, containing 3*5 = 15 floats:

```
myArray[0][0]
myArray[0][1]
myArray[0][2]
myArray[0][3]
myArray[0][4]
myArray[1][0]
myArray[1][1]
myArray[1][2]
myArray[1][3]
myArray[1][4]
```

```
myArray[2][0]
myArray[2][1]
myArray[2][2]
myArray[2][3]
myArray[2][4]
```

Think of a two-dimensional array as an array of arrays. Thus, `myArray[0]` is an array of five `floats`, as are `myArray[1]` and `myArray[2]`.

Here's a three-dimensional array:

```
float    myArray[ 3 ][ 5 ][ 10 ];
```

How many `floats` does this array contain? Tick, tick, tick. . . . Got it? The answer: 3*5*10 = 150. This version of `myArray` contains 150 `floats`.

By the Way

C allows you to create arrays of any dimension, although you'll rarely have a need for more than a single dimension.

So why would you ever want a multidimensional array? If you haven't already guessed, the answer to this question is going to lead us back to our CD tracking example.

Here are the declarations for our three CD tracking arrays:

```
#define kMaxCDs              300
#define kMaxArtistLength     50
#define kMaxTitleLength      50

char   rating[ kMaxCDs ];
char   artist[ kMaxCDs ][ kMaxArtistLength + 1 ];
char   title[ kMaxCDs ][ kMaxTitleLength + 1 ];
```

Once again, `rating` contains one `char` for each CD; `artist`, on the other hand, contains an array of `chars` for each CD. Each CD gets an array of `chars` whose length is `kMaxArtistLength` + 1. Each array is large enough to hold an artist's name up to 50 bytes long, with one byte left over to hold the terminating zero byte. To restate this, the two-dimensional array `artist` is large enough to hold up to 300 artist names, each of which can be up to 50 characters long, not including the terminating byte.

A Sample Program: `multiArray.µ`

The sample program `multiArray` brings this concept to life. The program defines the two-dimensional array `artist` (as described earlier), prompts you to type in a series of artists, stores their names in the two-dimensional `artist` array, then prints out the contents of `artist`.

Open the `Learn C Projects` folder, go inside the folder `09.01 – multiArray`, and open the project `multiArray.µ`. Run `multiArray` by selecting **Run** from the **Project** menu. The program will first tell you how many bytes of memory are allocated for the entire `artist` array:

```
The artist array takes up 15300 bytes of memory.
```

As a reminder, here's the declaration of `artist`:

```
#define kMaxCDs              300
#define kMaxArtistLength     50

char  artist[ kMaxCDs ][ kMaxArtistLength + 1 ];
```

By performing the `#define` substitution yourself, you can see that `artist` is defined as a 300-by-51 array; 300 times 51 is 15,300, matching the result reported by `multiArray`.

After `multiArray` reports the `artist` array size, it enters a loop, prompting you for your list of favorite musical artists:

```
Artist #1 (return to exit):
```

Enter an artist name, then enter a return. You'll be prompted for a second artist name. Type in a few more names, then enter an extra return. The extra return tells `multiArray` that you are done entering names.

The program will step through the array, using `printf()` to list the artists you've entered. In case your entire music collection consists of a slightly warped vinyl copy of Leonard Nimoy singing some old Dylan classics, feel free to use my list, shown in Figure 9.1.

Let's take a look at the source code.

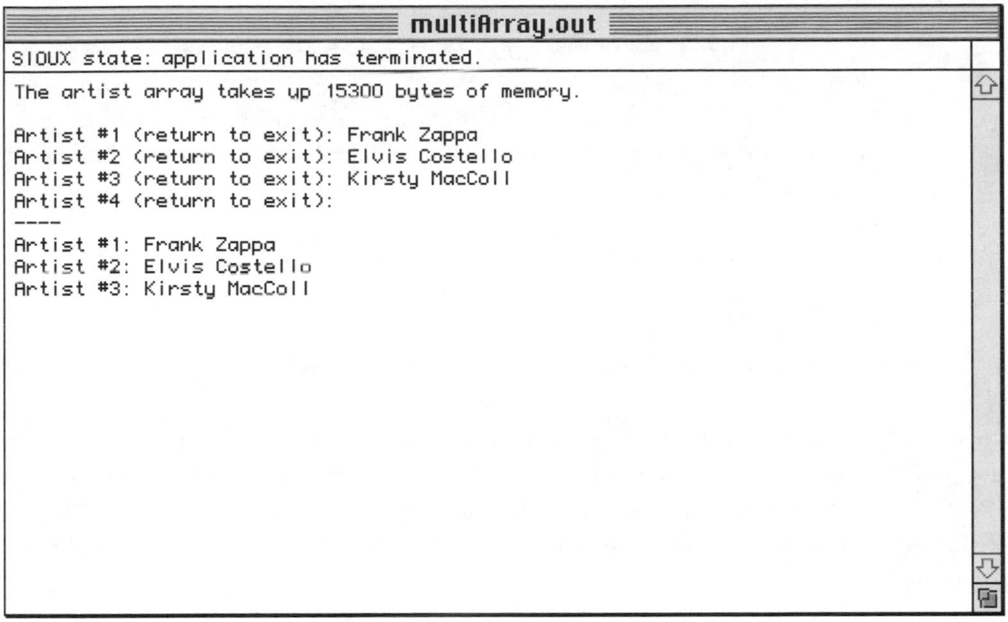

```
╔══════════════════ multiArray.out ══════════════════╗
SIOUX state: application has terminated.
─────────────────────────────────────────────────────
The artist array takes up 15300 bytes of memory.

Artist #1 (return to exit): Frank Zappa
Artist #2 (return to exit): Elvis Costello
Artist #3 (return to exit): Kirsty MacColl
Artist #4 (return to exit):
────
Artist #1: Frank Zappa
Artist #2: Elvis Costello
Artist #3: Kirsty MacColl
```

Figure 9.1 `multiArray` in action.

Stepping Through the Source Code

The program starts off with a standard #include; `<stdio.h>` gives us access to both `printf()` and `gets()`. After reading a line of text from the input buffer, `gets()` converts it into a zero-terminated string.

```
#include <stdio.h>
```

You've seen these two #defines before:

```
#define kMaxCDs              300
#define kMaxArtistLength     50
```

Here's the function prototype for `PrintArtists()`, the function we'll use to print out the `artist` array. Notice anything unusual about the declaration of `artist`? More on that in a bit.

```
/*********************/
/* Function Prototypes */
/*********************/
```

```
void   PrintArtists( short numArtists,
          char artist[][ kMaxArtistLength + 1 ] );
```

First, `main()` defines `artist`, our two-dimensional array, which is large enough to hold 300 artists. The name of each artist can be up to 50 bytes long, plus the zero terminating byte.

```
/**************************************************> main <*/
int    main( void )
{
   char   artist[ kMaxCDs ][ kMaxArtistLength + 1 ];
```

The number of artist names you've typed in is contained in `numArtists`. Notice that `numArtists` is a `short`. Since `kMaxCDs` is 300, even an `unsigned char` would not be large enough for `numArtists`. Since the maximum value of a `signed short` is 32767 (an implementation-dependent value), a `short` will be plenty big enough.

```
   short numArtists;
```

Beginning as `false`, `doneReading` will get set to `true` once we are ready to drop out of our artist-reading loop; `result` will hold the result returned by `gets()`:

```
   char   doneReading, *result;
```

This `printf()` prints out the size of the `artist` array. Notice that we've used the `%ld` format specifier to print the result returned by `sizeof`; `%ld` indicates that the type you are printing is the size of a `long`, which is true for `size_t`, the type returned by `sizeof`. If you use `%ld`, you won't need the `(int)` typecast we used in earlier programs.

```
printf( "The artist array takes up %ld bytes of memory.\n\n",
        sizeof( artist ) );

doneReading = false;
numArtists = 0;
```

Note that `size_t` is not guaranteed to be an `unsigned long`, although it usually is. The only guarantee is that `size_t` is the same size as that returned by the `sizeof` operator. In our case, `size_t` is defined as an unsigned long, so the `%ld` format specifier will work just fine.

Here's the loop that reads in the artist names. We'll drop out of the loop once `doneReading` is set to `true`.

```
while ( ! doneReading )
{
```

Inside the loop, we'll start off by printing a prompt that includes the artist number. We want the artist number to start at 1, but we don't want to increment `numArtists` until we are sure that the user has entered an artist number, so we'll just use `numArtists+1` in this `printf()`.

```
printf( "Artist #%d (return to exit): ", numArtists+1 );
```

Next, we'll call `gets()`; `gets()` is pretty much the same as the `ReadLine()` function from the `wordCount` program in Chapter 8. This `gets()` reads characters from the input buffer until it encounters a `'\n'`, then converts the read characters into a zero-terminated string. `gets()` takes a single parameter, a `char` pointer that points to the first byte of the memory where the finished string will be written:

```
result = gets( artist[ numArtists ] );
```

Once it is done, `gets()` returns a pointer to the beginning of the string (essentially the same pointer you passed in as a parameter), allowing you to use the result of `gets()` as a parameter to another function, such as `printf()`.

If an error occurs while reading from the input buffer, `gets()` returns the constant `NULL`, C's symbol for an invalid pointer. In all the time I've been writing C code, I've never seen this happen, but you never know.

Take a look at the parameter we passed to `gets()`:

```
artist[ numArtists ]
```

What type is this parameter? Remember, `artist` is a two-dimensional array, and a two-dimensional array is an array of arrays. Thus, `artist` is an array of an array of `chars`; `artist[numArtists]` is an array of `chars`, and so is exactly suited as a parameter to `gets()`.

Imagine an array of `chars` named `blap`:

```
char  blap[ 100 ];
```

You'd have no problem passing `blap` as a parameter to `gets()`, right? In that case, `gets()` would read the characters from the input buffer and place them in `blap`. Our `artist[0]` is just like `blap`. Both are pointers to an array of `chars`. `blap[0]` is the first `char` of the array `blap`; likewise, `artist[0][0]` is the first `char` of the array `artist[0]`.

OK, back to the code. If `gets()` fails (which it won't) or if the first byte of the string we just read in is the zero terminator (more on this in a sec), we'll set `doneReading` to `true` so we drop out of the loop. If the read was successful and we got a string bigger than 0 bytes long, we'll increment `numArtists` and go back to the top of the loop.

```
    if ( (result == NULL) ||
         (result[0] == '\0') )
         doneReading = true;
    else
         numArtists++;
}
```

Important

There are two important questions, both relating to this expression:

```
(result[0] == '\0')
```

What is `'\0'`, and why are we comparing it against the first byte of the string stored in `result`? Just like `'\n'`, `'\0'` is a character constant, a shorthand for a `char` with specific meaning. Here, `'\0'` is the zero terminator C places at the end of its strings. In earlier programs, when we wanted to add a zero terminator at the end of a string, we used the constant 0; `'\0'` is a character that has a value of 0 and works just as well.

Using '\0' makes it pretty clear that you are talking about the zero terminator instead of just an arbitrary numerical value. Once again, choose a style that makes sense to you and be consistent.

To answer the second question, we compare '\0' with the first byte of the string returned by gets() to see whether the string contains more than zero characters. A string that starts with the terminator is said to be a zero-length string. That's what gets() returns if the first character it encounters is a carriage return ('\n').

By the way, a zero-length string is represented in C as two consecutive double-quotes: "".

Once we drop out of the loop, we print a dividing line, then call PrintArtists() to print the contents of our array of artist names. The second parameter, artist, is a pointer to the first element of the artist array, that is, &(artist[0]).

```
printf( "----\n" );

PrintArtists( numArtists, artist );

return 0;
}
```

Take a look at the definition of the second parameter of PrintArtists(). Notice that the first of the two dimensions is missing (the first pair of brackets is empty). Although we could have included the first dimension (kMaxCDs), the fact that we were able to leave it out makes a really interesting point. When memory is allocated for an array, it is allocated as one big block. To access a specific element of the array, the compiler uses the dimensions of the array, as well as the specific element requested, to calculate an offset into this block.

```
/*************************************************> PrintArtists <*/
void  PrintArtists( short numArtists,
        char artist[][ kMaxArtistLength + 1 ] )
{
```

In the case of artist, the compiler allocated a block of memory 300 * 51 = 15,300 bytes long. Think of this block as 300 char arrays, each of which is 51 bytes long. To get to the first byte of the first array, we just use the pointer that was passed in (artist points to the first byte of the first of the 300 arrays). To access the first byte of the second array (in C notation, artist[1][0]), the compiler adds 51 to the pointer artist. In other words, the start of the second array is 51 bytes farther in memory than the start of the first array. The start of the 10th array is 9*51 = 459 bytes farther in memory than the start of the first array.

Although it is nice to know how to compute array offsets in memory, the point is that the compiler calculates the artist array offsets using the second dimension and not the first dimension of artist (51 is used; 300 is not used).

Important

> The compiler could use the first array bound (300) to verify that you don't reference an array element that is **out of bounds**. For example, the compiler could complain if it sees this line of code:
>
> ```
> artist[305][0] = '\0';
> ```
>
> The compiler would tell you that you are trying to reference a memory location outside the block of memory allocated for artist.
>
> Guess what. C compilers don't do bounds checking of any kind. If you want to access memory beyond the bounds of your array, no one will stop you. This is part of the "charm" of C. C gives you the freedom to write programs that crash in spectacular ways. Your job is to learn how to avoid such pitfalls.

OK, let's finish up this code. PrintArtists() first checks to see whether numArtists is zero or less. If it is, an appropriate message is printed:

```
/*****************************************> PrintArtists <*/
void  PrintArtists( short numArtists,
        char artist[][ kMaxArtistLength + 1 ] )
{
   short i;

   if ( numArtists <= 0 )
      printf( "No artists to report.\n" );
```

If we've got at least one artist to print, we'll step through the array, printing the artist number followed by the zero-terminated artist string. Notice that we used %s to print each string; %s is designed to print a '\0' terminated string:

```
else
{
    for ( i=0; i<numArtists; i++ )
        printf( "Artist #%d: %s\n",
            i+1, artist[i] );
}
}
```

Although I tried to make this code reasonably safe, there is definitely a bug in this program. Take a look at the output shown in Figure 9.2. I ran multiArray and then typed the digits "1234567890" five times (for a total of 50 characters. I then typed "12" to put the grand total at 52 characters. When I entered a return, gets() read all 52 characters from the input buffer, copied them into the array artist[0], and then stuck a '\0' at the end of the string. Do you see the problem here? Here's a hint. Each artist subarray is exactly 51 bytes long.

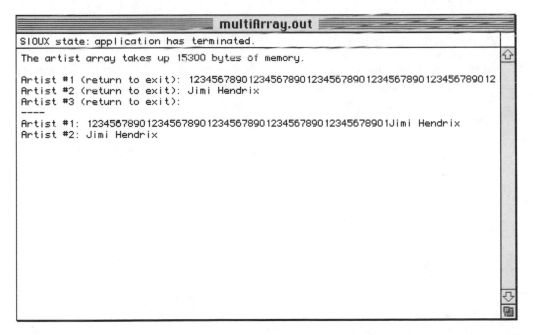

Figure 9.2 This output results from a bug in the program. Look at the end of both lines labeled Artist #1.

When `gets()` wrote the 53 bytes (52 bytes plus the '\0') starting at `artist[0][0]`, the first 51 bytes fit just fine. The extra 2 bytes (the character '2' and the '\0') were written to the next 2 bytes of memory, which happen to correspond to the memory locations `artist[1][0]` and `artist[1][1]`. When `gets()` read the second artist name, it copied the string "Jimi Hendrix" starting at `artist[1][0]`. Here's where things start to get skoongy. The string "Jimi Hendrix" overwrites the last two bytes of the first string (the character '2' and the '\0'). Horrors! We just overwrote the first string's terminator.

When `PrintArtists()` prints the first string, it keeps printing until it comes to a terminating '\0', which doesn't happen until the end of "Jimi Hendrix". This is a pretty subtle bug. One solution is to make the "width" of the array larger. Instead of 51 bytes for each artist, how about 100 bytes? Although this solution reduces the chances of an out-of-bounds error, it has the disadvantage of requiring more memory and is still not perfect.

A better solution is to read each artist name from the input buffer one character at a time. If you get 50 bytes of data and still haven't reached the end of a name, slap a '\0' in the 51st byte and drop the rest of the name in the **bit bucket** (that is, ignore the rest of the name). Hmmm. . . . Something tells me that you'll be implementing this solution as an exercise in the back of this chapter. Am I clairvoyant? Could be.

Arrays and Memory

At the beginning of the chapter, we described a program that would track your CD collection. The goal was to look at two different approaches to solving the same problem. The first approach, Model A, uses three arrays to hold a rating, artist name, and title for each CD in the collection:

```
#define kMaxCDs              300
#define kMaxArtistLength      50
#define kMaxTitleLength       50

char   rating[ kMaxCDs ];
char   artist[ kMaxCDs ][ kMaxArtistLength + 1 ];
char   title[ kMaxCDs ][ kMaxTitleLength + 1 ];
```

Before we move on to Model B, let's take a closer look at the memory used by the Model A arrays.

- The array `rating` uses 1 byte for each CD (enough for a 1-byte rating from 1 to 10).

- The array `artist` uses 51 bytes for each CD (enough for a text string holding the artist's name, up to 50 bytes in length, plus the terminating byte).

- The array `title` also uses 51 bytes for each CD (enough for a text string holding the CD's title, up to 50 bytes in length, plus the terminating byte).

Add those three, and you find that Model A allocates 103 bytes for each CD. Since Model A allocates space for 300 CDs when it declares its three key arrays, it uses 300 * 103 = 30,900 bytes.

Since the program really needs only 103 bytes for each CD, wouldn't it be nice if you could allocate the memory for a CD when you need it? With this type of approach, if your collection consisted of only 50 CDs, you'd have to use only 50 * 103 = 5150 bytes of memory instead of 30,900.

As you'll see by the end of the chapter, C provides a mechanism for allocating memory as you need it. Model B takes a first step toward memory efficiency by creating a single data structure that contains all the information relevant to a single CD. Later in the chapter, you'll learn how to allocate just enough memory for a single structure.

Designing Data Structures (Model B)

As stated earlier, our CD program must keep track of a rating (from 1 to 10), the CD artist's name, and the CD's title:

```
#define kMaxCDs              300
#define kMaxArtistLength     50
#define kMaxTitleLength      50

char   rating[ kMaxCDs ];
char   artist[ kMaxCDs ][ kMaxArtistLength + 1 ];
char   title[ kMaxCDs ][ kMaxTitleLength + 1 ];
```

The struct Keyword

C provides the perfect mechanism for wrapping all three of these variables into one tidy bundle. A `struct` allows you to associate any number of variables together under a single name. Here's an example of a `struct` declaration:

```
#define kMaxArtistLength        50
#define kMaxTitleLength         50

struct CDInfo
{
   char   rating;
   char   artist[ kMaxArtistLength + 1 ];
   char   title[ kMaxTitleLength + 1 ];
}
```

This `struct` type declaration creates a new type, called `CDInfo`. Just as you'd use a type such as `short` or `float` to declare a variable, you can use this new type to declare an individual `struct`. Here's an example:

```
struct CDInfo  myInfo;
```

This line of code uses the previous type declaration as a template to create an individual `struct`. The compiler uses the type declaration to tell it how much memory to allocate for the `struct`, then allocates a block of memory large enough to hold all of the individual variables that make up the `struct`.

The variables that form the `struct` are known as **fields**. A `struct` of type `CDInfo` has three fields: a `char` named `rating`, an array of `chars` named `artist`, and an array of `chars` named `title`. To access the fields of a `struct`, use the `.` operator:

```
struct CDInfo  myInfo;

myInfo.rating = 7;
```

Notice the `.` between the `struct` name (`myInfo`) and the field name (`rating`). The `.` following a `struct` name tells the compiler that a field name is to follow.

A Sample Program: structSize.μ

Here's a program that demonstrates the declaration of a `struct` type, as well as the definition of an individual `struct`. Open the `Learn C Projects` folder, go inside the folder `09.02 - structSize`, and open the project `structSize.μ`. Run `structSize` by selecting **Run** from the **Project** menu.

Compare your output with the console window shown in Figure 9.3. They should be the same. The first three lines of output show the `rating`, `artist`, and

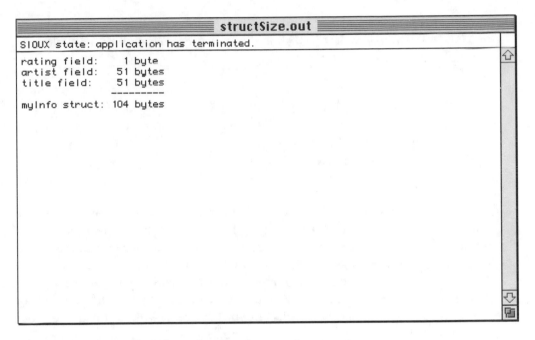

Figure 9.3 `structSize` shows the size of a `CDInfo struct`.

`title` fields. To the right of each field name, you'll find printed the number of bytes of memory allocated to that field. The last line of output shows the memory allocated to the entire `struct`. Notice that the sum of the three individual fields is not equal to the memory allocated to the entire `struct`. What gives? You'll find out in the next section, when we step through the source code.

Stepping Through the Source Code

If you haven't done so already, quit `structSize` and take a minute to look over the source code in `structSize.c`. Once you feel comfortable with it, read on.

The program `structSize.c` starts off with our standard #include, along with a brand new one:

```
#include <stdio.h>
#include "structSize.h"
```

Notice the double quotes around `"structSize.h"`; they tell the compiler to look for this include file in the same folder as the source code file. The compiler compiles the source code it finds in `"structSize.h"` as if it were inside `structSize.c`.

In general, angle brackets (<>) are used for system include files (such as <stdio.h>). Double quotes (" ") should be used for include files that belong to your application.

Important

> As you've already seen, C include files typically end in the two characters .h. Though you *can* give your include files any name you like, the .h convention is one you should definitely stick with. Include files are also known as **header files**, which is where the h comes from.

Let's take a look at structSize.h. There are three ways you can do this. The first way is to select **Open** from the **File** menu, then select and open structSize.h. The second way is to double-click on the word structSize to select it, then either type ⌘**D** or select **Open Selection** from the **File** menu. Go ahead, try it! Notice that this second method doesn't work if you select only part of the word structSize or if you select "structSize.h" instead of structSize. It will work if you select structSize.h (without the quotes), but why bother when "double-click, ⌘**D**" is so much easier?

The third method for opening include files works only if you've already gotten your code to compile. CodeWarrior builds a list of all the files included by a specific source code file and attaches the list to a pop-up menu (look for the label ▶). Selecting a file from the pop-up menu opens that file. You'll find the ▶ pop-up label in the lower-left corner of each of your source code files and to the right of each source code file in the project window.

Important

> Include files typically contain things like #defines, global variables, global declarations, and function prototypes. By embedding these things in an include file, you declutter your source code file and, more important, make this common source code available to other source code files through a single #include.

The structSize.h header file starts off with two #defines you've seen before:

```
#define kMaxArtistLength    50
#define kMaxTitleLength     50
```

Next comes the declaration of the struct type, CDInfo:

```
/**********************/
/* Struct Declarations */
/**********************/
struct CDInfo
{
    char  rating;
    char  artist[ kMaxArtistLength + 1 ];
    char  title[ kMaxTitleLength + 1 ];
};
```

By including the header file at the top of the file (where we might place our globals), we've made the CDInfo struct type available to all of the functions inside structSize.c. If we placed the CDInfo type declaration inside of main( ) instead, our program would still have worked (as long as we placed the type declaration before the definition of myInfo), but we would then not have access to the CDInfo type outside of main( ).

That's all that was in the header file structSize.h. Back in structSize.c, main( ) starts by defining a CDInfo struct named myInfo, which has three fields: myInfo.rating, myInfo.artist, and myInfo.title.

```
/***********************************************> main <*/
int   main( void )
{
    struct CDInfo  myInfo;
```

The next three statements print the size of the three myInfo fields. Notice that we are again using the %ld format specifier to print the value returned by sizeof:

```
printf( "rating field:    %ld byte\n",
        sizeof( myInfo.rating ) );

printf( "artist field:    %ld bytes\n",
        sizeof( myInfo.artist ) );

printf( "title field:    %ld bytes\n",
        sizeof( myInfo.title ) );
```

This next printf( ) prints a separator line, purely for aesthetics. Notice the way everything lines up in Figure 9.3?

```
printf( "                        ---------\n" );
```

Here's where the surprise kicks in. If the `rating` field is 1 byte, `artist` 51 bytes, and `title` also 51 bytes, you'd expect the size of the entire `struct` to be 1+51+51 = 103 bytes long. As you can see by the output shown in Figure 9.3, 104 bytes of memory were allocated for `myInfo`.

```
printf( "myInfo struct: %ld bytes",
        sizeof( myInfo ) );

return 0;
}
```

Here's why. Some computers have rules they follow to keep various data types lined up a certain way. For example, 680x0 compilers force all data larger than a `char` to start on an even-byte boundary (at an even memory address). A `long` will always start at an even address. A `short` will always start at an even address. A `struct`, no matter its size, will always start at an even address. Conversely, a `char` or array of `chars` can start at either an odd or an even address. In addition, a `struct` must always have an even number of bytes.

In our example, the three `struct` fields are all either `chars` or arrays of `chars`, so they are all allowed to start at either an odd or an even address. The three fields total 103 bytes. Since a `struct` on a 680x0 must always have an even number of bytes, the compiler adds an extra byte (known as **padding,** or a **pad byte**) at the end of the `struct`. We won't ever use this byte of padding, but it's important to know it's there.

Important

> Remember that these data alignment rules vary from machine to machine and are not specific to the C language. When in doubt, write some code and try it out.

Data Alignment: PowerPC Versus 680x0

This section talks about the difference in data alignment between computers based on the 680x0 and those based on the PowerPC. If the last example brought tears to your eyes, feel free to skim this section or to skip it entirely.

The previous example demonstrated the data alignment rules for a 680x0-based computer. To restate them:

- All data larger than a `char` must start at an even address.

- All `struct`s must start at an even address.

- All `struct`s must contain an even number of bytes.

On the PowerPC, things aren't quite as simple. The specifics may vary from compiler to compiler, but in general, a variable's alignment in memory (and within a `struct`) depends on its size. For example, the compiler will allocate a 1-byte variable anywhere in memory but will start a 2-byte variable only at an even address. A 4-byte variable starts at an address that is a multiple of 4, and an 8-byte variable starts at an address that is a multiple of 8.

Within a `struct`, the compiler follows these same rules, with two slight provisos. The first is that the size of the largest data type in the `struct` determines where the `struct` begins in memory. For example, if a `struct` contains a `long`, a `short`, and an array of `chars`, the compiler uses the `long` to determine where the `struct` begins in memory (in this case, at an address that is a multiple of 4). Note that this is true even for an array of 100 `chars`. It's the size of the type that counts, not the total size of a field.

The second proviso is that the compiler will use padding bytes to make sure that the size of the `struct` is also a multiple of the largest data size within. For example, if the largest data type in a `struct` is an 8-byte `double`, the `struct` will start at an address that is a multiple of 8 and will be a multiple of 8 bytes in size.

Some examples should make this clearer. Take a look at this struct:

```
struct LongShortShort
{
    long   myLong;
    short  myShort1;
    short  myShort2;
};
```

Since this `struct` starts with a 4-byte `long`, the `struct` will start at an address that is a multiple of 4. The compiler will allocate the `long` and the two `shorts` one after another in memory, with no padding required. The `long` starts at an address that is a multiple of 4, and the two `shorts` naturally follow at two even addresses. The `struct` takes up a total of 8 bytes.

Here's a slightly scrambled version of the same `struct`:

```
struct ShortLongShort
{
    short myShort1;
    long  myLong;
    short myShort2;
};
```

This version also starts off at an address that is a multiple of 4, because the largest type in the `struct` is a `long`. This time, however, some padding bytes are required. The compiler starts the first `short` at the multiple-of-4 address. Next comes the `long`, but in order for it to start at a multiple-of-4 address, 2 padding bytes must be placed after the `short`. Next, the second `short` is allocated immediately following the `long` (it's OK there, since a `short` requires only an even address).

So far, our `struct` is 10 bytes long (the 2-byte `short`, 2 padding bytes, a 4-byte `long`, and a 2-byte `short`). Since the largest data size in the `struct` is a 4-byte `long`, the compiler adds 2 padding bytes, bringing the size of the `struct` up to 12 bytes, a multiple of 4.

Here's another example:

```
struct DoubleChar
{
    double   myDouble;
    char   myChar;
};
```

This one is based on an 8-byte alignment (its largest data size is an 8-byte `double`) and starts at a memory address that is a multiple of 8. The `char` is allocated immediately after the `double`, since a `char` can fit anywhere. So far, the `struct` weighs in at 9 bytes. To ensure that the size of the `struct` is a multiple of 8, 7 padding bytes are added. The `struct` ends up at 16 bytes in size.

If you are interested in learning more about 680x0 and PowerPC data alignment, check out the program `structSize2` in the `Learn C Projects` folder, in the subfolder named `09.03 - structSize2`. You'll find three different projects, each of which declares a series of `struct`s and then prints the size of each `struct` according to the current data alignment model.

The first two projects were built using the 680x0 version of CodeWarrior. The project `structSize2.68K.`μ has its preferences set so that CodeWarrior will use the 680x0 data alignment model. The second project, `structSize2.PPCon68K.`μ, has its preferences set so that CodeWarrior uses the PowerPC data alignment model (even though the project generates 68000 object code).

The third project is in the subfolder labeled `PowerPC Native Version` and, as its name implies, was built using the PowerPC native version of CodeWarrior. This project also uses the PowerPC data alignment model. Although you can get a sense of the PowerPC data alignment model by running the PowerPC setting on a 680x0-based machine, there's no substitute for the real thing. If you want to learn more about data alignment on the Macintosh, check out the book *Inside Macintosh: PowerPC System Software*.

Passing a struct as a Parameter

Think back to the CD tracking program we've been discussing throughout the chapter. We started off with three separate arrays, each of which tracked a separate element: the rating field, the CD artist, and the title of each CD.

We then introduced the concept of a structure that would group all the elements of one CD together, in a single `struct`. One advantage of a `struct` is that you can use a single pointer to pass all the information about a CD. Imagine a routine called `PrintCD()`, designed to print the three elements that describe a single CD. Using the original array-based model, we'd have to pass three parameters to `PrintCD()`:

```
void  PrintCD( char rating, char *artist, char *title )
{
    printf("rating: %d\n", rating );
    printf("artist: %s\n", artist );
    printf("title: %s\n", title );
}
```

Using the `struct`-based model, however, we could pass the info by using a single pointer. As a reminder, here's the `CDInfo` struct declaration again:

```
#define kMaxArtistLength        50
#define kMaxTitleLength         50

struct CDInfo
```

```
{
    char   rating;
    char   artist[ kMaxArtistLength + 1 ];
    char   title[ kMaxTitleLength + 1 ];
};
```

This version of `main()` defines a `CDInfo` struct and passes its address to a new version of `PrintCD()` (we'll get to it next).

```
int    main( void )
{
    struct CDInfo   myInfo;

    PrintCD( &myInfo );

    return 0;
}
```

Just as has been the case in earlier programs, passing the address of a variable to a function gives that function the ability to modify the original variable. Passing the address of `myInfo` to `PrintCD()` gives `PrintCD()` the ability to modify the three `myInfo` fields. Although our new version of `PrintCD()` doesn't modify `myInfo`, it's important to know that that opportunity exists. Here's the new, struct-based version of `PrintCD()`:

```
void  PrintCD( struct CDInfo *myCDPtr )
{
    printf( "rating: %d\n", (*myCDPtr).rating );
    printf( "artist: %s\n", myCDPtr->artist );
    printf( "title: %s\n", myCDPtr->title );
}
```

Notice that `PrintCD()` receives its parameter as a pointer to (address of) a `CDInfo` struct. The first `printf()` uses the * operator to turn the struct pointer back to the struct it points to, then uses the . operator to access the rating field:

```
(*myCDPtr).rating
```

C features a special operator, ->, that lets you accomplish the same thing. The -> operator is binary, that is, it requires both a left and a right operand. The left operand is a pointer to a `struct`, and the right operand is the `struct` field. The notation `myCDPtr->artist` is exactly the same as `(*myCDPtr).rating`.

Use whichever form you prefer. In general, most C programmers use the -> operator to get from a `struct`'s pointer to one of the `struct`'s fields.

Passing a Copy of the `struct`

Here's a version of `main()` that passes the `struct` itself, instead of its address:

```
int    main( void )
{
    struct CDInfo  myInfo;

    PrintCD( myInfo );
}
```

Whenever the compiler encounters a function parameter, it passes a copy of the parameter to the receiving routine. The previous version of `PrintCD()` received a copy of the address of a `CDInfo struct`.

In this new version of `PrintCD()`, the compiler passes a copy of the entire `CDInfo struct`, not just a copy of its address. This copy of the `CDInfo struct` includes copies of the `rating` field and the `artist` and `title` arrays:

```
void  PrintCD( struct CDInfo myCD )
{
    printf( "rating: %d\n", myCD.rating );
    printf( "artist: %s\n", myCD.artist );
    printf( "title: %s\n", myCD.title );
}
```

Important

> When a function exits, all of its local variables (except for `static` variables, which we'll cover in Chapter 11) are no longer available. This means that any changes you make to a local parameter are lost when the function returns. If this version of `PrintCD()` made changes to its local copy of the `CDInfo struct`, those changes would be lost when `PrintCD()` returned.

Sometimes, you'll want to pass a copy of a `struct`. One advantage this technique offers is that there's no way that the receiving function can modify the original `struct`. Another advantage is that it offers a simple mechanism for making a copy of a `struct`. A disadvantage of this technique is that copying a `struct` takes time and uses memory. Time won't usually be a problem, but memory usage might be, especially if your `struct` gets pretty large. Just be aware that whatever you pass as a parameter is going to get copied by the compiler.

Important

There's a sample program in the `Learn C Projects` folder, inside a subfolder named `09.04 - paramAddress,` that should help show the difference between passing the address of a `struct` and passing a copy of the `struct`. Basically, here's how the program works.

First, `main()` defines a `CDInfo struct` named `myCD`, then prints the address of `myCD`'s `rating` field:

```
printf( "Address of myCD.rating in main():      %ld\n",
     &(myCD.rating) );
```

Notice that we print an address using the `%ld` format specifier. Although there are other ways to print a variable's address, this works just fine for our purposes. Here's the output of this `printf()`:

```
Address of myCD.rating in main():            26352526
```

Next, `main()` passes the address of `myCD` and `myCD` as parameters to a routine named `PrintParamInfo()`:

```
PrintParamInfo( &myCD, myCD );
```

Here's the prototype for `PrintParamInfo()`:

```
void    PrintParamInfo( struct CDInfo *myCDPtr,
                struct CDInfo myCDCopy );
```

The first parameter is a copy of the address of `main()`'s `myCD struct`. The second parameter is a copy of the same `struct`. `PrintParamInfo()` prints the address of the `rating` field of each version of `myCD`:

```
printf( "Address of myCDPtr->rating in PrintParamInfo(): %ld\n",
        &(myCDPtr->rating) );
printf( "Address of myCDCopy.rating in PrintParamInfo(): %ld\n",
        &(myCDCopy.rating) );
```

Here are the results, including the line of output generated by `main()`:

```
Address of myCD.rating in main():           26352526
Address of myCDPtr->rating in PrintParamInfo(): 26352526
Address of myCDCopy.rating in PrintParamInfo(): 26352414
```

Notice that the `rating` field accessed with a pointer has the same address as the original `rating` field in `main()`'s `myCD` struct. If `PrintParamInfo()` uses the first parameter to modify the `rating` field, it will, in effect, be changing `main()`'s `rating` field. If `PrintParamInfo()` uses the second parameter to modify the `rating` field, the `rating` field will remain untouched.

By the way, most programmers use **hexadecimal** (or **hex**) **notation** when they print addresses. Hex notation represents numbers as base 16 instead of the normal base 10 you are used to. Instead of the 10 digits 0 through 9, hex features the 16 digits 0, 1, 2, 3, 4, 5, 6, 7, 8, 9, a, b, c, d, e, and f. Each digit of a number represents a successive power of 16 instead of successive powers of 10.

For example, the number 532 in base 10 is equal to $5*10^2 + 3*10^1 + 2*10^0 =$ 5*100+3*10+2*1. The number 532 in hex is equal to $5*16^2 + 3*16^1 + 2*16^0 =$ 5*256+3*16+2*1 = 1330 in base 10. The number `ff` in hex is equal to 15*16 + 15*1 = 255 in base 10. Remember, the hex digit `f` has a decimal (base 10) value of 15.

To represent a hex constant in C, precede it by the characters `0x`. The constant `0xff` has a decimal value of 255. The constant `0xFF` also has a decimal value of 255. C doesn't distinguish between upper- and lowercase when representing hex digits.

To print an address in hex, use the format specifier `%p` instead of `%ld`. Modify `paramAddress` by using `%p`, just to get a taste of hex.

struct Arrays

Just as you can declare an array of chars or ints, you can also declare an array of structs:

```
#define kMaxCDs                    300

struct CDInfo  myCDs[ kMaxCDs ];
```

This declaration creates an array of 300 structs of type CDInfo. The array is named myCDs. Each of the 300 structs will have the three fields rating, artist, and title. You access the fields of the structs as you might expect. Here's an example (note the use of the all-important . operator):

```
myCDs[ 10 ].rating = 9;
```

We now have an equivalent to our first CD-tracking data structure. Whereas Model A used three arrays, we now have a solution that uses a single array. As you'll see when you start writing your own programs, packaging your data in a struct makes life a bit simpler. Instead of passing three parameters each time you need to pass a CD to a function, you can simply pass a struct.

From a memory standpoint, both CD tracking solutions cost about the same. With three separate arrays, the cost is:

```
              300 bytes /* rating array */
300 * 51 = 15,300 bytes /* artist array */
300 * 51 = 15,300 bytes /* artist array */
          ------------
Total      30,900 bytes
```

With an array of structs, the cost is:

```
300 * 104 = 31,200 bytes  /* Cost of array of 300 CDInfo structs */
```

Why does the array of structs take up 300 more bytes than the three separate arrays? Easy. Each struct contains a byte of padding to bring its size from an odd number (103) to an even number (104). Since the array contains 300 structs, we accumulate 300 bytes of padding. Since 300 bytes is pretty negligible, these two methods are reasonably close in terms of memory cost.

So what can we do to cut this memory cost down? Thought you'd never ask!

Allocating Your Own Memory

One of the limitations of an array-based CD tracking model is that arrays are not resizable. When you define an array, you have to specify exactly how many elements make up your array. For example, this code defines an array of 300 `CDInfo` structs:

```
#define kMaxCDs              300


struct CDInfo  myCDs[ kMaxCDs ];
```

As we calculated earlier, this array will take up 31,200 bytes of memory, whether we use 1 array or 300 to track a CD. If you know in advance exactly how many elements your array requires, arrays are just fine. In the case of our CD tracking program, this just isn't practical. For example, if my CD collection consists entirely of a test CD that came with my stereo and a rare soundtrack recording of *Gilligan's Island* outtakes, a 300-`struct` array is overkill. Even worse, what happens if I've got more than 300 CDs? No matter what number I pick for `kMaxCDs`, there's always the chance that it won't prove large enough.

The problem here is that arrays are just not flexible enough to do what we want. Instead of trying to predict the amount of memory we'll need in advance, what we need is a method that will allow us to get a chunk of memory the size of a `CDInfo` `struct`, as we need it. In more technical terms, we need to allocate and manage our own memory.

When your program starts running, the Macintosh operating system (the software that controls your Macintosh) sets aside a block of memory dedicated to your application. To find out how much memory gets set aside for a particular application, go to the Finder, click on the application's icon, and select **Get Info** from the **File** menu. An info window will appear, similar to the one shown in Figure 9.4. In the lower-right corner of the window, you'll see a series of fields labeled `Suggested size`, `Minimum size`, and `Preferred size`. The numbers to the right of each of these fields tells the operating system how much memory is suggested, is required (at a minimum), and—in an ideal memory-rich world—how much memory the application would prefer. The application shown in Figure 9.4, eWorld, requires a minimum of 1100K in order to run. Since 1K is equal to 1024 bytes, that's equal to 1,126,400 bytes.

When your application starts, some of this memory is used to hold the object code that makes up your application. Still more memory is used to hold such things as your application's global variables. As your application runs, some of this memory will be allocated to `main()` local variables. When `main()` calls a

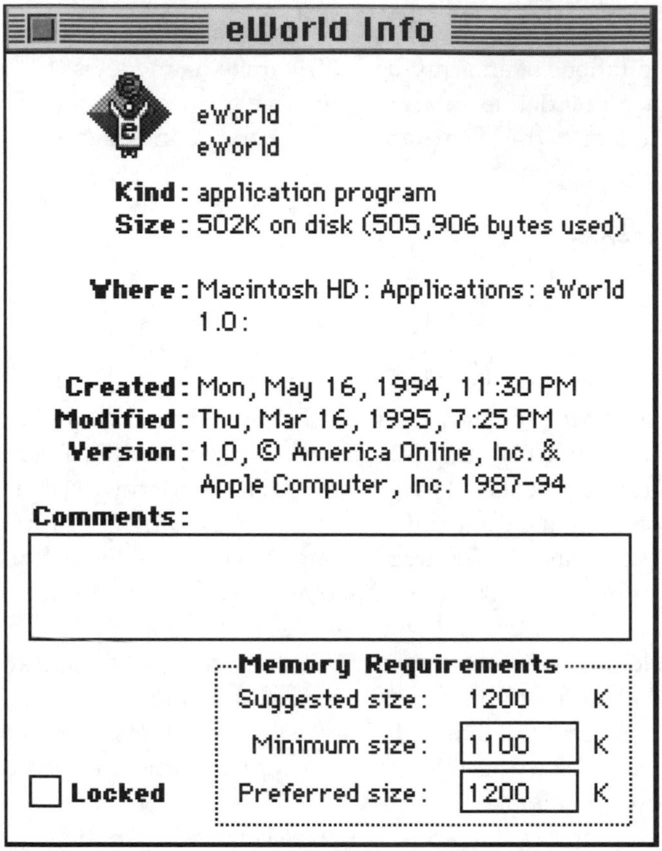

Figure 9.4 The **Get Info** window for the eWorld application. This application requires 1100K of memory to run but prefers 1200K.

function, memory is allocated for that function's local variables. When that function returns, the memory allocated for its local variables is freed up, or made available to be allocated again.

In the next few sections, you'll learn about some functions you can call to allocate a block of memory and to free the memory (to return it to the pool of available memory). Ultimately, we'll combine these functions with a special data structure to provide a memory-efficient, more flexible alternative to the array.

Using Standard Library Functions

malloc()

The Standard Library function `malloc()` allows you to to allocate a block of memory of a specified size. To access `malloc()`, you'll need to include the file `<stdlib.h>`:

```
#include <stdlib.h>
```

The function `malloc()` takes a single parameter, the size of the requested block, in bytes. `malloc()` returns a pointer to the newly allocated block of memory. Here's the function prototype:

```
void *malloc( size_t size );
```

By the Way

> Note that the parameter is declared to be of type `size_t`, the same type returned by `sizeof`. Think of `size_t` as equivalent to an `unsigned long`. Note also that `malloc()` returns the type (`void *`), a pointer to a `void`. A void pointer is essentially a generic pointer. Since there's no such thing as a variable of type `void`, the type (`void *`) is used to declare a pointer to a block of memory whose type has not been determined.
>
> In general, you'll convert the (`void *`) returned by `malloc()` to the pointer type you really want. Read on to see an example of this.

If `malloc()` can't allocate a block of memory the size you requested, it returns a pointer with the value NULL. NULL, a constant, is usually defined to have a value of 0 and is used to specify an invalid pointer. In other words, a pointer with a value of NULL does not point to a legal memory address. You'll learn more about NULL and (`void *`) as we use them in our examples.

Here's a code fragment that allocates a single `CDInfo struct`:

```
struct CDInfo  *myCDPtr;

myCDPtr = malloc( sizeof( struct CDInfo ) );
```

The first line of code declares a new variable, `myCDPtr`, which is a pointer to a `CDInfo struct`. At this point, `myCDPtr` doesn't point to a `CDInfo struct`.

You've just told the compiler that `myCDPtr` is designed to point to a `CDInfo` struct.

The second line of code calls `malloc()` to create a block of memory the size of a `CDInfo` struct; `sizeof` returns its result as a `size_t`, the type we need to pass as a parameter to `malloc()`. How convenient!

By the Way

On the right side of the = operator is a (`void *`) and on the left side a (`struct CDInfo *`). The compiler automatically resolves this type difference for us. We could have used a typecast here to make this more explicit:

```
myCDPtr = (struct CDInfo *)malloc(sizeof(struct CDInfo ));
```

It really isn't necessary, however, and besides, we won't get into typecasting until Chapter 11!

If `malloc()` was able to allocate a block of memory the size of a `CDInfo` struct, `myCDPtr` contains the address of the first byte of this new block. If `malloc()` was unable to allocate our new block (perhaps there wasn't enough unallocated memory left), `myCDPtr` will be set to `NULL`.

```
if ( myCDPtr == NULL )
    printf( "Couldn't allocate the new block!\n" );
else
    printf( "Allocated the new block!\n" );
```

If `malloc()` succeeded, `myCDPtr` points to a struct of type `CDInfo`. For the duration of the program, we can use `myCDPtr` to access the fields of this newly allocated struct:

```
myCDPtr->rating = 7;
```

It is important to understand the difference between a block of memory allocated using `malloc()` and a block of memory that corresponds to a local variable. When a function declares a local variable, the memory associated with that variable is temporary. As soon as the function exits, the block of memory associated with that memory is returned to the pool of available memory. A block of memory that you allocate using `malloc()`, by contrast, sticks around until you specifically return it to the pool of available memory.

free()

The Standard Library function `free()` returns a previously allocated block of memory back to the pool of available memory. Here's the function prototype:

```
void  free( void *ptr );
```

This function takes a single argument, a pointer to the first byte of a previously allocated block of memory, for example:

```
free( myCDPtr );
```

This line returns the block allocated earlier to the free-memory pool. Use `malloc()` to allocate a block of memory. Use `free()` to free up a block of memory allocated with `malloc()`. When a program exits, the operating system automatically frees up all allocated memory.

Warning

Never pass an address to `free()` that didn't come from `malloc()`. Never put a fork in an electrical outlet. Both will make you extremely unhappy!

Keep Track of That Address!

The address returned by `malloc()` is critical. If you lose it, you've lost access to the block of memory you just allocated. Even worse, you can never free up the block, and it will just sit there, wasting valuable memory, for the duration of your program.

By the Way

One great way to lose a block's address is to call `malloc()` inside a function, saving the address returned by `malloc()` in a local variable. When the function exits, your local variable goes away, taking the address of your new block with it!

One way to keep track of a newly allocated block of memory is to place the address in a global variable. Another way is to place the pointer inside a special data structure known as a **linked list**.

Working with Linked Lists

The linked list is one of the most widely used data structures in C. A linked list is a series of `structs`, each of which contains, as a field, a pointer. Each `struct` in the series uses its pointer to point to the next `struct` in the series. Figure 9.5 shows a linked list containing three elements.

A linked list starts with a **master pointer**. The master pointer is a pointer variable, typically a global, that points to the first `struct` in the list. This first `struct` contains a field, also a pointer, that points to the second `struct` in the linked list. The second `struct` contains a pointer field that points to the third element. The linked list in Figure 9.5 ends with the third element. The pointer field in the last element of a linked list is typically set to `NULL`.

By the Way

> The notation used at the end of the linked list in Figure 9.5 is borrowed from our friends in electrical engineering. The funky three-line symbol at the end of the last pointer represents a `NULL` pointer.

Why Use Linked Lists?

Linked lists allow you to be extremely memory efficient. Using a linked list, you can implement our CD-tracking data structure, allocating exactly the number of `structs` that you need. Each time a CD is added to your collection, you'll allocate a new `struct` and add it to the linked list.

A linked list starts out as a single master pointer. When you want to add an element to the list, call `malloc()` to allocate a block of memory for the new element. Next, make the master pointer point to the new block. Finally, set the new block's next element pointer to `NULL`.

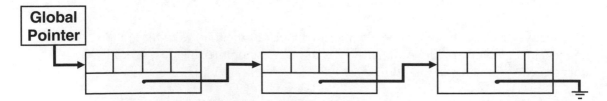

Figure 9.5 A linked list containing three elements.

Creating a Linked List

The first step in creating a linked list is to design the main link, the linked list `struct`. Here's a sample:

```
#define kMaxArtistLength        50
#define kMaxTitleLength         50

struct CDInfo
{
   char            rating;
   char            artist[ kMaxArtistLength + 1 ];
   char            title[ kMaxTitleLength + 1 ];
   struct CDInfo   *next;
}
```

The change here is the addition of a fourth field, a pointer to a `CDInfo` `struct`. The `next` field is the key to connecting two `CDInfo` `structs`. If `myFirstPtr` is a pointer to one `CDInfo` `struct` and `mySecondPtr` is a pointer to a second `struct`, the following line connects the two `structs`:

```
myFirstPtr->next = mySecondPtr;
```

Once they are connected, you can use a pointer to the first `struct` to access the fields in the second `struct`! For example:

```
myFirstPtr->next->rating = 7;
```

This line sets the `rating` field of the second `struct` to 7. Using the `next` field to get from one `struct` to the next is also known as **traversing a linked list.**

Our next (and final) program for this chapter will incorporate the new version of the `CDInfo` `struct` to demonstrate a more memory-efficient CD tracking program. This program is pretty long, so you may want to take a few moments to let the dog out and answer your mail.

By the Way

There are many variants of the linked list. If you connect the last element of a linked list to the first element, you create a never-ending, circular list. You can add a `prev` field to the `struct` and use it to point to the previous element in the list (as opposed to the next one). This technique allows you to traverse the linked list in two directions and creates a doubly linked list.

> As you gain more programming experience, you'll want to check out some books on data structures. Three books well worth exploring are *Algorithms in C* by Robert Sedgewick, *Data Structures and C Programs* by Christopher J. Van Wyk, and Volume 1 (subtitled *Fundamental Algorithms*) of Donald Knuth's Computer Science series. As always, these books are listed in the bibliography in Appendix G.

A Sample Program: cdTracker.μ

This program implements Model B of our CD tracking system. The program uses a text-based menu, allowing you to quit, add a new CD to the collection, or list all of the currently tracked CDs.

Open the `Learn C Projects` folder, go inside the folder `09.05 – cdTracker`, and open the project `cdTracker.μ`. Run `cdTracker` by selecting **Run** from the **Project** menu. The console window will appear, showing the prompt:

```
Enter command (q=quit, n=new, l=list):
```

At this point, you have three choices. You can type a q, followed by a carriage return, to quit the program. You can type an n, followed by a carriage return, to add a new CD to your collection. Finally, you can type an l, followed by a carriage return, to list all the CDs in your collection.

Start by typing an l, followed by a carriage return. You should see the message:

```
No CDs have been entered yet...
```

Next, the original command prompt should reappear:

```
Enter command (q=quit, n=new, l=list):
```

This time, type an n, followed by a carriage return. You will be prompted for the artist's name and the title of a CD you'd like added to your collection:

```
Enter Artist's Name:  Frank Zappa
Enter CD Title:  Anyway the Wind Blows
```

Next, you'll be prompted for a rating for the new CD. The program expects a number between 1 and 10. Try typing something unexpected, such as the letter x, followed by a carriage return:

```
Enter CD Rating (1-10):   x
Enter CD Rating (1-10):   10
```

The program checks your input, discovers it isn't in the proper range, and repeats the prompt. This time, type a number between 1 and 10, followed by a carriage return. The program returns you to the main command prompt:

```
Enter command (q=quit, n=new, l=list):
```

Type the letter l, followed by a carriage return. The single CD you just entered will be listed, and the command prompt will again be displayed:

```
Artist:   Frank Zappa
Title:    Anyway the Wind Blows
Rating:   10


----------
Enter command (q=quit, n=new, l=list):
```

Type an n, followed by a carriage return, and enter another CD. Repeat the process one more time, adding a third CD to the collection. Now enter the letter l, followed by a carriage return, to list all three CDs. Here's my list:

```
Enter command (q=quit, n=new, l=list):   l


----------
Artist:   Frank Zappa
Title:    Anyway the Wind Blows
Rating:   10


----------
Artist:   XTC
Title:    The Big Express
Rating:   8


----------
```

```
Artist:   Jane Siberry
Title:    Bound by the Beauty
Rating:   9


----------
Enter command (q=quit, n=new, l=list):
```

Finally, enter a q, followed by a carriage return, to quit the program. Let's hit the source code.

Stepping Through the Source Code

The code for `cdTracker.c` starts by including three different files: `<stdlib.h>` gives us access to `malloc()` and `free()`; `<stdio.h>` gives us access to such routines as `printf()`, `getchar()`, and `gets()`:

```
#include <stdlib.h>
#include <stdio.h>
```

The third include file is our own `"cdTracker.h"`, which starts off with three `#define`s that you should know pretty well by now:

```
/***********/
/* Defines */
/***********/
#define kMaxCDs              300
#define kMaxArtistLength     50
#define kMaxTitleLength      50
```

Next comes the new and improved `CDInfo struct` declaration:

```
/**********************/
/* Struct Declarations */
/**********************/
struct CDInfo
{
   char        rating;
   char        artist[ kMaxArtistLength + 1 ];
   char        title[ kMaxTitleLength + 1 ];
   struct CDInfo   *next;
} *gFirstPtr, *gLastPtr;
```

Notice the two variables hanging off the end of this `struct` declaration. This is a shorthand declaration of two globals, each of which is a pointer to a `CDInfo` `struct`. We'll use these two globals to keep track of our linked list.

The global `gFirstPtr` will always point to the first `struct` in the linked list; the global `gLastPtr` will always point to the last `struct` in the linked list. We'll use `gFirstPtr` when we want to step through the linked list, starting at the beginning. We'll use `gLastPtr` when we want to add an element to the end of the list. As long as we keep these pointers around, we'll have access to the linked list of memory blocks we'll be allocating.

By the Way

We could have split this declaration into two parts, like this:

```
struct CDInfo
{
        char            rating;
        char            artist[ kMaxArtistLength + 1 ];
        char            title[ kMaxTitleLength + 1 ];
        struct CDInfo   *next;
};

struct CDInfo*gFirstPtr, *gLastPtr;
```

Either form is fine, although the shorthand version in `cdTracker.h` does a better job of showing that `gFirstPtr` and `gLastPtr` belong with the `CDInfo` struct declaration.

The header file `cdTracker.h` ends with a series of function prototypes:

```
/**********************/
/* Function Prototypes */
/**********************/
char        GetCommand( void );
struct CDInfo   *ReadStruct( void );
void        AddToList( struct CDInfo *curPtr );
void        ListCDs( void );
void        Flush( void );
```

Let's get back to `cdTracker.c`; `main()` defines a char named `command`, which will be used to hold the single-letter command typed by the user:

```
/*****************************************************> main <*/
int    main( void )
{
   char          command;
```

Next, the variables `gFirstPtr` and `gLastPtr` are set to a value of `NULL`. As defined earlier, `NULL` indicates that these pointers do not point to valid memory addresses. Once we add an item to the list, these pointers will no longer be `NULL`:

```
   gFirstPtr = NULL;
   gLastPtr = NULL;
```

Next, `main()` enters a `while` loop, calling the function `GetCommand()`. `GetCommand()` prompts you for a one-character command: a 'q', 'n', or 'l'. Once `GetCommand()` returns a 'q', we drop out of the `while` loop and exit the program.

```
   while ( (command = GetCommand() ) != 'q' )
   {
```

If `GetCommand()` returns an 'n', the user wants to enter information on a new CD. First, we call `ReadStruct()`, which allocates space for a `CDInfo` struct, then prompts the user for the information to place in the fields of the new struct. Once the struct is filled out, `ReadStruct()` returns a pointer to the newly allocated struct.

The pointer returned by `ReadStruct()` is passed on to `AddToList()`, which adds the new struct to the linked list:

```
      switch( command )
      {
         case 'n':
            AddToList( ReadStruct() );
            break;
```

If `GetCommand()` returns an 'l', the user wants to list all the CDs in his or her collection. That's what the function `ListCDs()` does:

```
       case 'l':
          ListCDs( );
          break;
    }
  }
```

Before the program exits, it says `"Goodbye..."`.

```
  printf( "Goodbye..." );
}
```

Next up on the panel is `GetCommand()`. `GetCommand()` declares a `char` named `command`, used to hold the user's command:

```
/*********************************************> GetCommand <*/
char  GetCommand( void )
{
  char  command;
```

Because we want to execute the body of this next loop at least once, we used a `do` loop instead of a `while` loop. We'll first prompt the user to enter a command, then use `scanf()` to read a character from the input buffer. The function `Flush()` will read characters, one at a time, from the input buffer until it reads in a carriage return. If we didn't call `Flush()`, any extra characters we typed after the command (including the `'\n'`) would be picked up the next time through this loop, and extra prompt lines would appear, one for each extra character. To see this effect, comment out the call to `Flush()` and type more than one character when prompted for a command:

```
  do
  {
    printf( "Enter command (q=quit, n=new, l=list):  " );
    scanf( "%c", &command );
    Flush( );
  }
  while ( (command != 'q') && (command != 'n')
          && (command != 'l') );
```

We'll drop out of the loop once we get a `'q'`, an `'n'`, or an `'l'`.

By the Way

Here's a cool trick Keith Rollin (C guru extraordinaire) showed me. Instead of ending the do loop with this statement:

```
while ( (command != 'q') && (command != 'n')
         && (command != 'l') );
```

try this code instead:

```
while ( ! strchr( "qnl", command ) );
```

The two parameters of `strchr()` are: a zero-terminated string and an int containing a character. First, `strchr()` searches the string for the character and, if it was found, returns a pointer to the character inside the string. If the character wasn't in the string, `strchr()` returns NULL. Pretty cool, eh?

Once we drop out of the loop, we'll print a separator line and return the single-letter command:

```
printf( "\n----------\n" );
return( command );
}
```

Next up is `ReadStruct()`. Notice the unusual declaration of the function name:

```
/*****************************************> ReadStruct <*/
struct CDInfo  *ReadStruct( void )
{
```

This line says that `ReadStruct()` returns a pointer to a CDInfo struct:

```
struct CDInfo  *ReadStruct( void )
```

`ReadStruct()` uses `malloc()` to allocate a block of memory the size of a CDInfo struct. The variable `infoPtr` will act as a pointer to the new block. We'll use the variable num to read in the rating, which we'll eventually store in `infoPtr->rating`.

```
struct CDInfo    *infoPtr;
int              num;
```

ReadStruct() calls malloc() to allocate a CDInfo struct, assigning the address of the block returned to infoPtr:

```
infoPtr = malloc( sizeof( struct CDInfo ) );
```

If malloc() cannot allocate a block of the requested size, it will return a value of NULL. If this happens, we'll print an appropriate message and call the Standard Library function exit(). As its name implies, exit() causes the program to immediately exit.

```
if ( infoPtr == NULL )
{
    printf( "Out of memory!!!  Goodbye!\n" );
    exit( 0 );
}
```

By the Way

The parameter you pass to exit() will be passed back to the operating system (or to whatever program launched your program).

If we're still here, malloc() must have succeeded. Next, we'll print a prompt for the CD artist's name, then call gets() to read a line from the input buffer and place that line in the artist field of the newly allocated struct.

We then repeat the process to prompt for and read in the CD title:

```
printf( "Enter Artist's Name:   " );
gets( infoPtr->artist );

printf( "Enter CD Title:   " );
gets( infoPtr->title );
```

This loop prompts the user to enter a number between 1 and 10. We then use scanf() to read an int from the input buffer. Note that we used a temporary int to read in the number instead of reading it directly into infoPtr->rating. We did this because the %d format specifier expects an int, and rating is declared as a char. Once we read the number, we call Flush() to get rid of any other characters (including the '\n'):

```
do
{
   printf( "Enter CD Rating (1-10):   " );
   scanf( "%d", &num );
   Flush();
}
while ( ( num < 1 ) || ( num > 10 ) );
```

Warning

This do loop is not as careful as it could be. If scanf() encounters an error of some kind, num will end up with an undefined value. If that undefined value happens to be between 1 and 10, the loop will exit, and an unwanted value will be entered in the rating field. Although that might not be such a big deal in our case, we probably would want to drop out of the loop or, at the very least, print some kind of error message if this happens.

Here's another version of the same code:

```
do
{
   printf( "Enter CD Rating (1-10):   " );
   if ( scanf( "%d", &num ) != 1 )
   {
      printf( "Error returned by scanf()!\n" );
      exit( -1 );
   };
   Flush();
}
while ( ( num < 1 ) || ( num > 10 ) );
```

Now, scanf() returns the number of items it read. Since we've asked it to read a single int, this version prints an error message and exits if we don't read exactly one item. This is a pretty simplistic error strategy, but it does make a point. Pay attention to error conditions and to function return values.

Once a number between 1 and 10 is read in, it is assigned to the rating field of the newly allocated struct:

```
infoPtr->rating = num;
```

Finally, a separating line is printed, and the pointer to the new `struct` is returned:

```
printf( "\n----------\n" );

return( infoPtr );
}
```

`AddToList()` takes a pointer to a `CDInfo` `struct` as a parameter. It uses the pointer to add the `struct` to the linked list:

```
/********************************************> AddToList <*/
void  AddToList( struct CDInfo *curPtr )
{
```

If `gFirstPtr` is `NULL`, the list must be empty. If it is, make `gFirstPtr` point to the new `struct`:

```
if ( gFirstPtr == NULL )
   gFirstPtr = curPtr;
```

If `gFirstPtr` is not `NULL`, there's at least one element in the linked list. In that case, make the `next` field of the very last element on the list point to the new `struct`:

```
else
   gLastPtr->next = curPtr;
```

In either case, set `gLastPtr` to point to the new "last element in the list." Finally, make sure that the `next` field of the last element in the list is `NULL`. You'll see why we did this in the next function, `ListCDs()`.

```
gLastPtr = curPtr;
curPtr->next = NULL;
}
```

`ListCDs()` lists all the CDs in the linked list. The variable `curPtr` is used to point to the link element currently being looked at:

```
/*********************************************> ListCDs <*/
void  ListCDs( void )
{
    struct CDInfo  *curPtr;
```

If no CDs have been entered yet, we'll print an appropriate message:

```
if ( gFirstPtr == NULL )
{
    printf( "No CDs have been entered yet...\n" );
    printf( "\n----------\n" );
}
```

Otherwise, we'll use a `for` loop to step through the linked list. The `for` loop starts by setting `curPtr` to point to the first element in the linked list and continues as long as `curPtr` is not NULL. Each time through the loop, `curPtr` is set to point to the next element in the list. Since we make sure that the last element's `next` pointer is always set to NULL, we know that when `curPtr` is equal to NULL, we have been through every element in the list and that we are done:

```
else
{
    for ( curPtr=gFirstPtr; curPtr!=NULL; curPtr = curPtr->next )
    {
```

Next, the first two `printf()` routines use the `%s` format specifier to print the strings in the fields `artist` and `title`:

```
        printf( "Artist:  %s\n", curPtr->artist );
        printf( "Title:   %s\n", curPtr->title );
```

Next, the `rating` field and a separating line are printed, and it's back to the top of the loop:

```
        printf( "Rating:  %d\n", curPtr->rating );

        printf( "\n----------\n" );
    }
  }
}
```

Flush() uses getchar() to read characters from the input buffer until it reads in a carriage return. Flush() is a good utility routine to have around:

```
/****************************************> Flush <*/
void  Flush( void )
{
   while ( getchar() != '\n' )
      ;
}
```

What's Next?

This chapter covered a wide range of topics, from #includes to linked lists. The intent of the chapter, however, was to attack a real-world programming problem: in this case, a program to catalog CDs. The chapter showed several design approaches, discussing the pros and cons of each. Finally, the chapter presented a prototype for a CD tracking program. The program allows you to enter information about a series of CDs and, on request, will present a list of all the CDs tracked.

One problem with this program, however, is that once you exit, you lose all of the data you entered. The next time you run the program, you have to start all over again.

Chapter 10 offers a solution to this problem. The chapter introduces the concept of files and file management, showing you how to save your data from memory out to your disk drive and how to read your data back in again. The chapter updates cdTracker, storing the CD information collected in a file on your disk drive.

Exercises

1. What's wrong with each of the following code fragments:

a. struct Employee
    {
          char name[20];

241

```
            int     employeeNumber
      };
```

b. `while ( getchar() == '\n' ) ;`

c. `#include "stdio.h"`

d.
```
struct Link
{
    name[ 50 ];
    Link  *next;
};
```

e.
```
struct Link
{
    struct Link    next;
    struct Link prev;
}
```

f.
```
StepAndPrint( char *line )
{
    while ( *line != 0 )
        line++;

    printf( "%s", line );
}
```

2. Update `multiArray` so it gets its input one byte at a time. If more characters are entered than will fit in the `struct`, terminate the string with as many bytes as will fit, and ignore the rest.

3. Update cdTracker.c so it maintains its linked list in order from the lowest rating to the highest rating. If two CDs have the same rating, the order is unimportant.

4. Update `cdTracker.c`, adding a `prev` field to the `CDInfo struct` so it maintains a doubly linked list. As before, the `next` field will point to the next link in the list. Now, however, the `prev` field should point to the previous link in the list. Add to the menu an option that prints the list backward, from the last `struct` in the list to the first.

Working with Files

Chapter 9 introduced `cdTracker`, a program designed to keep track of your compact disc collection. The program `cdTracker` allowed you to enter a new CD, as well as to list all existing Cds. However, `cdTracker` didn't save the CD information when it exited. If you ran `cdTracker`, entered information on 10 CDs, and then quit, your information would be gone. The next time you ran `cdTracker`, you'd have to start from scratch.

The solution to this problem is somehow to save all of the CD information before you quit the program. This chapter will show you how. Chapter 10 introduces the concept of **files** for the long-term storage of your program's data.

What Is a File?

A file is a series of bytes residing in some storage media. Files can be stored on your hard drive, on a floppy disk, or even on a CD-ROM. The word processor you keep on your hard drive resides in a file. Each document you create with your word processor also resides in a file.

The CD that came with this book contains many different files. The CodeWarrior compiler lives in its own file. Each of the Learn C projects consists of at least two files: a project file and at least one source code file. When you compile and link a project, you produce a new kind of file, an application file. All of these are examples of the same thing: a collection of bytes known as a file.

All of the files on your computer share a common set of traits. For example, each file has a size. The file `Finder` in my `System Folder` has a size of 453,467 bytes. The file `SimpleText` in my `Applications` folder has a size of 53,589 bytes. Each of these files resides on a hard disk drive attached to my computer.

Working with Files, Part One

In the C world, each file consists of a **stream** of consecutive bytes. When you want to access the data in a file, you first **open** the file using a Standard Library function named `fopen()`, pronounced eff-open. Once your file is open, you can **read** data from the file or **write** new data back into the file, using Standard Library functions, such as `fscanf()` and `fprintf()`. Once you are done working with your file, you'll close it by using the Standard Library function `fclose()`.

Opening and Closing a File

Here's the function prototype for `fopen()`, found in the file `<stdio.h>`:

```
FILE *fopen( const char *name, const char *mode );
```

By the Way

The `const` keyword marks a variable or a parameter as read-only. In other words, `fopen()` is not allowed to modify the array of characters pointed at by `name` or `mode`. Here's another example:

```
const int myInt = 27;
```

This declaration creates an `int` named `myInt` and assigns it a value of 27 (we'll talk in Chapter 11 about definitions that also initialize). More important, the value of `myInt` is now permanently set, and `myInt` is now read-only. As long as `myInt` remains in scope, you can't change its value.

The first parameter, `name`, tells `fopen()` which file you want to open. For example, the file name `"My Data File"` tells `fopen()` to look in the current folder (the folder containing the currently running application) for a file named `My Data File`.

Important

The colon character (`:`) has a special meaning in a Macintosh file. A single colon refers to the current folder, and a pair of colons refers to a folder's parent folder. For example, the file name `::My Data File` refers to a file named `My Data File` in the folder containing the current folder. The file name `:folder:file` refers to a file named `file` in a folder named `folder`, which is in the current folder.

Be aware that different operating systems use different file-naming conventions. UNIX uses a `/` instead of a `:` and `//` instead of `::`. DOS and Windows use `\` and `\\` instead of `:` and `::`. Check with your operating system's technical manuals and experiment for yourself!

The second parameter, mode, tells fopen() how you'll be accessing the file. The three basic file modes are "r", "w", and "a", for read, write, and **append**, respectively.

Using "r" tells fopen() that you want to read data from the file and that you won't be writing to the file at all. The file must already exist in order to use this mode. In other words, you can't use the mode "r" to create a file.

The mode "w" tells fopen() that you want to write to the specified file. If the file doesn't exist yet, a new file with the specified name is created. If the file does exist, fopen() deletes it and creates a new empty file for you to write into.

Warning

This last point bears repeating. Calling fopen() with a mode of "w" will delete the contents of an existing file, essentially starting you over from the beginning of the file. Be careful!

The mode "a", similar to "w", tells fopen() that you want to write to the specified file and to create the file if it doesn't exist. If the file does exist, however, the data you write to the file is appended to the end of the file.

If fopen() successfully opens the specified file, it allocates a struct of type FILE and returns a pointer to the FILE struct, which contains information about the open file, including the current mode ("r", "w", "a", or whatever), as well as the current **file position**. The file position, acting like a bookmark in a book, is a pointer into the file. When you open a file for reading, for example, the file position points to the first byte in the file. When you read the first byte, the file position moves to the next byte.

It's not really important to know the details of the FILE struct. All you need to do is keep track of the FILE pointer returned by fopen(). By passing the pointer to a Standard Library function that reads or writes, you'll be sure that the read or write takes place in the right file and at the right file position. You'll see how all this works as we go through the chapter sample code.

Here's a sample fopen() call:

```
FILE  *fp;

if ( (fp = fopen( "My Data File", "r")) == NULL )
{
   printf( "File doesn't exist!!!\n" );
   exit(1);
}
```

This code first calls fopen(), attempting to open the file named My Data File for reading. If fopen() cannot open the file for some reason (perhaps you've asked it to open a file that doesn't exist or you've already opened the maximum number of files), it returns NULL. In that case, we'll print an error message and exit.

By the Way

There is a limit to the number of simultaneously open files. This limit is implemented as a constant, FOPEN_MAX, defined in the file <stdio.h>.

If fopen() does manage to open the file, it will allocate the memory for a FILE struct, and fp will point to that struct. We can then pass fp to routines that read from the file. Once we're done with the file, we'll pass fp to the function fclose():

```
int fclose( FILE *stream );
```

Next, fclose() takes a pointer to a FILE as a parameter and attempts to close the specified file. If the file is closed successfully, fclose() frees up the memory allocated to the FILE struct and returns a value of 0. It is very important that you match every fopen() with a corresponding fclose(); otherwise, you'll end up with unneeded FILE structs floating around in memory.

In addition, once you've passed a FILE pointer to fclose(), that FILE pointer no longer points to a FILE struct. If you want to access the file again, you'll have to make another fopen() call.

By the Way

If fclose() fails, it returns a value of –1. Many programmers ignore the value returned by fclose(), since there's not a whole lot you can do about it. On the other hand, you can never have too much error checking in your code, so you might consider checking the value returned by fclose() and, at the very least, printing an appropriate error message if fclose() fails.

Reading a File

Once you open a file for reading, the next step is to read data from the file. There are several Standard Library functions to help you do just that. For starters, the function fgetc() reads a single character from a file's input buffer. Here's the function prototype:

```
int fgetc( FILE *fp );
```

The single parameter is the FILE pointer returned by fopen(). After reading a single character from the file, fgetc() advances the file position pointer. If the file position pointer is already at the end of the file, fgetc() returns the constant EOF.

By the Way

> Although fgetc() returns an int, the following also works just fine:
>
> ```
> char    c;
>
> c = fgetc( fp );
> ```
>
> When the C compiler encounters two different types on each side of an assignment operator, it does its best to convert the value on the right-hand side to the type of the left-hand side before doing the assignment. As long as the type of the right-hand side is no larger than the type of the left-hand side (as is the case here, as an int is at least as large as a char), this won't be a problem.
> We'll get into the specifics of typecasting in Chapter 11.

The function fgets() reads a series of characters into an array of chars. Here's the function prototype:

```
char *fgets( char *s, int n, FILE *tp );
```

The first parameter is a pointer to an array of chars that you've already allocated. Don't just declare a (char *) and pass it in to fgets(). Instead, allocate an array of chars large enough to hold the largest block of chars you might end up reading in, then pass a pointer to that array as the first parameter (you'll see an example in a second).

The second parameter is the maximum number of characters you'd like to read. The function fgets() stops reading once it reads in n–1 chars or if it encounters an end-of-file or a '\n' before it reads n–1 chars. If fgets() successfully reads n–1 chars, it appends a 0 terminator to the char array (that's why the array has to be at least n chars in size). If fgets() encounters a '\n' before it reads n–1 chars, it stops reading after the '\n' is read, then adds the 0 terminator to the array, right after the '\n'. If fgets() encounters an end-of-file before it reads n–1 chars, it adds the 0 terminator to the array, right after the last character read. If fgets() encounters an end-of-file before it reads in any chars, it returns NULL. Otherwise, fgets() returns a pointer to the char array.

Finally, the third parameter is the `FILE` pointer returned by `fopen()`. Here's an example:

```
#define kMaxBufferSize          200

FILE        *fp;
char        buffer[ kMaxBufferSize ];

if ( (fp = fopen( "My Data File", "r")) == NULL )
{
   printf( "File doesn't exist!!!\n" );
   exit(1);
}

if ( fgets( buffer, kMaxBufferSize, fp ) == NULL )
{
   if ( feof( fp ) )
      printf( "End-of-file!!!\n" );
   else
      printf( "Unknown error!!!\n" );
}
else
   printf( "File contents: %s\n", buffer );
```

Notice that the example calls a function named `feof()` if `fgets()` returns `NULL`. `NULL` is returned no matter what error `fgets()` encounters. The function `feof()` returns `true` if the last read on the specified file resulted in an end-of-file and a `false` otherwise.

The function `fscanf()` is similar to `scanf()`, reading from a file instead of the keyboard. Here's the prototype:

```
int   fscanf( FILE *fp, const char* format, ... );
```

The first parameter is the `FILE` pointer returned by `fopen()`. The second parameter is a format specification embedded inside a character string. The format specification tells `fscanf()` what kind of data you want read from the file. The `...` operator in a parameter list tells the compiler that zero or more parameters may follow the second parameter. Like `scanf()` and `printf()`, `fscanf()` uses the format specification to determine the number of parameters it expects to see. Be sure to pass the correct number of parameters; otherwise, your program will get confused.

These are a few of the file-access functions provided by the Standard Library. Check out the Standard Library function summaries found in Appendix D in this book and in electronic form on the book's CD (search for the file name C Library Reference.) Even better, get yourself a copy of *C: A Reference Manual* by Harbison and Steele and check out Chapter 15, "Input/Output Facilities."

In the meantime, the next section provides an example that uses the functions fopen() and fgetc() to open a file and display its contents.

printFile.μ

This program opens a file named My Data File, reads in all the data from the file, one character at a time, and prints each character in the console window. Open the Learn C Projects folder, go inside the folder 10.01 - printFile, and open the project printFile.μ. Run printFile by selecting **Run** from the **Project** menu. Compare your output with the console window shown in Figure 10.1. They should be the same.

Quit the application and return to CodeWarrior. Let's take a look at the data file read in by printFile. Select **Open...** from the **File** menu. CodeWarrior will prompt you for a text file to open. Select the file named My Data File. A window will open, allowing you to edit the contents of the file named My Data File.

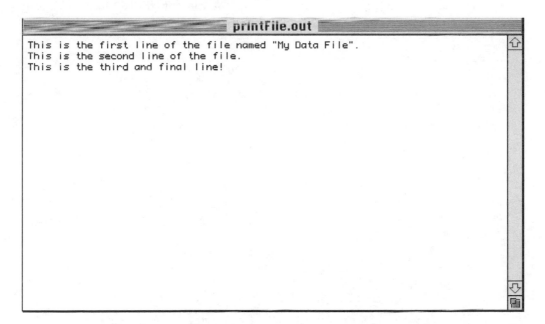

Figure 10.1 The printFile output, showing the contents of the file My Data File.

Feel free to make some changes to the file and run the program again. Make sure not to change the name of the file, however.

Let's take a look at the source code.

Stepping Through the Source Code

Open the source code file `printFile.c` by double-clicking on its name in the project window. Take a minute to look over the source code. Once you feel comfortable with it, read on.

The source code starts off with the usual `#include`:

```
#include <stdio.h>
```

Then, `main()` defines two variables: `fp` is our `FILE` pointer, and `c` is an `int` that will hold the `chars` we read from the file:

```
int    main( void )
{
    FILE      *fp;
    int        c;
```

This call of the function `fopen()` opens the file named `My Data File` for reading, returning the file pointer to the variable `fp`:

```
fp = fopen( "My Data File", "r" );
```

If `fp` is not `NULL`, the file was opened successfully:

```
if ( fp != NULL )
{
```

The `while` loop continuously calls `fgetc()`, passing it the file pointer `fp`. Next, `fgetc()` returns the next character in `fp`'s input buffer. The returned character is assigned to `c`. If `c` is not equal to `EOF`, `putchar()` is called, taking `c` as a parameter:

```
while ( (c = fgetc( fp )) != EOF )
    putchar( c );
```

Now, `putchar()` prints the specified character to the console window. We could have accomplished the same thing by using `printf()`:

```
printf( "%c", c );
```

By the Way

> As you program, you'll often find two different solutions to the same problem. Should you use `putchar()` or `printf()`? If performance is critical, pick the option that is more specific to your particular need. In this case, `printf()` is designed to handle many different data types, whereas `putchar()` is designed to handle one data type, an `int`. Chances are, the source code for `putchar()` is simpler and more efficient than the source code for `printf()` *when it comes to printing an int*. If performance is critical, you might want to use `putchar()` instead of `printf()`. If performance isn't critical, go with your own preference.

Once we are done, we'll close the file by calling `fclose()`. Remember to always balance each call of `fopen()` with a corresponding call to `fclose()`.

```
    fclose( fp );
}

    return 0;
}
```

stdin, stdout, and stderr

C provides you with three `FILE` pointers that are always available and always open. `stdin` represents the keyboard, `stdout` represents the console window, and `stderr` represents the file where the user wants all error messages sent. These three pointers are normally associated with command line–oriented operating systems, such as UNIX and DOS, and are rarely used on the Macintosh, but it's definitely worth knowing about them.

In `printFile`, we used the function `fgetc()` to read a character from a previously opened file. The following line will read the next character from the keyboard's input buffer:

```
c = fgetc( stdin );
```

Thus, `fgetc( stdin )` is equivalent to calling `getchar()`.

As you'll see in the next few sections, whenever C provides a mech-anism for reading or writing to a file, C also provides a similar mechanism for reading from `stdin` or writing to `stdout`. You probably won't use `stdin` and `stdout` in your code, but it's good to know what they are and what they do.

Working with Files, Part Two

So far, you've learned how to open a file by using `fopen()` and how to read from a file by using `fgetc()`. You've seen, once again, that you can often use two different functions to solve the same problem. Now let's look at some functions that allow you to write data out to a file.

Writing to a File

The Standard Library offers several functions that write data out to a previously opened file. This section will introduce three of them: `fputc()`, `fputs()`, and `fprintf()`.

The first, `fputc()`, takes an `int` holding a character value and writes the character out to the specified file. The function `fputc()` is declared as follows:

```
int    fputc( int c, FILE *fp );
```

If `fputc()` successfully writes the character out to the file, it returns the value passed to it in the parameter c. If the write fails for some reason, `fputc()` returns the value EOF.

By the Way

Note that:

```
fputc( c, stdout );
```

is the same as calling:

```
putchar( c );
```

The function `fputs()` is similar to `fputc()` but writes out a zero-terminated string instead of a single character. This function is declared as follows:

```
int    fputs( const char *s, FILE *fp );
```

`fputs()` writes out all the characters in the string but does not write out the terminating 0. If the write succeeds, `fputs()` returns a 0. If the write fails, `fputs()` returns EOF.

The third function, `fprintf()`, works just like `printf()`. Instead of sending its output to the console window, `fprintf()` writes its output to the specified file. It is declared as follows:

```
int    fprintf( FILE *fp, const char *format, ... );
```

The first parameter specifies the file to be written to. The second is the format-specification text string. Any further parameters depend on the contents of that string.

A Sample Program: cdFiler.μ

In Chapter 9, we ran cdTracker, a program designed to help you track your compact disc collection. The big shortcoming of cdTracker is its inability to save your carefully entered CD data. As you quit the program, the CD information you entered gets discarded, forcing you to start over the next time you run cdTracker.

Our next program, cdFiler, solves this problem by adding two special functions to cdTracker. ReadFile() opens a file named cdData, reads in the CD data in the file, and uses the data to build a linked list of cdInfo structs. WriteFile() writes the linked list back out to the file.

Open the Learn C Projects folder, go inside the folder 10.02 - cdFiler, and open the project cdFiler.μ. Check out the cdFiler.μ project window shown in Figure 10.2. Notice that there are two separate source code files. Your project can contain as many source code files as you like. Just make sure that only one of the files has a function named main(), since that's where your program will start.

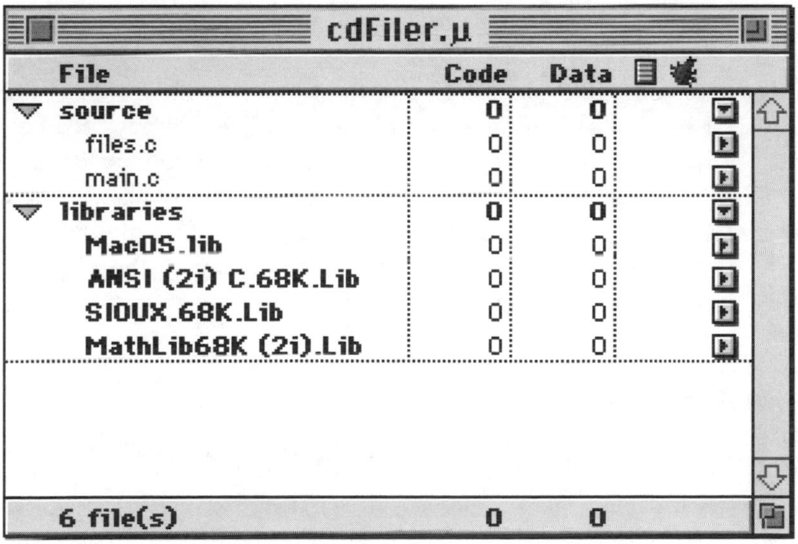

File	Code	Data		
▽ source	0	0		▽
files.c	0	0		▶
main.c	0	0		▶
▽ libraries	0	0		▽
MacOS.lib	0	0		▶
ANSI (2i) C.68K.Lib	0	0		▶
SIOUX.68K.Lib	0	0		▶
MathLib68K (2i).Lib	0	0		▶
6 file(s)	0	0		

Figure 10.2 The cdFiler.μ project window.

The file main.c is almost identical to the file cdTracker.c from Chapter 9. The file files.c contains the functions that allow cdFiler to read and write the file cdData.

Exploring *cdData*

Before you run the program, take a quick look at the file cdData. Select **Open...** from the **File** menu. When prompted for a text file to open, select the file cdData. A text editing window for cdData will appear on the screen. At first glance, the contents of the file may not make much sense, but the text does follow a well-defined pattern:

```
Frank Zappa
Anyway the Wind Blows
8
Edith Piaf
The Voice of the Sparrow
10
Joni Mitchell
For the Roses
9
```

The file is organized in three-line clusters. Each cluster contains a one-line CD artist, a one-line CD title, and a one-line numerical CD rating.

Important

The layout of your data files is as important a part of the software design process as the layout of your program's functions. The file described here follows a well-defined pattern. As you lay out a file for your next program, think about the future. Can you live with one-line CD titles? Do you want the ability to add a new CD field, perhaps the date of the CD's release?

The time to think about these types of questions is at the beginning of your program's life, during the design phase.

Running *cdFiler*

Before you run cdFiler, close the cdData text editing window.

To create this window, CodeWarrior had to open the file `cdData`. If you don't close the window before you run the program, the file will remain open. When you run `cdFiler`, it will also open the file. You'll have the same file open in two places. That is not a good idea. Although CodeWarrior allows you to do this, your results can be somewhat unpredictable.

Once the window is closed, run `cdFiler` by selecting **Run** from the **Project** menu. The console window will appear, prompting you for a 'q', 'n', or 'l':

```
Enter command (q=quit, n=new, l=list): l
```

Type l, followed by a carriage return. This will list the CDs currently in the program's linked list. If you need a refresher on linked lists, now would be a perfect time to turn back to Chapter 9.

```
Enter command (q=quit, n=new, l=list):  l

----------
Artist:  Frank Zappa
Title:   Anyway the Wind Blows
Rating:  8

----------
Artist:  Edith Piaf
Title:   The Voice of the Sparrow
Rating:  10

----------
Artist:  Joni Mitchell
Title:   For the Roses
Rating:  9

----------
Enter command (q=quit, n=new, l=list):
```

Whereas Chapter 9's `cdTracker` started with an empty linked list, `cdFiler` starts with a linked list built from the contents of the `cdData` file. The CDs you just listed should match the CDs you saw when you edited the `cdData` file.

Let's add a fourth CD to the list. Type n, followed by a carriage return:

```
Enter command (q=quit, n=new, l=list): n

----------
Enter Artist's Name: Adrian Belew
Enter CD Title: Mr. Music Head
Enter CD Rating (1-10): 8

----------
Enter command (q=quit, n=new, l=list):
```

Next, type l to make sure that your new CD made it into the list:

```
Enter command (q=quit, n=new, l=list): l

----------
Artist:  Frank Zappa
Title:   Anyway the Wind Blows
Rating:  8

----------
Artist:  Edith Piaf
Title:   The Voice of the Sparrow
Rating:  10

----------
Artist:  Joni Mitchell
Title:   For the Roses
Rating:  9

----------
Artist: Adrian Belew
Title:  Mr. Music Head
Rating: 8

----------
Enter command (q=quit, n=new, l=list):
```

Finally, type q, followed by a carriage return. This causes the program to write the current linked list back out to the file **cdData**. To prove that this worked, run **cdFiler** one more time. When prompted for a command, type 1 to list your current CDs. You should find your new CD nestled at the bottom of the list. Let's see how this works.

Stepping Through the Source Code

The file **cdFiler.h** contains source code that will be included by both **main.c** and **files.c**. The first two #defines should be familiar to you. The third creates a constant containing the name of the file containing our CD data:

```
/***********/
/* Defines */
/***********/
#define kMaxArtistLength      50
#define kMaxTitleLength       50

#define kCDFileName                    "cdData"
```

This **CDInfo** struct is identical to the one found in **cdTracker**:

```
/**********************/
/* Struct Declarations */
/**********************/
struct CDInfo
{
    char        rating;
    char        artist[ kMaxArtistLength + 1 ];
    char        title[ kMaxTitleLength + 1 ];
    struct CDInfo  *next;
};
```

Just as we did in **cdTracker**, we've declared two globals to keep track of the beginning and end of our linked list. The **extern** keyword at the beginning of the declaration tells the C compiler to link this declaration to the definition of these two globals, which can be found in **main.c**. If you removed the **extern** keyword from this line, the compiler would first compile **files.c**, defining space for both pointers. When the compiler went to compile **main.c**, it would complain that these globals were already declared.

The `extern` mechanism allows you to declare a global without allocating memory for it. Since the `extern` declaration doesn't allocate memory for your globals, you'll need another declaration (usually found in the same file as `main()`) that does allocate memory for the globals. You'll see that declaration in `main.c`:

```
/**********************/
/* Global Declarations */
/**********************/
extern struct CDInfo    *gFirstPtr, *gLastPtr;
```

Next comes the list of function prototypes. By listing all the functions in this `#include` file, we make all functions available to be called from all other functions. As your programs get larger and more sophisticated, you might want to create a separate include file for each of your source code files. Some programmers create one include file for globals, another for defines, and another for function prototypes.

```
/*******************************/
/* Function Prototypes - main.c */
/*******************************/
char        GetCommand( void );
struct CDInfo  *ReadStruct( void );
void        AddToList( struct CDInfo *curPtr );
void        ListCDs( void );
void        ListCDsInReverse( void );
void        Flush( void );


/*******************************/
/* Function Prototypes - files.c */
/*******************************/
void  WriteFile( void );
void  ReadFile( void );
char  ReadStructFromFile( FILE *fp, struct CDInfo *infoPtr
);
```

The file `main.c` is almost exactly the same as the file `cdTracker.c` from Chapter 9. There are four differences, however. First, we include the file `cdFiler.h` instead of `cdTracker.h`:

```
#include <stdlib.h>
#include <stdio.h>
#include "cdFiler.h"
```

Next, we include the definitions of our two globals directly in this source code file, to go along with the `extern` declarations in `cdFiler.h`. This definition is where the memory gets allocated for these two global pointers:

```
/**********************/
/* Global Definitions */
/**********************/
struct CDInfo  *gFirstPtr, *gLastPtr;
```

The last two differences are contained in `main()`. Before we enter the command-processing loop, we call `ReadFile()` to read in the `cdData` file and turn the contents into a linked list:

```
/***********************************************> main <*/
int   main( void )
{
    char         command;

    gFirstPtr = NULL;
    gLastPtr = NULL;

    ReadFile();

    while ( (command = GetCommand() ) != 'q' )
    {
        switch( command )
        {
            case 'n':
                AddToList( ReadStruct() );
                break;
            case 'l':
                ListCDs();
                break;
        }
    }
```

Once we drop out of the loop, we call `WriteFile()` to write the linked list out to the file `cdData`:

```
WriteFile();

printf( "Goodbye..." );

return 0;
}
```

For completeness, here's the remainder of `cdMain.c`. Each of these functions is identical to its `cdTracker.c` counterpart:

```
/*****************************************> GetCommand <*/
char  GetCommand( void )
{
    char   command;

    do
    {
        printf( "Enter command (q=quit, n=new, l=list):  " );
        scanf( "%c", &command );
        Flush();
    }
    while ( (command != 'q') && (command != 'n')
                && (command != 'l') );

    printf( "\n----------\n" );
    return( command );
}


/*****************************************> ReadStruct <*/
struct CDInfo  *ReadStruct( void )
{
    struct CDInfo   *infoPtr;
    int             num;

    infoPtr = malloc( sizeof( struct CDInfo ) );
```

```
   if ( infoPtr == NULL )
   {
      printf( "Out of memory!!!  Goodbye!\n" );
      exit( 0 );
   }

   printf( "Enter Artist's Name:  " );
   gets( infoPtr->artist );

   printf( "Enter CD Title:  " );
   gets( infoPtr->title );

   do
   {
      printf( "Enter CD Rating (1-10):  " );
      scanf( "%d", &num );
      Flush();
   }
   while ( ( num < 1 ) || ( num > 10 ) );

   infoPtr->rating = num;

   printf( "\n----------\n" );

   return( infoPtr );
}


/*********************************************> AddToList <*/
void  AddToList( struct CDInfo *curPtr )
{
   if ( gFirstPtr == NULL )
      gFirstPtr = curPtr;
   else
      gLastPtr->next = curPtr;

   gLastPtr = curPtr;
   curPtr->next = NULL;
}
```

```
/******************************************> ListCDs <*/
void  ListCDs( void )
{
    struct CDInfo  *curPtr;

    if ( gFirstPtr == NULL )
    {
        printf( "No CDs have been entered yet...\n" );
        printf( "\n----------\n" );
    }
    else
    {
        for ( curPtr=gFirstPtr; curPtr!=NULL; curPtr = curPtr->next )
        {
            printf( "Artist:  %s\n", curPtr->artist );
            printf( "Title:   %s\n", curPtr->title );
            printf( "Rating:  %d\n", curPtr->rating );

            printf( "\n----------\n" );
        }
    }
}



/******************************************> Flush <*/
void  Flush( void )
{
    while ( getchar() != '\n' )
        ;
}
```

The file files.c starts out with the same #includes as main.c:

```
#include <stdlib.h>
#include <stdio.h>
#include "cdFiler.h"
```

WriteFile() first checks to see whether there are any CDs to write out. If gFirstPtr is NULL (the value it was set to in main()), no CDs have been entered yet, and we can just return:

```
/**********************************************> WriteFile <*/
void  WriteFile( void )
{
   FILE          *fp;
   struct CDInfo  *infoPtr;
   int            num;

   if ( gFirstPtr == NULL )
      return;
```

Next, we'll open the file **cdData** for writing. If **fopen()** returns NULL, we know that it couldn't open the file, and we'll print out an error message and return:

```
   if ( ( fp = fopen( kCDFileName, "w" ) ) == NULL )
   {
      printf( "***ERROR: Could not write CD file!" );
      return;
   }
```

This **for** loop steps through the linked list, setting **infoPtr** to point to the first **struct** in the list, then moving it to point to the next **struct**, and so on, until **infoPtr** is equal to NULL. Since the last **struct** in our list sets its **next** pointer to NULL, **infoPtr** will be equal to NULL when it points to the last **struct** in the list and the third **for** statement is executed:

```
   for ( infoPtr=gFirstPtr; infoPtr!=NULL; infoPtr=infoPtr->next )
   {
```

Each time through the list, we call **fprintf()** to print the **artist** string, followed by a carriage return, and then the **title** string, followed by a carriage return. Remember, each of these strings was zero-terminated, a requirement if you plan on using the **%s** format specifier:

```
      fprintf( fp, "%s\n", infoPtr->artist );
      fprintf( fp, "%s\n", infoPtr->title );
```

Finally, we convert the **rating** field to an **int** by assigning it to the **int** num, then print it (as well as a following carriage return) to the file by using **fprintf()**. We converted the **char** to an **int** because the **%d** format specifier was designed to work with an **int**, not a **char**:

```
      num = infoPtr->rating;
      fprintf( fp, "%d\n", num );
   }
}
```

Once we finish writing the linked list into the file, we'll close the file by calling `fclose()`:

```
   fclose( fp );
}
```

`ReadFile()` starts by opening the file `cdData` for reading. If we can't open the file, we'll print an error message and return, leaving the list empty:

```
/*********************************************> ReadFile <*/
void  ReadFile( void )
{
   FILE           *fp;
   struct CDInfo  *infoPtr;
   int            i;

   if ( ( fp = fopen( kCDFileName, "r" ) ) == NULL )
   {
      printf( "***ERROR: Could not read CD file!" );
      return;
   }
```

With the file open, we'll enter a loop that continues as long as `ReadStructFromFile()` returns true. By using the do-while loop, we'll execute the body of the loop before we call `ReadStructFromFile()` for the first time. This is what we want. The body of the loop attempts to allocate a block of memory the size of a `CDInfo` `struct`. If the `malloc()` fails, we'll bail out of the program:

```
   do
   {
      infoPtr = malloc( sizeof( struct CDInfo ) );

      if ( infoPtr == NULL )
      {
         printf( "Out of memory!!!  Goodbye!\n" );
```

```
        exit( 0 );
    }
}
while ( ReadStructFromFile( fp, infoPtr ) );
```

`ReadStructFromFile()` will return `false` when it reaches the end of the file, when it can't read another set of `CDInfo` fields. In that case, we'll close the file and free up the last block we just allocated, since we have nothing to store in it:

```
fclose( fp );
free( infoPtr );
}
```

`ReadStructFromFile()` uses a funky form of `fscanf()` to read in the first two `CDInfo` fields. Notice the use of the format descriptor `"%[^\n]\n"`. This tells `fscanf()` to read characters from the specified file until it reaches an `'\n'`, then to read the `'\n'` character and stop. The characters `[^\n]` represent the set of all characters except `'\n'`. Note that the `%[` format specifier places a zero-terminating byte at the end of the characters it reads in:

```
/*********************************> ReadStructFromFile <*/
char  ReadStructFromFile( FILE *fp, struct CDInfo *infoPtr )
{
    int       num;

    if ( fscanf( fp, "%[^\n]\n", infoPtr->artist ) != EOF )
    {
```

By the Way

> The square brackets inside a format specifier give you much greater control over `scanf()`. For example, the format specifier `"%[abcd]"` would tell `scanf()` to keep reading as long as it was reading an `'a'`, a `'b'`, a `'c'`, or a `'d'`. The first non-[abcd] character would be left in the input buffer for the next part of the format specifier or for the next read operation to pick up.
>
> If the first character in the set is the character `^`, the set represents the characters that do not belong to the set. In other words, the format specifier `"%[^abcd]"` tells `scanf()` to continue reading as long as it doesn't encounter any of the characters `'a'`, `'b'`, `'c'`, or `'d'`.

If `fscanf()` reaches the end of the file, we'll return `false`, letting the calling function know that there are no more fields to read. If `fscanf()` succeeds, we'll move on to the `title` field, using the same technique. If this second `fscanf()` fails, we've got a problem, since we read an `artist` but couldn't read a `title`.

```
if ( fscanf( fp, "%[^\n]\n", infoPtr->title ) == EOF )
{
    printf( "Missing CD title!\n" );
    return false;
}
```

If we got both the `artist` and `title`, we'll use a more normal format specifier to pick up an `int` and the third carriage return:

```
else if ( fscanf( fp, "%d\n", &num ) == EOF )
{
    printf( "Missing CD rating!\n" );
    return false;
}
```

If we picked up the `int`, we'll use the assignment operator to convert the `int` to a `char` and add the now complete `struct` to the list by passing it to `AddToList()`:

```
    else
    {
        infoPtr->rating = num;
        AddToList( infoPtr );
        return true;
    }
}
else
    return false;
}
```

Working with Files, Part Three

Now that you've mastered the basics of file reading and writing, there are a few more topics worth exploring before we leave this chapter. We'll start off with a look at some additional file-opening modes.

The "Update" Modes

So far, you've encountered the three basic file-opening modes: `"r"`, `"w"`, and `"a"`. Each of these modes has a corresponding **update mode,** specified by adding + to the mode. The three update modes—`"r+"`, `"w+"`, and `"a+"`—allow you to open a file for both reading and writing.

Important

Alhough the three update modes do allow you to switch between read and write operations without reopening the file, you must first call `fsetpos()`, `fseek()`, `rewind()`, or `fflush()` before you make the switch. (See Appendix C or the *C Library Reference* on the book's CD.)

In other words, if your file is opened using one of the update modes, you can't call `fscanf()` and then call `fprintf()` (or call `fprintf()` followed by `fscanf()`) unless you call `fsetpos()`, `fseek()`, `rewind()`, or `fflush()` in between.

In Harbison and Steele's *C: A Reference Manual,* there's a great chart that summarizes these modes quite nicely. My version of the chart is shown in Figure 10.3. Before you read on, take a minute to look the chart over to be sure you understand the different file modes.

By the Way

C also allows a file mode to specify whether a file is limited to ASCII characters (text mode) or is allowed to hold any type of data at all (binary mode). To open a file in text mode, just append a `t` at the end of the mode string (as in `"rt"` or `"w+t"`). To open a file in binary mode, append a `b` at the end of the mode string (as in `"rb"` or `"w+b"`).

If you use a file mode that doesn't include a `t` or a `b`, check your development environment manuals to find out which of the two types is the default.

Random File Access

So far, each of the examples presented in this chapter has treated files as a **sequential stream of bytes**. When `cdFiler` read from a file, it started at the beginning of the file and read the contents, one byte at a time or in larger chunks, but from the beginning straight through until the end. This sequential approach works fine if

Mode Rules	"r"	"w"	"a"	"r+"	"w+"	"a+"
Named file must already exist	yes	no	no	yes	no	no
Existing file's contents are lost	no	yes	no	no	yes	no
Read OK	yes	no	no	yes	yes	yes
Write OK	no	yes	yes	yes	yes	yes
Write begins at end of file	no	no	yes	no	no	yes

Figure 10.3 My version of the Harbison and Steele file mode chart showing the rules associated with the six basic file-opening modes.

you intend to read or write the entire file all at once. As you might have guessed, there is another model.

Instead of starting at the beginning and streaming through a file, you can use a technique called **random file access**. The Standard Library provides a set of functions that let you reposition the file position indicator to any location within the file, so that the next read or write you do occurs exactly where you want it to.

Imagine a file filled with 100 longs, each 4 bytes long. The file would be 400 bytes long. Now suppose that you wanted to retrieve the 10th long in the file. Using the sequential model, you would have to do 10 reads to get the 10th long into memory. Unless you read the entire file into memory, you'll continually be reading a series of longs to get to the long you want.

Using the random-access model, you would first calculate where in the file the 10th long starts, jump to that position in the file, and then just read that long. To move the file position indicator just before the 10th long, you'd skip over the first nine longs (9*4 = 36 bytes).

The `fseek()`, `ftell()`, and `rewind()` Functions

There are five functions that you'll need to know about in order to randomly access your files. One of those functions, `fseek()`, moves the file position indicator to an offset you specify, relative to the beginning of the file, the current file position, or the end of the file:

```
int    fseek( FILE *fp, long offset, int wherefrom );
```

You'll pass your FILE pointer as the first parameter, a long offset as the second parameter, and one of SEEK_SET, SEEK_CUR, or SEEK_END as the third parameter. SEEK_SET represents the beginning of the file, SEEK_CUR represents the current position, and SEEK_END represents the end of the file (in which case you'll probably use a negative `offset`).

The function `ftell()` takes a `FILE` pointer as a parameter and returns a `long` containing the value of the file position indicator:

```
long  ftell( FILE *fp );
```

The function `rewind()` takes a `FILE` pointer as a parameter and resets the file position indicator to the beginning of the file:

```
void  rewind( FILE *fp );
```

The functions `fsetpos()` and `fgetpos()` were introduced as part of ISO C and allow you to work with file offsets that are larger than will fit in a `long`. You can look these two functions up in the usual places.

By the Way

A Sample Program: `dinoEdit.µ`

The last sample program in this chapter, `dinoEdit` is a simple example of random file access. The program allows you to edit a series of dinosaur names stored in a file named `My Dinos`. Each dinosaur name in this file is 20 characters long. If the dinosaur name is shorter than 20 characters, the appropriate number of spaces is added to the name to bring the length up to 20. This is done to make the size of each item in the file a fixed length. You'll see why this is important as we go through the source code. For now, let's take `dinoEdit` for a spin.

Open the `Learn C Projects` folder, go inside the folder `10.03 - dinoEdit`, and open the project `dinoEdit.µ`. Run `dinoEdit` by selecting **Run** from the **Project** menu. The program will count the number of dinosaur names in the file `My Dinos` and will use that number to prompt you for a dinosaur number to edit:

```
Enter number from 1 to 5 (0 to exit):
```

Since the file `My Dinos` on your CD has five dinosaur names, enter a number from 1 to 5:

```
Enter number from 1 to 5 (0 to exit): 3
```

If you enter the number 3, for example, `dinoEdit` will fetch the third dinosaur name from the file, then ask you to enter a new name for the third dinosaur. If you enter a return without typing a new name, the existing name will remain untouched. If you type a new name, `dinoEdit` will overwrite the existing name with the new name:

```
Dino #3: Galimimus
Enter new name: Euoplocephalus
```

Either way, `dinoEdit` will prompt you to enter another dinosaur number. Reenter the same number, so you can verify that the change was made in the file:

```
Enter number from 1 to 5 (0 to exit): 3
Dino #3: Euoplocephalus
Enter new name:
Enter number from 1 to 5 (0 to exit): 0
Goodbye...
```

Let's take a look at the source code.

Stepping Through the Source Code

The file `dinoEdit.h` starts off with a few #defines: `kDinoRecordSize` defines the length of each dinosaur record; `kMaxLineLength` defines the length of an array of `chars` we'll use to read in any new dinosaur names; `kDinoFileName` is the name of the dinosaur file. Note that the dinosaur file doesn't contain any carriage returns, just 5 * 20 = 100 bytes of pure dinosaur pleasure!

```
/**********/
/* Defines */
/**********/
#define kDinoRecordSize      20
#define kMaxLineLength       100
#define kDinoFileName        "My Dinos"
```

Next come the function prototypes for the functions in `main.c`:

```
/*****************************/
/* Function Prototypes - main.c */
/*****************************/
int   GetNumber( void );
int   GetNumberOfDinos( void );
void  ReadDinoName( int number, char *dinoName );
```

```
char   GetNewDinoName( char *dinoName );
void   WriteDinoName( int number, char *dinoName );
void   Flush( void );
void   DoError( char *message );
```

First, `main.c` starts with four #includes: `<stdlib.h>` gives us access to the function `exit()`; `<stdio.h>` gives us access to a number of functions, including `printf()` and all the file-manipulation functions, types, and constants; and `<string.h>` gives us access to the function `strlen()`. You've already seen what "dinoEdit.h" brings to the table:

```
#include <stdlib.h>
#include <stdio.h>
#include <string.h>
#include "dinoEdit.h"
```

By the Way

If you ever want to find out which of the functions you call are dependent on which of your include files, just comment out the #include statement in question and recompile. The compiler will spew out an error message (or a whole bunch of messages) telling you it couldn't find a prototype for a function you called.

`main()` basically consists of a loop that first prompts for a dinosaur number at the top of the loop, then processes the selection in the body of the loop:

```
/*************************************************> main <*/
int    main( void )
{
   int      number;
   FILE    *fp;
   char     dinoName[ kDinoRecordSize+1 ];
```

`GetNumber()` prompts for a dinosaur number between 0 and the number of dinosaur records in the file. If the user types 0, we'll drop out of the loop and exit the program:

```
   while ( (number = GetNumber() ) != 0 )
   {
```

If we made it here, `GetNumber()` must have returned a legitimate record number. `ReadDinoName()` takes the dinosaur number and returns the corresponding dinosaur name from the file. The returned dinosaur name is then printed:

```
ReadDinoName( number, dinoName );

printf( "Dino #%d: %s\n", number, dinoName );
```

`GetNewDinoName()` prompts the user for a new dinosaur name to replace the existing name. `GetNewDinoName()` returns `true` if a name is entered and `false` if the user just entered a return. If the user entered a name, we'll pass it on to `WriteDinoName()`, which will write the name in the file, overwriting the old name:

```
    if ( GetNewDinoName( dinoName ) )
        WriteDinoName( number, dinoName );
}

printf( "Goodbye..." );

return 0;
}
```

`GetNumber()` starts off with a call to `GetNumberOfDinos()`. As its name implies, `GetNumberOfDinos()` goes into the dinosaur file and returns the number of records in the file:

```
/**********************************************> GetNumber <*/
int    GetNumber( void )
{
    int        number, numDinos;

    numDinos = GetNumberOfDinos();
```

`GetNumber()` then continuously prompts for a dinosaur number until the user enters a number between 0 and `numDinos`:

```
    do
    {
```

```
      printf( "Enter number from 1 to %d (0 to exit): ",
         numDinos );
      scanf( "%d", &number );
      Flush();
   }
   while ( (number < 0) || (number > numDinos) );

   return( number );
}
```

GetNumberOfDinos() starts our file-management adventure. First, we'll open My Dinos for reading only:

```
/********************************> GetNumberOfDinos <*/
int    GetNumberOfDinos( void )
{
   FILE   *fp;
   long      fileLength;

   if ( (fp = fopen( kDinoFileName, "r" )) == NULL )
      DoError( "Couldn't open file...Goodbye!" );
```

Important

Notice that we've passed an error message to a function called DoError() instead of printing it with printf(). There are several reasons for doing this. First, since DoError() executes two lines of code (calls of printf() and exit()), each DoError() call saves a bit of code.

More important, this approach encapsulates all our error handling in a single function. If we want to send all error messages to a log file, all we have to do is edit DoError() instead of hunting down all the error messages and attaching a few extra lines of code.

Next, we'll call fseek() to move the file position indicator to the end of the file. Can you see what's coming?

```
   if ( fseek( fp, 0L, SEEK_END ) != 0 )
      DoError( "Couldn't seek to end of file...Goodbye!" );
```

Now, we'll call ftell() to retrieve the current file position indicator, which also happens to be the file length! Cool!

```
if ( (fileLength = ftell( fp )) == -1L )
    DoError( "ftell() failed...Goodbye!" );
```

Now that we have the file length, we can close the file:

```
fclose( fp );
```

Finally, we'll calculate the number of dinosaur records by dividing the file length by the number of bytes in a single record. For simplicity's sake, we'll convert the number of records to an `int` before we return it. That means that we can't deal with a file that contains more than 32,767 dinosaur records. How many dinosaurs can you name?

```
    return( (int)(fileLength / kDinoRecordSize) );
}
```

`ReadDinoName()` first opens the file for reading only.

```
/*******************************> ReadDinoName <*/
void  ReadDinoName( int number, char *dinoName )
{
    FILE   *fp;
    long   bytesToSkip;

    if ( (fp = fopen( kDinoFileName, "r" )) == NULL )
        DoError( "Couldn't open file...Goodbye!" );
```

Since we'll be reading the `number`th dinosaur, we have to move the file position indicator to the end of the (`number`–1)th dinosaur. That means that we'll need to skip over (`number`–1) dinosaur records:

```
bytesToSkip = (long)((number-1) * kDinoRecordSize);
```

We'll use `fseek()` to skip that many bytes from the beginning of the file (that's what the constant `SEEK_SET` is for):

```
if ( fseek( fp, bytesToSkip, SEEK_SET ) != 0 )
    DoError( "Couldn't seek in file...Goodbye!" );
```

Finally, we'll call `fread()` to read the dinosaur record into the array of `chars` pointed to by `dinoName`. The first `fread()` parameter is the pointer to the block of memory where the data will be read. The second parameter is the number of bytes in a single record. Since `fread()` expects both the second and third parameters to be of type `size_t`, we'll use a typecast to make the compiler happy. (Gee, by the time we talk about typecasting in Chapter 11, you'll already be an expert!) The third parameter is the number of records to read in. We want to read in one record of `kDinoRecordSize` bytes. The last parameter is the `FILE` pointer we got from `fopen()`.

Because `fread()` returns the number of records read, we expect to return a value of 1, since we asked `fread()` to read one record. If that doesn't happen, something is dreadfully wrong (perhaps the file got corrupted or that Pepsi you spilled in your hard drive is finally starting to take effect).

```
if ( fread( dinoName, (size_t)kDinoRecordSize,
    (size_t)1, fp ) != 1 )
    DoError( "Bad fread()...Goodbye!" );
```
Once again, we close the file when we're done working with it.
```
fclose( fp );
}
```

`GetNewDinoName()` starts by prompting for a new dinosaur name, then calling `gets()` to read in a line of text:

```
/****************************> GetNewDinoName <*/
char   GetNewDinoName( char *dinoName )
{
    char   line[ kMaxLineLength ];
    int    i, nameLen;

    printf( "Enter new name: " );

    gets( line );
```

If the line was empty (if the user just entered a carriage return), we'll return `false`, letting the calling function know that the user has, in effect, decided not to replace the dinosaur name:

```
if ( line[0] == '\0' )
    return false;
```

Our next step is to fill the `dinoName` array with spaces. We'll then call `strlen()` to find out how many characters the user typed in. We'll copy those characters back into the `dinoName` array, leaving `dinoName` with a dinosaur name, followed by a bunch of spaces:

```
for ( i=0; i<kDinoRecordSize; i++ )
    dinoName[i] = ' ';
```

`strlen()` takes a pointer to a zero-terminated string and returns the length of the string, not including the 0 terminator:

```
nameLen = strlen( line );
```

If the user typed a dinosaur name larger than 20 characters long, we'll copy only the first 20 characters:

```
if ( nameLen > kDinoRecordSize )
    nameLen = kDinoRecordSize;
```

Here's where we copy the characters from `line` into `dinoName`:

```
for ( i=0; i<nameLen; i++ )
    dinoName[i] = line[i];
```

Finally, we'll return `true` to let the calling function know that the name is ready:

```
    return true;
}
```

`WriteDinoName()` opens the file for reading and writing. Since we used a mode of `"r+"` instead of `"w+"`, we won't lose the contents of `My Dinos` (in other words, `My Dinos` won't be deleted and recreated):

```
/*******************************> WriteDinoName <*/
void  WriteDinoName( int number, char *dinoName )
{
    FILE  *fp;
    long  bytesToSkip;
```

```
if ( (fp = fopen( kDinoFileName, "r+" )) == NULL )
   DoError( "Couldn't open file...Goodbye!" );
```

Next, we calculate the number of bytes we need to skip to place the file position indicator at the beginning of the record we want to overwrite, then call `fseek()` to move the file position indicator:

```
bytesToSkip = (long)((number-1) * kDinoRecordSize);

if ( fseek( fp, bytesToSkip, SEEK_SET ) != 0 )
   DoError( "Couldn't seek in file...Goodbye!" );
```

We then call `fwrite()` to write the dinosaur record back out. Note that `fwrite()` works exactly the same way as `fread()`, including returning the number of records written:

```
if ( fwrite( dinoName, (size_t)kDinoRecordSize,
   (size_t)1, fp ) != 1 )
   DoError( "Bad fwrite()...Goodbye!" );

fclose( fp );
}
```

You've seen this function before:

```
/*****************************************> Flush <*/
void  Flush( void )
{
   while ( getchar() != '\n' )
      ;
}
```

`DoError()` prints the error message, adding a carriage return, then exits:

```
/*****************************************> DoError <*/
void  DoError( char *message )
{
   printf( "%s\n", message );
   exit( 0 );
}
```

What's Next?

Chapter 11 tackles a wide assortment of programming topics. We'll look at typecasting, the technique used to translate from one type to another. We'll cover recursion, the ability of a function to call itself. We'll also examine function pointers, variables that can be used to pass a function as a parameter.

Exercises

1. What's wrong with each of the following code fragments:

a.
```
FILE   *fp;

fp = fopen( "w", "My Data File" );
if ( fp != NULL )
         printf( "The file is open." );
```

b.
```
char myData = 7;
FILE   *fp;

fp = fopen( "r", "My Data File" );
fscanf( "Here's a number: %d", &myData );
```

c.
```
FILE   *fp;
char   *line;

fp = fopen( "My Data File", "r" );
fscanf( fp, "%s", &line );
```

d.
```
FILE   *fp;
char   line[100];

fp = fopen( "My Data File", "w" );
fscanf( fp, "%s", line );
```

2. Write a program that reads in and prints a file with the following format:

• The first line in the file contains a single int. Call it x.

• All subsequent lines contain a list of x ints separated by tabs.

If the first number in the file is 6, all subsequent lines will have six `int`s per line. There is no limit to the number of lines in the file. Keep reading and printing lines until you reach the end of the file.

You can print each `int` as you encounter it or, for extra credit, allocate an array of `int`s large enough to hold one line's worth of `int`s, then pass that array to a function that prints an `int` array.

3. Modify `cdFiler.`π so that memory for the `artist` and `title` lines is allocated as the lines are read in. First, you'll need to change the `CDInfo struct` declaration as follows:

```
struct CDInfo
{
    char          rating;
    char          *artist
    char          *title;
    struct CDInfo *next;
};
```

In addition to calling `malloc()` to allocate a `CDInfo struct`, you'll call `malloc()` to allocate space for the `artist` and `title` strings. Don't forget to leave enough space for the terminating 0 at the end of each string.

Advanced Topics

Congratulations! By now, you've mastered most of the fundamental C programming concepts. This chapter will fill you in on some useful C programming tips, tricks, and techniques that will enhance your programming skills. We'll start with a look at typecasting, C's mechanism for translating one data type to another.

What Is Typecasting?

There often will be times when you find yourself trying to convert a variable of one type to a variable of another type. For example, the following code fragment causes the line i is equal to 3 to appear in the console window:

```
float f;
int     i;

f = 3.5;
i = f;

printf( "i is equal to %d", i );
```

Notice that the original value assigned to f was truncated from 3.5 to 3 when the value in f was assigned to i. This truncation was caused when the compiler saw an int on the left side and a float on the right side of this assignment statement:

```
i = f;
```

The compiler automatically translated the float to an int. In general, the right-hand side of an assignment statement is always translated to the type on the left-hand side when the assignment occurs. In this case, the compiler handled the type conversion for you.

Typecasting is a mechanism you can use to translate the value of an expression from one type to another. A typecast, or just plain **cast**, always takes this form:

```
(type) expression
```

The `type` is any legal C type. Look at the following code fragment:

```
float f;
```

```
f = 1.5;
```

The variable `f` gets assigned a value of 1.5. Now look at this code fragment:

```
float f;
```

```
f = (int)1.5;
```

The value of 1.5 is cast as an `int` before being assigned to `f`. Just as you might imagine, casting a `float` as an `int` truncates the `float`, turning the value 1.5 into 1. In this example, two casts were performed. First, the `float` value 1.5 was cast to the `int` value 1. When this `int` value was assigned to the `float` `f`, the value was cast to the `float` value 1.0.

Cast with Care

Use caution when you cast from one type to another. Problems can arise when casting between types of a different size. Consider this example:

```
int      i;
char  c;
```

```
i = 500;
c = i;
```

Here, the value 500 is assigned to the `int` i. So far, so good. Next, the value in i is cast to a `char` as it is assigned to the `char` c. See the problem? Since a `char` can hold values only between –128 and 127, assigning a value of 500 to c doesn't make sense.

So what happens to the extra byte or bytes when a larger type is cast to a smaller type? The matching bytes are typecast, and the value of any extra bytes is lost.

For example, when a 2-byte int is cast to a 1-byte char, the leftmost byte of the int (the byte with the more significant bits, the bits valued 2^8 through 2^{15}) is dropped, and the rightmost byte (the bits valued 2^0 through 2^7) is copied into the char.

Look at this:

```
int        i;
char    c;

i = 500;
c = i;
```

The int i has a value of 0x01E4, which is hex for 500. After the second assignment, the char ends up with the value 0xE4, which has a value of 244 if the char was unsigned or –12 if the char is signed.

To learn more about type conversions, check out Section 6.2 of Harbison and Steele's *C: A Reference Manual*.

Casting with Pointers

Typecasting can also be used when working with pointers. The notation (int *) myPtr casts the variable myPtr as a pointer to an int. Casting with pointers allows you to link structs of different types. For example, suppose that you declared two struct types, as follows:

```
struct Dog
{
    struct Dog  *next;
} ;

struct Cat
{
    struct Cat *next;
} ;
```

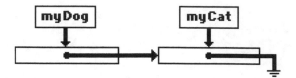

Figure 11.1 `myDog.next` points to `myCat`, and `myCat.next` points to `NULL`.

By using typecasting, you could create a linked list that contains both `Cats` and `Dogs`. Figure 11.1 shows a `Dog` whose `next` field points to a `Cat`. Imagine the source code you'd need to implement such a linked list.

Consider this source code:

```
struct Dog   myDog;
struct Cat   myCat;

myDog.next = &myCat; /* <—Compiler complains */
myCat.next = NULL;
```

In the first assignment statement, a pointer of one type is assigned to a pointer of another type: `&myCat` is a pointer to a `struct` of type `Cat`; `myDog.next` is declared to be a pointer to a `struct` of type `Dog`. To make this code compile, we'll need a typecast:

```
struct Dog   myDog;
struct Cat   myCat;

myDog.next = (struct Dog *)(&myCat);
myCat.next = NULL;
```

If both sides of an assignment operator are arithmetic types (such as `float`, `int`, and `char`), the compiler will automatically cast the right-hand side of the assignment to the type of the left-hand side. If both sides are pointers, you'll have to perform the typecast yourself.

There are a few exceptions to this rule. If the pointers on both sides of the assignment are the same type, no typecast is necessary. If the pointer on the right-hand side is either `NULL` or of type (`void *`), no typecast is necessary. Finally, if the pointer on the left-hand side is of type (`void *`), no typecast is necessary.

The type (`void *`) is sort of a wild card for pointers. It matches up with any pointer type. For example, here's a new version of the `Dog` and `Cat` code:

```
struct Dog
{
   void  *next;
} ;

struct Cat
{
   void  *next;
} ;

struct Dog  myDog;
struct Cat  myCat;

myDog.next = &myCat;
myCat.next = NULL;
```

This code lets `Dog.next` point to a `Cat struct` without a typecast. If you are not sure what type your pointers will be pointing to, declare your pointers as `(void *)`.

By the Way

The rules for typecasting are fairly complex and beyond the scope of this book. To learn more about type conversions, check out Sections 6.2 through 6.4 in *C: A Reference Manual* by Harbison and Steele. If you plan on moving on to C++ (and you should), check out the discussion of type conversions in *Learn C++ on the Macintosh* by yours truly.

Unions

C offers a special data type, known as a **union**, which allows a single variable to disguise itself as several different data types. A union data type is declared just like a `struct`. Here's an example:

```
union Number
{
   int      i;
   float    f;
   char     *s;
}  myNumber;
```

This declaration creates a `union` type named `Number`, as well as an individual `Number` named `myNumber`. If this were a `struct` declaration, you'd be able to store three different values in the three fields of the `struct`. A `union`, on the other hand, lets you store one and only one of the `union`'s fields in the `union`. Here's how this works.

When a `union` is declared, the compiler allocates the space required by the largest of the `union`'s fields, sharing that space with all of the `union`'s fields. If an `int` requires 2 bytes, a `float` 4 bytes, and a pointer 4 bytes, `myNumber` is allocated exactly 4 bytes. You can store an `int`, a `float`, or a `char` pointer in `myNumber`. The compiler allows you to treat `myNumber` as any of these types. To refer to `myNumber` as an `int`, refer to:

```
myNumber.i
```

To refer to `myNumber` as a `float`, refer to:

```
myNumber.f
```

To refer to `myNumber` as a `char` pointer, refer to:

```
myNumber.s
```

You are responsible for remembering which form the `union` is currently occupying.

Warning

> If you store an `int` in `myUnion` by assigning a value to `myUnion.i`, you'd best remember that fact. If you proceed to store a `float` in `myUnion.f`, you've just trashed your `int`. Remember, there are only 4 bytes allocated to the entire `union`.
>
> In addition, storing a value as one type and then reading it as another can produce unpredictable results. For example, if you stored a `float` in `myNumber.f`, the field `myNumber.i` would *not* be the same as `(int)(myNumber.f)`.

One way to keep track of the current state of the `union` is to declare an `int` to go along with the `union`, as well as a `#define` for each of the `union`'s fields:

```
#define kUnionContainsInt          1
#define kUnionContainsFloat        2
```

```
#define kUnionContainsPointer          3

union Number
{
    int        i;
    float f;
    char   *s;
} myNumber;

int    myUnionTag;
```

If you are currently using myUnion as a float, assign the value kUnionContainsFloat to myUnionTag. Later in your code, you can use myUnionTag when deciding which form of the union you are dealing with:

```
if ( myUnionTag == kUnionContainsInt )
    DoIntStuff( myUnion.i );
else if ( myUnionTag == kUnionContainsFloat )
    DoFloatStuff( myUnion.f );
else
    DoPointerStuff( myUnion.s );
```

Why Use Unions?

In general, a union is most useful when dealing with two data structures that share a set of common fields but differ in some small way. For example, consider these two struct declarations:

```
struct Pitcher
{
    char   name[ 40 ];
    int        team;
    int        strikeouts;
    int        runsAllowed;
} ;

struct Batter
{
    char   name[ 40 ];
    int        team;
```

```
    int       runsScored;
    int       homeRuns;
} ;
```

These `structs` might be useful if you were tracking the pitchers and batters on your favorite baseball team. Both `structs` share a set of common fields: the array of `chars` named `name` and the `int` named `team`. Both `structs` have their own unique fields as well. The `Pitcher` struct contains a pair of fields appropriate for a pitcher: `strikeouts` and `runsAllowed`. The `Batter` struct contains a pair of fields appropriate for a batter: `runsScored` and `homeRuns`.

One solution to your program would be to maintain two types of `structs`: a `Pitcher` and a `Batter`. There is nothing wrong with this approach. There is an alternative, however. You can declare a single `struct` that contains the fields common to `Pitcher` and `Batter`, with a `union` for the unique fields:

```
#define kMets      1
#define kReds      2

#define kPitcher   1
#define kBatter2

struct Pitcher
{
   int       strikeouts;
   int       runsAllowed;
} ;

struct Batter
{
   int       runsScored;
   int       homeRuns;
} ;

struct Player
{
   int       type;
   char   name[ 40 ];
   int       team;
   union
   {
```

```
        struct Pitcher     pStats;
        struct Batter      bStats;
    } u;
};
```

Here's an example of a `Player` declaration:

```
struct Player  myPlayer;
```

Once you created the `Player` struct, you would initialize the `type` field with one of either `kPitcher` or `kBatter`:

```
myPlayer.type = kBatter;
```

You would access the `name` and `team` fields like this:

```
myPlayer.team = kMets;
printf( "Stepping up to the plate:  %s", myPlayer.name );
```

Finally, you'd access the `union` fields like this:

```
if ( myPlayer.type == kPitcher )
   myPlayer.u.pStats.strikeouts = 20;
```

The u was the name given to the `union` in the declaration of the `Player` type. Every `Player` you declare will automatically have a `union` named u built into it. The `union` gives you access to either a `Pitcher` struct named `pStats` or a `Batter` struct named `bStats`. The preceding example references the `strikeouts` field of the `pStats` field.

`union`s provide an interesting alternative to maintaining multiple data structures. Try them. Write your next program using a `union` or two. If you don't like them, you can return them for a full refund.

Function Recursion

Some programming problems are best solved by repeating a mathematical process. For example, to learn whether a number is prime (see Chapter 6), you might step through each of the even integers between 2 and the number's square root, one at a time, searching for a factor. If no factor is found, you have a prime. The process of stepping through the numbers between 2 and the number's square root is called **iteration**.

In programming, iterative solutions are fairly common. Almost every time you use a `for` loop, you are applying an iterative approach to a problem. An alternative to the iterative approach is known as **recursion**. In a recursive approach, instead of repeating a process in a loop, you embed the process in a function and have the function call itself until the process is complete. The key to recursion is a function calling itself.

Suppose that you wanted to calculate 5 factorial (also known as 5 !). The factorial of a number is the product of each integer from 1 up to the number. For example, 5 factorial is:

```
5! = 5 * 4 * 3 * 2 * 1 = 120
```

Using an iterative approach, you might write some code like this:

```c
#include <stdio.h>


int main( void )
{
    int     i, num;
    long  fac;

    num = 5;
    fac = 1;

    for ( i=1; i<=num; i++ )
        fac *= i;

    printf( "%d factorial is %ld.", num, fac );

    return 0;
}
```

By the Way

> If you are interested in trying this code, it is provided on disk in the `Learn C Projects` folder, under the subfolder named `11.01 – iterate`.

If you ran this program, you'd see this line printed in the console window:

```
5 factorial is 120.
```